TOP 10 OF EVERYTHING

2009

TOP 10

OF EVERYTHING

Russell Ash **2009**

hamlyn

Produced for Hamlyn by
Palazzo Editions Ltd, 2 Wood Street, BA1 2JQ

Publishing director: Colin Webb
Art director: Bernard Higton
Project editor: Sonya Newland
Picture researcher: Sophie Hartley

First published in Great Britain in 2008 by
Hamlyn, a division of
Octopus Publishing Group Ltd
2–4 Heron Quays, London E14 4JP

Copyright © Octopus Publishing
Group Ltd 2008
Text copyright © Russell Ash 2008

Distributed in the United States and Canada
by Sterling Publishing Co., Inc.
387 Park Avenue South,
New York, NY 10016-8810

ISBN-13: 9780600618164

A CIP catalogue record for this book is
available from the British Library

Printed and bound in China

10 9 8 7 6 5 4 3 2 1

Contents

Introduction

MAGIC NUMBERS

Although 10 is the magic number as far as this book is concerned, the number 20 is not without its appeal: there were 20 days in an Aztec month, there are 20 bottles in a Nebuchadnezzar, and 20 numbers on a dartboard; we refer to 20/20 vision and the "Roaring '20s," and play the quiz 20 Questions, while 2020 is widely predicted as the year the world hits peak oil production. And 20 is now the number of years *Top 10 of Everything* has been published.

When I compiled the first edition in 1989, it was not intended to be an annual, but it has been ever since. A shelf of the complete set with one copy of each year's would be over 20 in (50 cm) long—mine, with all the versions now published around the world, is considerably longer!

IT WAS 20 YEARS AGO...

Alongside the array of Top 10 lists, the often dramatic changes over the past 20 years or so are reflected in the "Now & Then" lists presented here for the first time. They show such developments as population changes, oil consumers, and car owners, the tallest skyscrapers, the largest cities and movie budgets, the busiest airports, longest life expectancy, most expensive paintings, and the most popular names of people and pets.

THIS EVER-CHANGING WORLD

While the "Now & Then" lists show what has altered over the past 20 years, pretty much every list changes from year to year—even "fixed" lists such as those of tallest mountains are revised as more sophisticated measuring techniques are used, or deepest caves, as deeper branches are discovered. The minimum entry requirements for Top 10 lists are in a constant state of flux as, for example, rich people get increasingly richer and build ever-bigger yachts, movies with bigger and bigger budgets are released and achieve higher-earning opening weekends (three movies have now made more than $1 billion worldwide). And just as the tallest building in the world nears completion, plans are announced for one more than twice as tall, the proposed 5,280-ft (1,609-m) Mile-High Tower in Jeddah, Saudi Arabia.

IT'S A FACT

Top 10 lists provide a shorthand glimpse at what is happening with the world economy, global warming, deforestation, the countries that will have the most people and the densest populations in the future, and other issues that concern us all. At the same time, it conveys a fascinating and entertaining overview of the amazing diversity of our planet and its people, with lists on such subjects as longest place names and the people on the FBI's "Most Wanted" list, the largest diamonds and the largest snails, the heaviest and the oldest people, the richest dead celebrities, the largest shopping malls and the most powerful computers, the most common and the most unusual phobias, the most borrowed and the most translated authors, the leading chocolate consumers and the most overweight countries.

MADE TO MEASURE

The ground rules are that all the Top 10s in the book are measurable: biggests, fastests, richests, firsts, oldests, and so on. There are no "bests," except bestsellers, and "worsts" are of disasters and murders where they are measured by numbers of victims. Unless otherwise stated, movie lists are based on cumulative global earnings, irrespective of production or marketing budgets and, as is standard in the industry, inflation is not taken into account—which inevitably means that recent releases feature more prominently.

"Countries" are independent countries, not dependencies or overseas territories. All the lists are all-time and global unless a specific year or territory is noted. If the USA does not figure in a country-based list, it is generally added as an extra entry.

SOURCES

My sources encompass international organizations, commercial companies and research bodies, specialized publications, and a network of people around the world who have shared their knowledge of everything from snakes and skyscrapers to ships and spiders. As ever, I gladly acknowledge their invaluable contribution (see page 255 for a full list of credits), as well as everyone who has been involved with the book at all stages of its development on this and the previous 19 annual editions.

OVER TO YOU

I hope you enjoy the book. Your comments, corrections and suggestions for new lists are always welcome. Please contact me via the publisher or visit the *Top 10 of Everything* website www.top10ofeverything.com or my own www.RussellAsh.com

Russell Ash

THE UNIVERSE
& THE EARTH

Elementary

TOP 10 **MOST COMMON ELEMENTS IN THE EARTH'S CRUST**

ELEMENT	SYMBOL	PARTS PER MILLION*
1 Oxygen	O	461,000
2 Silicon	Si	282,000
3 Aluminum	Al	82,300
4 Iron	Fe	56,300
5 Calcium	Ca	41,500
6 Sodium	Na	23,600
7 Magnesium	Mg	23,300
8 Potassium	K	20,900
9 Titanium	Ti	5,650
10 Hydrogen	H	1,400

* Mg per kg, based on average percentages of elements in igneous rock

At an atomic level, out of every million atoms, some 200,000 are silicon, 63,000 aluminum, and 31,000 hydrogen—although in the Universe as a whole, hydrogen is by far the most common element, comprising some 930,000 out of every million atoms, followed by helium at 72,000 per million.

TOP 10 **MOST COMMON ELEMENTS ON THE MOON**

ELEMENT	SYMBOL	%
1 Oxygen	O	40.0
2 Silicon	Si	19.2
3 Iron	Fe	14.3
4 Calcium	Ca	8.0
5 Titanium	Ti	5.9
6 Aluminum	Al	5.6
7 Magnesium	Mg	4.5
8 Sodium	Na	0.33
9 Potassium	K	0.14
10 Chromium	Cr	0.002

This list is based on the analysis of the 45.8 lb (20.77 kg) of rock samples brought back to Earth by the crew of the 1969 *Apollo 11* lunar mission. One of the minerals they discovered at Tranquility Base was named Armalcolite in honour of the three astronauts **Arm**strong, **Al**drin, and **Col**lins. It contains magnesium, iron, titanium, and oxygen. In all, the six *Apollo* missions brought back 842 lb (382 kg) of lunar rocks and other samples.

TOP 10 **MOST COMMON ELEMENTS IN THE SUN**

ELEMENT	SYMBOL	% OF ATOMS
1 Hydrogen	H	92.1
2 Helium	He	7.8
3 Oxygen	O	0.061
4 Carbon	C	0.030
5 Nitrogen	N	0.0084
6 Neon	Ne	0.0076
7 Iron	Fe	0.0037
8 Silicon	Si	0.0031
9 Magnesium	Mg	0.0024
10 Sulfur	S	0.0015

A total of 99.9 percent of all the atoms in the Sun are made up of two elements, hydrogen and helium. Helium was in fact discovered in the Sun before it was detected on Earth, its name coming from *helios*, the Greek word for "Sun." More than 70 elements have been detected in the Sun, the most common of which correspond closely to those found in the Universe as a whole, but with some variations in their ratios, including a greater proportion of the principal element, hydrogen. The atoms of hydrogen in the Universe outnumber those of all the other elements combined.

TOP 10 **MOST COMMON ELEMENTS IN THE OCEANS**

	ELEMENT	SYMBOL	AMOUNT (TONS PER CU KM)
1	Oxygen*	O	857,000,000
2	Hydrogen*	H	107,800,000
3	Chlorine	Cl	19,870,000
4	Sodium	Na	11,050,000
5	Magnesium	Mg	1,326,000
6	Sulfur	S	928,000
7	Calcium	Ca	422,000
8	Potassium	K	416,000
9	Bromine	Br	67,300
10	Carbon	C	28,000

* Combined as water

A typical cubic kilometer (a billion tonnes) of seawater is a treasury of often valuable elements—there are reckoned to be 5,000 million million tons of solids dissolved in the world's oceans, but sodium and chlorine (combined as sodium chloride—common salt) are the only two that are extracted in substantial quantities. The costs of extracting elements such as gold (even though as much as 500 kilos of it may be found in the average cubic kilometer of seawater) would be so expensive that with current technology it is not economic to do so.

TOP 10 **MOST COMMON ELEMENTS IN THE UNIVERSE**

	ELEMENT	SYMBOL	PARTS PER MILLION*
1	Hydrogen	H	750,000
2	Helium	He	230,000
3	Oxygen	O	10,000
4	Carbon	C	5,000
5	Neon	Ne	1,300
6	Iron	Fe	1,100
7	Nitrogen	N	1,000
8	Silicon	Si	700
9	Magnesium	Mg	600
10	Sulfur	S	500

* Mg per kg

In his element
Einsteinium was named after Albert Einstein, winner of the 1921 Nobel Prize for Physics.

THE 10 **FIRST ELEMENTS TO BE NAMED AFTER REAL PEOPLE**

	ELEMENT	SYMBOL	NAMED AFTER	YEAR
1	Samarium*	Sm	Vasili Samarsky-Bykhovets (Russia, 1803–70)	1879
2	Gadolinium#	Gd	Johan Gadolin (Finland, 1760–1852)	1880
3	Curium	Cm	Pierre† and Marie Curie† (France, 1859–1906; Poland, 1867–1934)	1944
4	Einsteinium	Es	Albert Einstein† (German, 1879–1955)	1952
5	Fermium	Fm	Enrico Fermi† (Italian, 1901–54)	1953
6	Nobelium	No	Alfred Nobel (Sweden, 1833–96)	1958
7	Lawrencium	Lr	Ernest Lawrence† (USA, 1901–58)	1961
8	Rutherfordium	Rf	Ernest Rutherford† (UK, 1871–1937)	1969
9	Seaborgium	Sg	Glenn T. Seaborg† (USA, 1912–99)	1974
10	Bohrium	Bh	Niels Bohr† (Denmark, 1885–62)	1981

* Named after mineral samarskite, which was named after Samarsky-Bykhovets
# Named after mineral gadolinite, which was named after Gadolin
† Awarded Nobel Prize

The Universe

TOP 10 BRIGHTEST GALAXIES

GALAXY/NO.	DISTANCE FROM EARTH (MILLIONS OF LIGHT YEARS)	APPARENT MAGNITUDE
1 Large Magellanic Cloud	0.17	0.91
2 Small Magellanic Cloud	0.21	2.70
3 Andromeda Galaxy/NGC 224 M31	2.6	4.36
4 Triangulum Galaxy/NGC 598 M33	2.8	6.27
5 Centaurus Galaxy/NGC 5128	12.0	7.84
6 Bode's Galaxy/NGC 3031 M81	12.0	7.89
7 Silver Coin Galaxy/NGC 253	8.5	8.04
8 Southern Pinwheel Galaxy/NGC 5236 M83	15.0	8.20
9 Pinwheel Galaxy/NGC 5457 M101	24.0	8.31
10 Cigar Galaxy/NGC 55	4.9	8.42

Messier (M) numbers are named after French astronomer Charles Messier, who compiled the first catalog of galaxies, nebulae, and star clusters in 1781. From 1888 onward, these were replaced by New General Catalog (NGC) numbers. As well as the official names that have been assigned to them, galaxies discovered prior to the change are identified by both M and NGC numbers.

TOP 10 MOST FREQUENTLY SEEN COMETS

COMET	YEARS BETWEEN APPEARANCES
1 Encke 1	3.29
2 NEAT (Near Earth Asteroid Tracking) 22	4.20
3 Helfenzrieder 1	4.35
4 Catalina 3	4.42
5 LINEAR (Lincoln Near-Earth Asteroid Research) 30	4.85
6 LINEAR 46	4.86
7 = Grigg-Skjellerup 1	4.98
= NEAT 10	4.98
9 LONEOS (Lowell Observatory Near-Earth-Object Search) 6	5.01
10 Blanpain 1	5.10

Source: NASA, Planetary Data System Small Bodies Node

The comets in the Top 10, and several others, return with regularity (although with some notable variations), while others have such long periods that they may not be seen again for many thousands, or even millions, of years. The most frequent visitor is Encke's Comet, named not after its 1786 discoverer (French astronomer Pierre Méchain), but the German astronomer Johann Franz Encke, who in 1818 calculated the period of its elliptical orbit. It had been first observed shortly before his birth, but without its orbit being calculated, and has been seen on almost all its subsequent returns.

TOP 10 STARS NEAREST EARTH

STAR*	LIGHT YEARS	DISTANCE FROM EARTH MILES (MILLIONS)	KM (MILLIONS)
1 Proxima Centauri	4.22	24,792,500	39,923,310
2 Alpha Centauri	4.39	25,791,250	41,531,595
3 Barnard's Star	5.94	34,897,500	56,195,370
4 Wolf 359	7.78	45,707,500	73,602,690
5 Lalande 21185	8.31	48,821,250	78,616,755
6 Sirius	8.60	50,525,000	81,360,300
7 Luyten 726-8	8.72	51,230,000	82,495,560
8 Ross 154	9.69	56,928,750	91,672,245
9 Ross 248	10.32	60,630,000	97,632,360
10 Epsilon Eridani	10.49	61,628,750	99,240,645

* Excluding the Sun

Source: Peter Bond, Royal Astronomical Society

A spaceship traveling at 25,000 mph (40,237 km/h)—faster than any human has yet reached in space—would take more than 113,200 years to reach Earth's closest star, Proxima Centauri. Even this distance and those of the others in this Top 10 are dwarfed by those of stars within the Milky Way up to 2,500 light years away, while our own galaxy may span as much as 100,000 light years.

TOP 10 LARGEST ASTEROIDS

NAME	NO.	DISCOVERED	MAX. DIAMETER* MILES	KM
1 Ceres	1	Jan 1, 1801	584	940
2 Vesta	4	Mar 29, 1807	357	576
3 Pallas	2	Mar 28, 1802	334	538
4 Hygeia	10	Apr 12, 1849	267	430
5 Interamnia	704	Oct 2, 1910	210	338
6 Davida	511	May 30, 1903	201	324
7 Cybele	65	Mar 8, 1861	191	308
8 Europa	52	Feb 4, 1858	181	292
9 Sylvia	87	May 16, 1866	175	282
10 Patienta	451	Dec 4, 1899	173	280

* Most asteroids are irregular in shape

Asteroids, now often known as "minor planets," are fragments of rock orbiting between Mars and Jupiter. Ceres is large enough to be regarded as a "dwarf planet" (bodies over 466 miles/750 km in diameter), along with Pluto and Eris. Up to August 2007, some 161,988 asteroids had been identified. Each of the four Beatles has an asteroid named after him (4,147–4,150), as do Elvis Presley (17,059), the Rolling Stones (19,383), James Bond (9,007), and the members of the Monty Python team (9,617–9,622).

TOP 10 **LARGEST BODIES IN THE SOLAR SYSTEM**

	BODY	MAX. DIAMETER		SIZE COMPARED WITH EARTH
		MILES	KM	
1	Sun	865,036	1,392,140	109.136
2	Jupiter	88,846	142,984	11.209
3	Saturn	74,898	120,536	9.449
4	Uranus	31,763	51,118	4.007
5	Neptune	30,775	49,528	3.883
6	Earth	7,926	12,756	1.000
7	Venus	7,521	12,104	0.949
8	Mars	4,228	6,805	0.533
9	Ganymede	3,270	5,262	0.413
10	Titan	3,200	5,150	0.404

Most of the planets are visible with the naked eye and have been observed since ancient times. The exceptions are Uranus, discovered on March 13, 1781 by the British astronomer Sir William Herschel; Neptune, found by German astronomer Johann Galle on September 23, 1846 (Galle was led to his discovery by the independent calculations of the French astronomer Urbain Le Verrier and the British mathematician John Adams); and, outside the Top 10, former planet Pluto, located using photographic techniques by American astronomer Clyde Tombaugh.

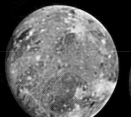
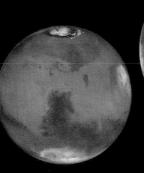

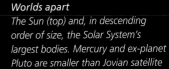

Worlds apart
The Sun (top) and, in descending order of size, the Solar System's largest bodies. Mercury and ex-planet Pluto are smaller than Jovian satellite Ganymede and Saturn's Titan.

To Boldly Go...

TOP 10 COUNTRIES WITH THE MOST SPACEFLIGHT EXPERIENCE

	COUNTRY	ASTRONAUTS/ COSMONAUTS	TOTAL DURATION OF MISSIONS* DAYS	HRS	MINS
1	USSR/Russia	211	17,738	17	4
2	USA	750	11,434	19	36
3	Germany	14	494	0	12
4	France	17	383	21	50
5	Kazakhstan	4	349	7	26
6	Canada	13	146	1	31
7	Japan	10	102	2	24
8	Italy	7	86	4	22
9	Ukraine	2	64	22	48
10	Switzerland	4	42	11	31

* To March 27, 2008

The USSR, and now Russia, has clocked up its considerable lead on the rest of the world—with 57.3 per cent of the total time spent by humans in space—largely through the long-duration stays of its cosmonauts on board the *Mir* space station. The USA has had more than three times as many astronauts in space—principally aboard the Space Shuttle—but its missions have been of shorter duration.

TOP 10 MOST EXPERIENCED US ASTRONAUTS*

	NAME	MISSIONS	TOTAL DURATION DAYS	HRS	MINS
1	C. Michael Foale	6	373	18	8
2	Michael López-Alegria	4	257	22	46
3	Carl E. Walz	4	230	13	4
4	Chiao Leroy	4	229	8	41
5	Daniel Bursch	4	226	22	16
6	William S. McArthur	4	224	22	19
7	Shannon Lucid	5	223	2	50
8	Kenneth Bowersox	5	211	14	12
9	Susan J. Helms	5	210	23	6
10	Edward Lu	3	205	23	18

* To March 27, 2008

TOP 10 MOST EXPERIENCED COSMONAUTS*

	COSMONAUT	MISSIONS	TOTAL DURATION DAYS	HRS	MINS
1	Sergei Krikalyov	6#	803	9	39
2	Sergei Avdeyev	3	747	14	14
3	Valeri Polyakov	2	678	16	32
4	Anatoly Solovyov	5#	651	0	2
5	Alexander Kaleri	4	609	21	53
6	Viktor Afanasyev	4	555	18	33
7	Yuri Usachev	4#	552	22	25
8	Musa Manarov	2	541	0	28
9	Alexander Viktorenko	4	489	1	33
10	Nikolai Budarin	3#	444	1	25

* To March 27, 2008; all Soviet/Russian
\# Including flights aboard US Space Shuttles

All the missions listed were undertaken by the USSR (and, latterly, Russia). In recent years a number of US astronauts added to their space logs by spending time on board the Russian *Mir* space station, and latterly on the International Space Station, but none has matched the endurance records set by Russian cosmonauts. Krikalyov established the cumulative record aboard the ISS during his sixth mission in 2005.

Mission patch
STS-102 carried Krikalyov, Helms, and Usachev, three of the most experienced of all astronauts and cosmonauts.

Walking round the world
During their record-duration spacewalk from the International Space Station, US astronaut James S. Voss, accompanied by Susan J. Helms, orbited the Earth more than five times.

TOP 10 **MOST EXPERIENCED NON-US AND NON-RUSSIAN ASTRONAUTS AND COSMONAUTS***

NAME / COUNTRY	MISSIONS	TOTAL DURATION DAYS	HRS	MINS
1 Thomas A. Reiter Germany	2	350	5	35
2 Talgat A. Musabayev Kazakhstan	3	341	9	48
3 Jean-Pierre Haigneré France	2	209	12	25
4 Léopold Eyharts France	2	69	21	31
5 Ulf D. Merbold Germany	3	49	21	36
6 Jean-Loup J. M. Chrétien France	3	43	11	19
7 Claude Nicollier Switzerland	4	42	12	5
8 Takao Doi Japan	2	31	10	45
9 Joseph J.-P. M. Garneau Canada	3	29	2	1
10 Dafydd Rhys Williams Canada	2	28	15	46

* To March 27, 2008

Claudie Haigneré, the wife of Jean-Pierre Haigneré, here in third place, has been on two Soyuz missions but just fails to make the list with a total time in space of 25 days 14 hours and 22 minutes. Asteroid 135268, discovered in France in 2001, was named Haigneré in honour of the country's most experienced space couple.

TOP 10 **LONGEST SPACEWALKS***

ASTRONAUTS[#] / SPACECRAFT	DATE	DURATION HR:MIN
1 James S. Voss, Susan J. Helms STS-102/ISS[†]	Mar 11, 2001	8:56
2 Thomas Akers, Richard Hieb, Pierre J. Thuot STS-49	May 13–14, 1992	8:29
3 John M. Grunsfeld, Steven L. Smith STS-103	Dec 22–23, 1999	8:15
4 C. Michael Foale, Claude Nicollier STS-103	Dec 23–24, 1999	8:10
5 John M. Grunsfeld, Steven L. Smith STS-103	Dec 24–25, 1999	8:08
6 = James F. Reilly, John D. Olivas STS-117	Jun 15–16, 2007	7:58
= Stanley G. Love, Rex J. Walheim STS-122	Feb 11, 2008	7:58
8 = Daniel Barry, Tamara Jernigan STS-96/ISS	May 30, 1999	7:55
= Michael López–Alegria, Sunita Williams Soyuz TMA-9/ISS	Jan 31, 2007	7:55
10 Jeffrey A. Hoffman, F. Story Musgrave STS-61	Dec 5, 1993	7:54

* To March 27, 2008
\# All US
† International Space Station

Bodies of Water

TOP 10 **DEEPEST OCEANS AND SEAS**

OCEAN/SEA	AVERAGE DEPTH FT	M
1 Southern Ocean	13,123–16,404	4–5,000
2 Pacific Ocean	13,215	4,028
3 Indian Ocean	13,002	3,963
4 Atlantic Ocean	12,999	3,926
5 Caribbean Sea	8,684	2,647
6 South China Sea	4,150	1,652
7 Red Sea	5,285	1,611
8 Bering Sea	5,075	1,547
9 Gulf of Mexico	4,875	1,486
10 Mediterranean Sea	4,688	1,429
World ocean average	*12,237*	*3,730*

TOP 10 **LARGEST OCEANS AND SEAS**

NAME	APPROX. AREA* SQ MILES	SQ KM
1 Pacific Ocean	60,060,900	155,557,000
2 Atlantic Ocean	29,637,977	76,762,000
3 Indian Ocean	26,469,622	68,556,000
4 Southern Ocean#	7,848,299	20,327,000
5 Arctic Ocean	5,427,053	14,056,000
6 Caribbean Sea	1,049,503	2,718,200
7 Mediterranean Sea	969,117	2,510,000
8 South China Sea	895,371	2,319,000
9 Bering Sea	884,908	2,291,900
10 Gulf of Mexico	614,984	1,592,800

* Excluding tributary seas
# Defined by the International Hydrographic Organization, 2000

The Shrinking Sea

Fifty years ago, the Aral Sea in Kazakhstan and Uzbekistan was the fourth-biggest inland sea in the world, with a water surface area of 25,521 sq miles (66,100 sq km) and islands of 2,200 sq km (849 sq miles), a total of 26,371 sq miles (68,300 sq km). By 2004, as a result of two feeder rivers being diverted to irrigate cotton crops, it had shrunk to 6,625 sq miles (17,158 sq km), with ships beached and former fishing villages 62 miles (100 km) inland, and it is heavily polluted. The recent construction of a dam has began the process of refilling the northern part, which has expanded by over 386 sq miles (1,000 sq km) since 2005.

TOP 10 **DEEPEST LAKES**

LAKE	LOCATION	GREATEST DEPTH FT	M
1 Baikal	Russia	5,712	1,741
2 Tanganyika	Burundi/Tanzania/Dem. Rep. of Congo/Zambia	4,825	1,471
3 Caspian Sea	Azerbaijan/Iran/ Kazakhstan/Russia/ Turkmenistan	3,363	1,025
4 Malawi (Nyasa)	Malawi/Mozambique/ Tanzania	2,316	706
5 Issyk-kul	Kyrgyzstan	2,191	668
6 Great Slave	Canada	2,015	614
7 Matana	Sulawesi, Indonesia	1,936	590
8 Crater	Oregon, USA	1,932	589
9 Toba	Sumatra, Indonesia	1,736	529
10 Hornindalsvatnet	Norway	1,686	514

TOP 10 **LARGEST LAKES**

LAKE	LOCATION	APPROX. AREA SQ MILES	SQ KM
1 Caspian Sea	Azerbaijan/Iran/ Kazakhstan/Russia/ Turkmenistan	143,244	371,000
2 Michigan/ Huron*	Canada/USA	45,342	117,436
3 Superior	Canada/USA	31,700	82,103
4 Victoria	Kenya/Tanzania/Uganda	26,828	69,485
5 Tanganyika	Burundi/Tanzania/ Dem. Rep. of Congo/ Zambia	12,700	32,893
6 Baikal	Russia	12,160	31,494
7 Great Bear	Canada	12,028	31,153
8 Malawi (Nyasa)	Malawi/Mozambique/ Tanzania	11,429	29,600
9 Great Slave	Canada	11,030	28,568
10 Erie	Canada/USA	9,940	25,745

* Now considered two lobes of the same lake

Regarded geologically and hydrologically as two lobes of the same lake, Michigan/Huron is the world's largest freshwater lake. A depth of 5,712 ft (1,741 m) near Olkhon, off Cape Ukhan, established Lake Baikal as the world's deepest, although subsequent research has failed to record soundings greater than 5,315 ft (1,620 m).

Victorious Victoria
The world's largest tropical lake, Victoria's fishing industry is a mainstay of the economy of the surrounding region. The lake was unknown to Europeans until its discovery by John Hanning Speke in 1858.

TOP 10 **LARGEST FRESHWATER LAKES IN THE USA***

LAKE	LOCATION	AREA SQ MILES	SQ KM
1 Michigan#	Illinois/Indiana/ Michigan/Wisconsin	22,300	57,700
2 Iliamna	Alaska	1,000	2,590
3 Okeechobee	Florida	700	1,813
4 Becharof	Alaska	458	1,186
5 Red	Minnesota	451	1,168
6 Teshepuk	Alaska	315	816
7 Naknek	Alaska	242	627
8 Winnebago	Wisconsin	215	557
9 Mille Lacs	Minnesota	207	536
10 Flathead	Montana	197	510

* Excluding those partly in Canada
# One lobe of Lake Michigan/Huron

Go with the Flow

TOP 10 LARGEST RIVER DRAINAGE BASINS

	RIVER BASIN	CONTINENT	APPROX. DRAINAGE AREA SQ MILES	SQ KM
1	Amazon	South America	2,372,492	6,144,727
2	Congo	Africa	1,440,344	3,730,474
3	Nile	Africa	1,256,591	3,254,555
4	Mississippi-Missouri	North America	1 236 388	3,202,230
5	Plata	South America	1,196,917	3,100,000
6	Ob'	Asia	1,147,688	2,972,497
7	Paraná	South America	997,175	2,582,672
8	Yenisei	Asia	986,291	2,554,482
9	Lena	Asia	890,650	2,306,772
10	Niger	Africa	873,272	2,261,763

Drainage basins are the areas of land into which water from rain or melting snow drain into a body of water, such as a river or lake, or to the sea. Endorheic basins are those where the water does not ultimately enter the sea. As they are important in providing water for agriculture, and domestic and industrial uses, the management of water resources is often based on defined drainage basins.

TOP 10 GREATEST* RIVER SYSTEMS

	RIVER SYSTEM	CONTINENT	AVERAGE DISCHARGE AT MOUTH (CU FT/SEC)	(CU M/SEC)
1	Amazon	South America	7,733,912	219,000
2	Congo (Zaïre)	Africa	1,476,153	41,800
3	Yangtze (Chang Jiang)	Asia	1,126,538	31,900
4	Orinoco	South America	1,059,440	30,000
5	Paraná	South America	907,587	25,700
6	Yenisei-Angara	Asia	692,168	19,600
7	Brahmaputra (Tsangpo)	Asia	678,042	19,200
8	Lena	Asia	603,881	17,100
9	Madeira-Mamoré	South America	600,349	17,000
10	Mississippi-Missouri	North America	572,098	16,200

* Based on rate of discharge at mouth

Frozen river
Discovered by Ernest Shackleton in 1908, the vast Beardmore glacier was named after Sir William Beardmore, the sponsor of his expedition.

TOP 10 LONGEST GLACIERS

	GLACIER / LOCATION	APPROX. LENGTH: MILES	KM
1	Lambert Antarctica	249	400
2	Bering Alaska, USA	118	190
3	Beardmore Antarctica	99	160
4	Byrd Antarctica	85	136
5	Nimrod Antarctica	84	135
6	Amundsen Antarctica	80	128
7	Hubbard Alaska, USA	76	122
8	Slessor Antarctica	75	120
9	Denman Antarctica	70	112
10	= Recovery Antarctica	62	100
	= Shackleton Antarctica	62	100

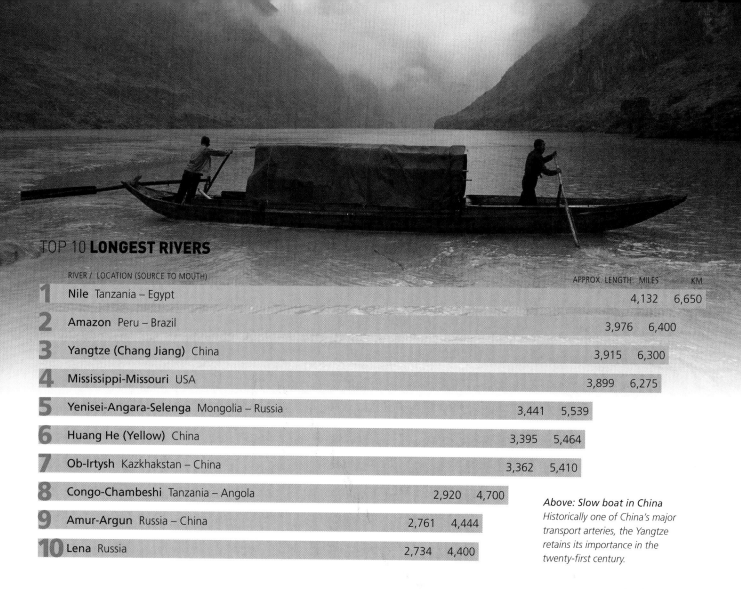

TOP 10 **LONGEST RIVERS**

	RIVER / LOCATION (SOURCE TO MOUTH)	APPROX. LENGTH: MILES	KM
1	Nile Tanzania – Egypt	4,132	6,650
2	Amazon Peru – Brazil	3,976	6,400
3	Yangtze (Chang Jiang) China	3,915	6,300
4	Mississippi-Missouri USA	3,899	6,275
5	Yenisei-Angara-Selenga Mongolia – Russia	3,441	5,539
6	Huang He (Yellow) China	3,395	5,464
7	Ob-Irtysh Kazkhakstan – China	3,362	5,410
8	Congo-Chambeshi Tanzania – Angola	2,920	4,700
9	Amur-Argun Russia – China	2,761	4,444
10	Lena Russia	2,734	4,400

Above: Slow boat in China
Historically one of China's major transport arteries, the Yangtze retains its importance in the twenty-first century.

TOP 10 **HIGHEST WATERFALLS**

	WATERFALL / RIVER	LOCATION	TOTAL DROP FT	M
1	Angel Carrao	Venezuela	3,212	979*
2	Tugela Tugela	South Africa	3,110	948
3	Ramnefjellsfossen Jostedal Glacier	Nesdale, Norway	2,625	800
4	Mongefossen Monge	Mongebekk, Norway	2,540	774
5	Gocta Cataracta Cocahuayco	Peru	2,531	771
6	Mutarazi Mutarazi River	Zimbabwe	2,499	762
7	Yosemite Yosemite Creek	California, USA	2,425	739
8	Østre Mardøla Foss Mardals	Eikisdal, Norway	2,152	656
9	Tyssestrengane Tysso	Hardanger, Norway	2,120	646
10	Cuquenán Arabopo	Venezuela	2,000	610

* Longest single drop 2,648 ft (807 m)

TOP 10 **WIDEST WATERFALLS**

	WATERFALL / RIVER / COUNTRY	WIDTH FT	M
1	Chutes de Khône, Mekong River, Laos	35,376	10,783
2	Salto Pará, Rio Caura, Venezuela	18,400	5,608
3 =	Salto del Guaíra, Rio Paraná, Brazil	15,840	4,828
=	Chutes de Livingstone, Congo River, Congo	15,840	4,828
5	Celilo Falls, Columbia River, USA	10,560	3,219
6	Kongou Falls, Ivindo River, Gabon	10,500	3,200
7	Salto de Iguaçu, Rio Iguaçu, Argentina/Brazil	8,858	2,700
8 =	Saltos dos Patos e Maribondo, Rio Grande, Brazil	6,600	2,012
=	Salto do Urubupungá, Rio Paraná, Brazil	6,600	2,012
10	Victoria Falls, Zambezi River, Zimbabwe/Zambia	5,700	1,737

Islands

TOP 10 **HIGHEST ISLANDS**

ISLAND / HIGHEST POINT	HIGHEST ELEVATION FT	M
1 New Guinea, Indonesia/Papua New Guinea; Puncak Jaya (Mount Carstensz)	16,023	4,884
2 Hawaii, USA; Mauna Kea	13,795	4,205
3 Borneo, Indonesia/Malaysia; Mount Kinabalu	13,454	4,101
4 Taiwan; Jade Mountain (Yu Shan)	12,965	3,952
5 Sumatra, Indonesia; Mount Kerinci	12,480	3,805
6 Ross, Antarctica; Mount Erebus	12,447	3,794
7 Honshu, Japan; Mount Fuji	12,388	3,776
8 New Zealand; Aorakim (Mount Cook)	12,319	3,755
9 Lombok, Indonesia; Mount Rinjani	12,224	3,726
10 Tenerife, Spain; Pico de Teide	12,198	3,718

Some of the tallest island mountains were formed by tectonic activity, while others are volcanic in origin, including dormant volcanoes Mauna Kea and Fuji, and active volcanoes Erebus and Rinjani, and Teide, the highest European island mountain.

TOP 10 **LARGEST ISLAND COUNTRIES**

COUNTRY	AREA SQ MILES	SQ KM
1 Indonesia	735,358	1,904,569
2 Madagascar	226,917	587,713
3 Papua New Guinea	178,703	462,840
4 Japan	145,897	377,873
5 Malaysia	127,354	329,847
6 Philippines	115,830	300,000
7 New Zealand	104,453	270,534
8 Cuba	42,803	110,861
9 Iceland	39,768	103,000
10 Sri Lanka	25,332	65,610

All the countries on this list are self-contained island countries. Because Ireland and Northern Ireland share an island, the UK and Ireland are both excluded from this list. Had it been included, the UK (excluding the Isle of Man and the Channel Islands) would take eighth place with an area of 93,784 sq miles (242,900 sq km). Although larger than all these islands, as a province of Denmark, Greenland is not eligible for this list.

TOP 10 **LARGEST CORAL ISLANDS**

ISLAND / LOCATION	AREA SQ MILES	SQ KM
1 Lifou, Loyalty Islands, New Caledonia	442.6	1,146.2
2 Muyua, Trobriand Islands, Papua New Guinea	337.4	873.9
3 Rennell, Solomon Islands	248.9	660.1
4 Mare, Loyalty Islands, New Caledonia	253.5	656.6
5 Grande Terre, Guadeloupe	246.7	639.0
6 Guam	208.9	541.0
7 Acklins, Bahamas	195.9	507.5
8 Crooked, Bahamas	109.9	282.1
9 Kiriwina, Trobriand Islands, Papua New Guinea	102.9	266.5
10 Niue	101.8	263.7

Source: United Nations Environment Program (UNEP)

These islands are all believed to be either raised coral or limestone atolls, although some may be combined with older volcanic structures—as is the largest, Lifou, which formed round a submerged volcano, and Guam, which comprises both a limestone plateau and dormant volcanoes.

TOP 10 **LARGEST GREAT LAKE ISLANDS**

ISLAND	LAKE	LOCATION	AREA SQ MILES	SQ KM
1 Manitoulin	Huron	Ontario	1,068	2,766
2 Isle Royale	Superior	Michigan	207	536
3 St. Joseph	Huron	Ontario	141	365
4 Drummond	Huron	Michigan	134	347
5 Saint Ignace	Superior	Ontario	106	274
6 Michipicoten	Superior	Ontario	71	184
7 Beaver	Michigan	Michigan	56	145
8 Cockburn	Huron	Ontario	54	139
9 Sugar	George/Nicolet	Michigan	49	128
10 Wolfe	Ontario	Ontario	48	124

Manitoulin, the largest of the Great Lakes' approximately 35,000 islands, is ranked 31st largest in Canada and 173rd in the world. It has more lakes within it than any other island in the world— a total of 110. Some of these, in turn, have their own islands. Manitoulin's 12,600 population expands to some 50,000 in the summer, making it the most populated lake island: other Great Lake islands have a low—or, in the case of Isle Royale no— permanent population.

Peak activity

Mount Kerinci, an active volcano, dominates the Kerinci Seblat National Park in Sumatra, the world's sixth-largest island.

TOP 10 **LARGEST ISLANDS**

ISLAND / LOCATION	SQ MILES	AREA* SQ KM
1 Greenland (Kalaatdlit Nunaat)	840,004	2,175,600
2 New Guinea, Papua New Guinea/ Indonesia	303,381	785,753
3 Borneo, Indonesia/Malaysia/Brunei	288,869	748,168
4 Madagascar	226,917	587,713
5 Baffin Island, Canada	194,574	503,944
6 Sumatra, Indonesia	171,068	443,065
7 Honshu, Japan	87,805	227,413
8 Great Britain	84,200	218,077
9 Victoria Island, Canada	83,897	217,292
10 Ellesmere Island, Canada	75,767	196,236

* Mainlands, including areas of inland water, but excluding offshore islands

Australia is regarded as a continental land mass rather than an island, otherwise it would rank first, at 2,941,517 sq miles (7,618,493 sq km).

TOP 10 **LARGEST VOLCANIC ISLANDS**

ISLAND / LOCATION / TYPE	AREA SQ MILES	SQ KM
1 Sumatra, Indonesia Active volcanic	171,068.7	443,065.8
2 Honshu, Japan Volcanic	87,182.0	225,800.3
3 Java, Indonesia Volcanic	53,588.5	138,793.6
4 North Island, New Zealand Volcanic	43,082.4	111,582.8
5 Luzon, Philippines Active volcanic	42,457.7	109,964.9
6 Iceland Active volcanic	39,315.2	101,826.0
7 Mindanao, Philippines Active volcanic	37,656.5	97,530.0
8 Hokkaido, Japan Active volcanic	30,394.7	78,719.4
9 New Britain, Papua New Guinea Volcanic	13,569.4	35,144.6
10 Halmahera, Indonesia Active volcanic	6,965.1	18,039.6

Source: United Nations Environment Program (UNEP)

Mountains & Land Features

TOP 10 **HIGHEST MOUNTAINS**

MOUNTAIN / LOCATION FIRST ASCENT / TEAM NATIONALITY	HEIGHT* FT	M
1 Everest, Nepal/China May 29, 1953, British/New Zealand	29,035	8,850
2 K2 (Chogori), Pakistan/China Jul 31, 1954, Italian	28,251	8,611
3 Kangchenjunga, Nepal/India May 25, 1955, British	28,169	8,586
4 Lhotse, Nepal/China May 18, 1956, Swiss	27,940	8,516
5 Makalu I, Nepal/China May 15, 1955, French	27,838	8,485
6 Cho Oyu, Nepal/China Oct 19, 1954, Austrian	26,864	8,188
7 Dhaulagiri I, Nepal May 13, 1960, Swiss/Austrian	26,795	8,167
8 Manaslu I (Kutang I), Nepal May 9, 1956, Japanese	26,781	8,163
9 Nanga Parbat (Diamir), Pakistan, Jul 3, 1953, German/Austrian	26,657	8,125
10 Anapurna I, Nepal Jun 3, 1950, French	26,545	8,091

* Height of principal peak; lower peaks of the same mountain are excluded

TOP 10 **LONGEST MOUNTAIN RANGES**

RANGE / LOCATION	LENGTH MILES	KM
1 Andes, South America	4,500	7,242
2 Rocky Mountains, North America	3,750	6,035
3 Himalayas/Karakoram/Hundu Kush, Asia	2,400	3,862
4 Great Dividing Range, Australia	2,250	3,621
5 Trans-Antarctic Mountains, Antarctica	2,200	3,541
6 Brazilian East Coast Range, Brazil	1,900	3,058
7 Sumatran/Javan Range, Sumatra, Java	1,800	2,897
8 Tien Shan, China	1,400	2,253
9 Eastern Ghats, India	1,300	2,092
10 = Altai, Asia	1,250	2,012
= **Central New Guinean Range**, Papua New Guinea	1,250	2,012
= **Urals**, Russia	1,250	2,012

This Top 10 includes only ranges that are continuous (the Sumatran/Javan Range is divided only by a short interruption between the two islands). The Aleutian Range extends for 1,650 miles (2,655 km), but is fragmented across numerous islands of the northwest Pacific. As well as these ranges that lie above the surface of the Earth, there are also several submarine ranges that are even longer.

TOP 10 **LARGEST DESERTS**

DESERT / LOCATION / APPROX. AREA (SQ MILES/SQ KM)

This Top 10 presents the approximate areas and ranking of the world's great deserts, which are often broken down into smaller desert regions—the Australian Desert into the Gibson, Great Sandy, Great Victoria, and Simpson, for example. The world total is more than double that of the Top 10, at some 13,616,000 sq miles (35,264,000 sq km), or about a quarter of the world's land area.

2 Australian
Australia*
1,300,000 / 3,400,000

3 Arabian Peninsula
Southwest Asia#
1,000,000 / 2,600,000

1 Sahara
Northern Africa
3,500,000 /
9,100,000

TOP 10 **LONGEST CAVES**

CAVE / LOCATION	TOTAL KNOWN LENGTH	
	MILES	KM
1 Mammoth Cave System, Kentucky, USA	367	590.6
2 Jewel Cave, South Dakota, USA	140	225.4
3 Optimisticeskaja, Ukraine	134	215.0
4 Wind Cave, South Dakota, USA	125	200.8
5 Lechuguilla Cave, New Mexico, USA	122	196.0
6 Hölloch, Switzerland	121	194.2
7 Fisher Ridge System, Kentucky, USA	110	177.3
8 Sistema Ox Bel Ha*, Mexico	102	164.4
9 Sistema Sac Actun*, Mexico	98	157.5
10 Siebenhengste-hohgant, Switzerland	96	154.0

* Underwater cave

Mammoth cave
The Mammoth Cave System, Kentucky, is the world's most extensive. It became a US National Park in 1941 and was designated a World Heritage Site in 1981.

The World's Deepest Cave

At 7,185 ft (2,190 m) the Voronya or Krubera Cave, Georgia, is the world's deepest cave. In January 2001 a team of Ukrainian cave explorers found a branch that extended to a record 5,610 ft (1,710 m). Progressively deeper penetrations have taken its extent to more than seven times the height of the Eiffel Tower.

* Includes Gibson, Great Sandy, Great Victoria, and Simpson
\# Includes an-Nafud and Rub al-Khali
† Includes Kara-Kum and Kyzylkum
§ Includes Great Basin, Mojave, Sonorah, and Chihuahuan

4 Turkestan
Central Asia†
750,000 / 1,900,000

5 = Gobi
central Asia
1,300,000 / 500,000

= North American Desert
USA/Mexico§
500,000 / 1,300,000

7 Patagonia
southern Argentina
260,000 / 670,000

8 Thar
Northwest India/ Pakistan
230,000 / 600,000

9 Kalahari
Southwest Africa
220,000 / 570,000

10 Takla Makan,
Northwest China
185,000 / 480,000

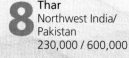

World Weather

TOP 10 **WETTEST PLACES—AVERAGE**

LOCATION* / AVERAGE ANNUAL RAINFALL# (IN / MM)

* Maximum of two places per country listed
# Annual rainfall total, averaged over a long period of years

Source: Philip Eden

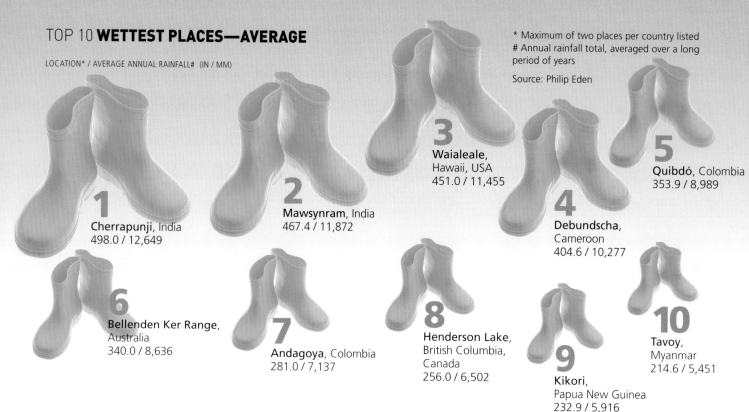

1 Cherrapunji, India
498.0 / 12,649

2 Mawsynram, India
467.4 / 11,872

3 Waialeale, Hawaii, USA
451.0 / 11,455

4 Debundscha, Cameroon
404.6 / 10,277

5 Quibdó, Colombia
353.9 / 8,989

6 Bellenden Ker Range, Australia
340.0 / 8,636

7 Andagoya, Colombia
281.0 / 7,137

8 Henderson Lake, British Columbia, Canada
256.0 / 6,502

9 Kikori, Papua New Guinea
232.9 / 5,916

10 Tavoy, Myanmar
214.6 / 5,451

TOP 10 **PLACES WITH THE HEAVIEST DAILY DOWNPOURS***

LOCATION# / HIGHEST RAINFALL RECORDED IN 24 HOURS (IN / MM)

* Based on limited data
# Maximum of two places per country listed

Source: Philip Eden

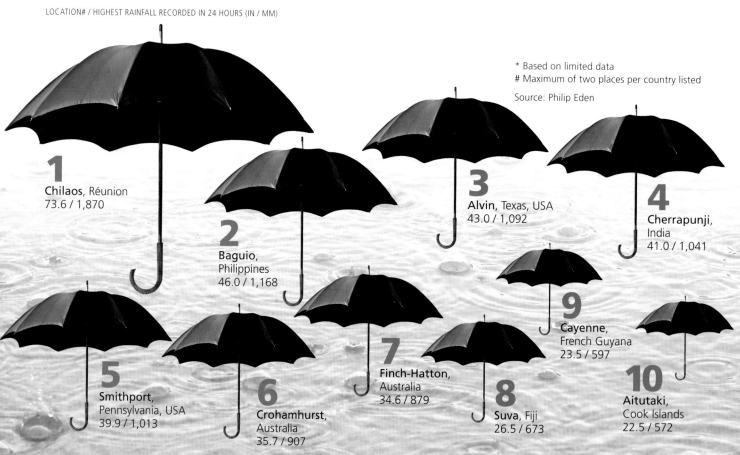

1 Chilaos, Réunion
73.6 / 1,870

2 Baguio, Philippines
46.0 / 1,168

3 Alvin, Texas, USA
43.0 / 1,092

4 Cherrapunji, India
41.0 / 1,041

5 Smithport, Pennsylvania, USA
39.9 / 1,013

6 Crohamhurst, Australia
35.7 / 907

7 Finch-Hatton, Australia
34.6 / 879

8 Suva, Fiji
26.5 / 673

9 Cayenne, French Guyana
23.5 / 597

10 Aitutaki, Cook Islands
22.5 / 572

TOP 10 **COLDEST PLACES— AVERAGE***

LOCATION#	AVERAGE TEMPERATURE °F	°C
1 Plateau†, Antarctica	-70.0	-56.7
2 Amundsen-Scott†, Antarctica	-56.2	-49.0
3 Northice†, Greenland	-22.0	-30.0
4 Eismitte†, Greenland	-20.5	-29.2
5 Resolute, NWT, Canada	-11.6	-24.2
6 Eureka, NWT, Canada	-3.5	-19.7
7 Ostrov Bol'shoy, Lyakhovskiy, Russia	5.5	-14.7
8 Barrow Point, Alaska, USA	9.8	-12.3
9 Barter Island, Alaska, USA	10.2	-12.1
10 Ostrov Vrangela, Russia	11.0	-11.7

* Lowest long-term temperature averaged throughout the year
# Maximum of two places per country listed
† Present or former scientific research base

Source: Philip Eden

TOP 10 **PLACES WITH THE MOST CONTRASTING SEASONS***

LOCATION#	WINTER °F	°C	SUMMER °F	°C	DIFFERENCE °F	°C
1 Verkhoyansk, Russia	-58.5	-50.3	56.5	13.6	115.0	63.9
2 Yakutsk, Russia	-49.0	-45.0	63.5	17.5	112.5	62.5
3 Manzhouli, China	-15.0	-26.1	69.0	20.6	84.0	46.7
4 Fort Yukon, Alaska, USA	-20.2	-29.0	61.4	16.3	81.6	45.3
5 Fort Good Hope, Northwest Territory, Canada	-21.8	-29.9	59.5	15.3	81.3	45.2
6 Brochet, Manitoba, Canada	-20.5	-29.2	59.7	15.4	80.2	44.6
7 Tunka, Mongolia	-16.0	-26.7	61.0	16.1	77.0	42.8
8 Fairbanks, Alaska, USA	-11.2	-24.0	60.1	15.6	71.3	39.6
9 Semipalatinsk, Kazakhstan	0.5	-17.7	69.0	20.6	68.5	38.3
10 Jorgen Bronlund Fjørd, Greenland	-23.6	-30.9	43.5	6.4	67.1	37.3

* Biggest differences between mean monthly temperatures in summer and winter
# Maximum of two places per country listed

Source: Philip Eden

TOP 10 **HOTTEST PLACES— AVERAGE**

LOCATION*	AVERAGE TEMPERATURE# °F	°C
1 Dalol, Ethiopia	94.3	34.6
2 Assab, Eritrea	86.8	30.4
3 Néma, Mauritania	86.5	30.3
4 Berbera, Somalia	86.2	30.1
5 Hombori, Mali	86.1	30.1
6 Perm Island, South Yemen	86.0	30.0
7 Djibouti, Djibouti	85.8	29.9
8 Atbara, Sudan	85.7	29.8
9 =Bender Qaasim, Somalia	85.5	29.7
=Kamaran Island, North Yemen	85.5	29.7

* Maximum of two places per country listed
# Highest long-term temperature averaged throughout the year

Source: Philip Eden

TOP 10 **DRIEST PLACES—AVERAGE**

LOCATION*	AVERAGE ANNUAL RAINFALL# IN	MM
1 Arica, Chile	0.7	0.03
2 =Al'Kufrah, Peru	0.8	0.03
=Aswân, Egypt	0.8	0.03
=Luxor, Egypt	0.8	0.03
5 Ica, Peru	2.3	0.09
6 Wadi Halfa, Sudan	2.6	0.10
7 Iquique, Chile	5.0	0.20
8 Pelican Point, Namibia	8.0	0.03
9 =Aoulef, Algeria	12.0	0.32
=Callao, Peru	12.0	0.32

* Maximum of two places per country listed
# Annual total averaged over a long period of years

Source: Philip Eden

Natural Disasters

THE 10 **COUNTRIES WITH THE MOST DEATHS FROM NATURAL DISASTERS***

COUNTRY / EST. DEATHS FROM NATURAL DISASTERS, 1900–2007

China
12,619,280

India
9,108,609

Soviet Union
3,868,434

Bangladesh
2,970,175

Ethiopia
415,837

Indonesia
237,091

Japan
221,719

Uganda
203,611

Niger
193,999

Pakistan
169,471

World total 31,849,838

* Includes deaths from drought, earthquakes, epidemics, extreme temperatures, floods, insect infestations, landslides, volcanoes, waves/surges, wildfires, windstorms

Source: EM-DAT, CRED, University of Louvain, Belgium

THE 10 **WORST HURRICANES, TYPHOONS, AND CYCLONES**

	LOCATION	DATE	ESTIMATED NO. KILLED
1	Ganges Delta, Bangladesh	Nov 13, 1970	500,000–1,000,000
2	Bengal, India	Oct 7, 1737	>300,000
3	= Coringa, India	Nov 25, 1839	300,000
	= Haiphong, Vietnam	Oct 8, 1881	300,000
5	Bengal, India	Oct 21, 1876	200,000
6	Ganges Delta, Bangladesh	Apr 29, 1991	138,000
7	Bombay, India	Jun 6, 1882	>100,000
8	Southern Japan	Aug 23, 1281	68,000
9	North-east China	Aug 2–3, 1922	60,000
10	Calcutta, India	Oct 5, 1864	50,000–70,000

The cyclone of 1970 hit the Bay of Bengal with winds of over 120 mph (190 km/h). Loss of life was worst in the Bhola region, as a result of which it is often known as the Bhola cyclone. The cyclone that struck India in 1737 churned the river and sea into a 40-ft (12-m) storm surge, flooding land and destroying 20,000 ships.

THE 10 **WORST EARTHQUAKES**

	LOCATION	DATE	ESTIMATED NO. KILLED
1	Near East/Mediterranean	May 20, 1202	1,100,000
2	Shenshi, China	Feb 2, 1556	820,000
3	Calcutta, India	Oct 11, 1737	300,000
4	Antioch, Syria	May 20, AD 526	250,000
5	Tang-shan, China	Jul 28, 1976	242,419
6	Nan-Shan, China	May 22, 1927	200,000
7	Yeddo, Japan	Dec 30, 1703	190,000
8	Kansu, China	Dec 16, 1920	180,000
9	Messina, Italy	Dec 28, 1908	160,000
10	Tokyo/Yokohama, Japan	Sep 1, 1923	142,807

There are some discrepancies between the "official" death tolls in many of the world's worst earthquakes and the estimates of other authorities. A figure of 750,000 is sometimes quoted for the Tang-shan earthquake of 1976. Several other earthquakes in China and Turkey resulted in deaths of 100,000 or more. In recent times, the Armenian earthquake of December 7, 1988 and that which struck northwest Iran on June 21, 1990 resulted in the deaths of over 55,000 (official estimate 28,854) and 50,000 respectively. One of the most famous earthquakes—that which destroyed San Francisco on April 18, 1906—killed between 500 and 1,000, mostly in the fires that followed the shock.

THE 10 **WORST VOLCANIC ERUPTIONS**

	LOCATION	DATE	ESTIMATED NO. KILLED
1	**Tambora**, Indonesia	Apr 5–12, 1815	92,000

The cataclysmic eruption of Tambora on the island of Sumbawa killed about 10,000 islanders immediately, with a further 82,000 dying subsequently from disease and famine resulting from crops being destroyed. An estimated 1.7 million tons of ash were hurled into the atmosphere.

2	**Krakatoa**, Sumatra/Java	Aug 26–27, 1883	36,380

After a series of eruptions over the course of several days, the uninhabited island of Krakatoa exploded with what may have been the biggest bang ever heard by humans, audible up to 3,000 miles (4,800 km) away.

3	**Mont Pelée**, Martinique	May 8, 1902	27,000

After lying dormant for centuries, Mont Pelée began to erupt in April 1902. Assured that there was no danger, the residents of the main city, St. Pierre, stayed in their homes and were there when at 7.30 a.m. on May 8 the volcano burst apart.

4	**Nevado del Ruiz**, Colombia	Nov 13, 1985	22,940

The Andean volcano gave warning signs of erupting, but by the time local inhabitants began to evacuate, it was too late.

5	**Mount Etna**, Sicily	Mar 11, 1669	up to 20,000

Europe's largest volcano (10,760 ft/3,280 m) has erupted frequently, but the worst instance occurred in 1669 when the lava flow engulfed the town of Catania—according to some accounts killing as many as 20,000.

6	**Mount Etna**, Sicily	1169	>15,000

Large numbers died in Catania cathedral, where they believed they would be safe, and more were killed when a tsunami caused by the eruption hit the port of Messina.

7	**Unzen**, Japan	Apr 1, 1792	14,300

During a period of intense volcanic activity in the area, the island of Unzen (or Unsen) completely disappeared, killing all its inhabitants.

8	**Laki**, Iceland	Jan–Jun 1783	9,350

Iceland is one the most volcanically active places on Earth, but being sparsely populated eruptions seldom result in major loss of life. The worst exception occurred at the Laki volcanic ridge, culminating on June 11, with the largest lava flow ever recorded.

9	**Kelut**, Indonesia	May 19, 1919	5,110

Dormant since 1901, Kelut erupted without warning, ejecting a crater lake that killed inhabitants by drowning or in resultant mudslides. The volcano remains active, erupting as recently as 2007.

10	**Galunggung**, Indonesia	Oct 8, 1882	4,011

Galunggung erupted suddenly, spewing boiling mud, burning sulfur, ash, and rocks before finally exploding, destroying a total of 114 villages. A further eruption in 1982 killed 68 people.

LIFE ON EARTH

Extinct & Endangered

TOP 10 **HEAVIEST DINOSAURS EVER DISCOVERED**

	NAME	ESTIMATED WEIGHT (TONS)
1	Bruhathkayosaurus	193–243
2	Amphicoelias	134
3	= Argentinosaurus	88–110
	= Puertasaurus	88–110
5	Argyrosaurus	>88
6	Paralititan	72–88
7	Antarctosaurus	76
8	Sauroposeidon	55–66
9	Brachiosaurus	52–62
10	Supersaurus	44–55

Right: Long leg
Femur of a gigantic Antarctosaurus dinosaur, found in Argentina.

Below: Jumbo sized
Another former inhabitant of Argentina, after which it is named, Argentinosaurus may have weighed as much as ten 10-ton elephants.

THE 10 **FIRST DINOSAURS TO BE NAMED**

	NAME / MEANING	NAMED BY	YEAR
1	Megalosaurus Great lizard	William Buckland	1824
2	Iguanodon Iguana tooth	Gideon Mantell	1825
3	Hylaeosaurus Woodland lizard	Gideon Mantell	1833
4	Macrodontophion Long tooth snake	A. Zborzewski	1834
5	Palaeosaurus Ancient lizard	Samuel Stutchbury and Henry Riley	1836
6	Thecodontosaurus Socket-toothed lizard	Henry Riley and Samuel Stutchbury	1836
7	Plateosaurus Flat lizard	Hermann von Meyer	1837
8	Poekilopleuron Varying side	Jacques Armand and Eudes-Deslongchamps	1838
9	Cetiosaurus Whale lizard	Richard Owen	1841
10	Cladeiodon Branch tooth	Richard Owen	1841

The name Megalosaurus was proposed by William Buckland (1784–1856), an English geologist. The Iguanodon was identified by Gideon Algernon Mantell (1790–1852). In 1822 he (or perhaps his wife Mary) found teeth that resembled enormous versions of those of the Central American iguana lizard, and hence—first in a letter dated November 12, 1824—and then in an article in *Philosophical Transactions*, suggested the name Iguanodon. A number of dinosaurs had been named before the word "dinosaur" itself had been coined: "dinosauria" ("fearfully great lizards") was proposed as a name for the group by Richard Owen in 1842.

Under threat
Indigenous to Borneo, Indonesia, orangutans (whose name means "man of the forest") are among the country's mammal species in danger of extinction as a result of poaching and habitat destruction.

THE 10 **COUNTRIES WITH THE MOST THREATENED BIRD SPECIES**

COUNTRY / TOTAL NO. OF THREATENED BIRDS

1. Brazil 122
2. Indonesia 116
3. Peru 94
4. Colombia 87
5. China 86
6. India 75
7. USA 74
8. New Zealand 70
9. Ecuador 68
10. Philippines 67

Source: 2007 IUCN Red List of Threatened Species

THE 10 **COUNTRIES WITH THE MOST THREATENED REPTILE AND AMPHIBIAN SPECIES**

	COUNTRY	THREATENED REPTILES	AMPHIBIANS	TOTAL
1	Mexico	95	198	293
2	Colombia	15	209	224
3	Ecuador	10	163	173
4	China	31	85	116
5	India	25	63	88
6	Peru	6	80	86
7	= Australia	38	47	85
	= USA	32	53	85
9	Madagascar	20	55	75
10	Malaysia	21	46	67

Source: 2007 IUCN Red List of Threatened Species

THE 10 **COUNTRIES WITH THE MOST THREATENED MAMMAL SPECIES**

COUNTRY / TOTAL NO. OF THREATENED MAMMALS

1. Indonesia 146
2. India 89
3. China 83
4. Brazil 73
5. Mexico 72
6. Australia 64
7. Papua New Guinea 58
8. Philippines 51
9. Malaysia 50
10. Madagascar 47

USA 41

Source: 2007 IUCN Red List of Threatened Species

The IUCN Red List system classifies the degree of threat posed to wildlife on a sliding scale from Vulnerable (high risk of extinction in the wild), through Endangered (very high risk of extinction in the wild), to Critically Endangered (facing an extremely high risk of extinction in the wild), with mammals in these countries under threat in any of these categories. The actual threats are many and varied, and include both human activities and natural events, ranging from habitat loss and degradation, invasions by alien species, hunting, and accidental destruction to persecution, pollution, and natural disasters.

Sea Creatures

TOP 10 **FASTEST FISH**

	FISH / SCIENTIFIC NAME	MAX. RECORDED SPEED MPH	KM/H
1	Sailfish (*Istiophorus platypterus*)	69	112
2	Striped marlin (*Tetrapturus audax*)	50	80
3	Wahoo (peto, jack mackerel) (*Acanthocybium solandri*)	48	77
4	Southern bluefin tuna (*Thunnus maccoyii*)	47	76
5	Yellowfin tuna (*Thunnus albacares*)	46	74
6	Blue shark (*Prionace glauca*)	43	69
7 =	Bonefish (*Albula vulpes*)	40	64
=	Swordfish (*Xiphias gladius*)	40	64
9	Tarpon (ox-eye herring) (*Megalops cyprinoides*)	35	56
10	Tiger shark (*Galeocerdo cuvier*)	33	53

Source: Lucy T. Verma

Jaws of death
The great white shark, star of the Jaws films, is rightly feared as the type responsible for 38 percent of all recorded attacks and 47 percent of fatalities.

TOP 10 **LONGEST-LIVED MARINE ANIMALS**

	ANIMAL / SCIENTIFIC NAME	MAX. LIFESPAN (YEARS)
1	Quahog (marine clam) (*Arctica islandica*)	220*
2	Bowhead whale (*Balaena mysticetus*)	200
3 =	Alligator snapping turtle (*Macrochelys temminckii*)	150
=	Whale shark (*Rhincodon typus*)	150
5	Sea anemone (*Actina mesembryanthemum*, etc.)	90
6	European eel (*Anguilla anguilla*)	88
7	Lake sturgeon (*Acipenser fulvescens*)	82
8	Freshwater mussel (*Palaeoheterodonta* – various)	80
9	Dugong (*Dugong dugon*)	73
10	Spiny dogfish (*Squalus acanthias*)	70

* Claim of 405-year old specimen caught off Iceland in 2007

At the other end of the scale, several fish have lifespans that are completed within a year, among them the white goby, top minnow, seahorse, dwarf pygmy goby, and ice fish, while the tropical killifish seldom lives for more than about eight months.

Ancient Ocean Quahog

Although a 220-year-old quahog clam found in 1982 holds the official record as the longest-lived animal, a specimen of *Arctica islandica*, the ocean quahog, discovered off the Iceland coast and studied at Bangor University, Wales, in 2007, was found to have some 405 annual growth rings, indicating it may have been alive when Shakespeare was writing *Hamlet*.

THE 10 **TYPES OF SHARK THAT HAVE KILLED THE MOST HUMANS**

SHARK SPECIES   UNPROVOKED ATTACKS*   TOTAL / FATALITIES#

1 Great white 237 / 64	2 Tiger 88 / 28	3 Bull 77 / 23	4 Requiem (species) 30 / 8
5 Blue 12 / 4	6 = Sand tiger 30 / 2	= Shortfin mako 8 / 2	
8 = Blacktip 28 / 1	= Oceanic whitetip 5 / 1	= Dusky 3 / 1	= Galapagos 1 / 1

* 1580–2007   # Where fatalities are equal, entries are ranked by total attacks

Source: International Shark Attack File, Florida Museum of Natural History

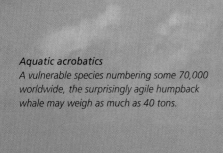

Aquatic acrobatics
A vulnerable species numbering some 70,000 worldwide, the surprisingly agile humpback whale may weigh as much as 40 tons.

TOP 10 **LARGEST WHALES**

	SPECIES / SCIENTIFIC NAME	LENGTH (RANGE) FT	M
1	Blue whale (*Balaenoptera musculus*)	69–88.5	21–27
2	Fin whale (*Balaenoptera physalus*)	59–72.25	18–22
3	Bowhead whale (*Balaena mysticetus*)	46–59	14–18
4	Sei whale (*Balaenoptera borealis*)	39.5–52.5	12–16
5	= Northern/Southern right whale (*Eubalaenaglacialis/Eubalaena australis*)	36–59	11–18
	= Sperm whale (*Physeter macrocephalus*)	36–59	11–18
7	Gray whale (*Eschrichtius robustus*)	39.5–46	12–14
8	Humpback whale (*Megaptera novaeangliae*)	37.75–49.25	11.5–15
9	Bryde's whale (*Balaenoptera brydei*)	37.75–47.5	11.5–14.5
10	Baird's beaked whale (*Berardius bairdii*)	35–42	10.7–12.8

TOP 10 **HEAVIEST SPECIES OF SALTWATER FISH CAUGHT**

	SPECIES / SCIENTIFIC NAME	ANGLER / LOCATION / DATE	WEIGHT LB	OZ	KG	G
1	Great white shark (*Carcharodon carcharias*)	Alfred Dean, Ceduna, South Australia, Apr 21, 1959	2,664	0	1,208	380
2	Tiger shark (*Galeocerdo cuvier*)	Kevin James Clapson, Ulladulla, Australia, Mar 28, 2004	1,785	11	809	975
3	Greenland shark (*Somniosus Microcephalus*)	Terje Nordtvedt, Trondheimsfjord, Norway, Oct 18, 1987	1,708	9	774	991
4	Black marlin (*Istiompax marlina*)	Alfred C. Glassell Jr., Cabo Blanco, Peru, Aug 4, 1953	1,560	0	707	610
5	Bluefin tuna (*Thunnus thynnus*)	Ken Fraser, Aulds Cove, Nova Scotia, Canada, Oct 26, 1979	1,496	0	678	580
6	Atlantic blue marlin (*Makaira nigricans*)	Paulo Amorim, Vitoria, Brazil, Feb 29, 1992	1,402	2	636	993
7	Pacific blue marlin (*Makaira nigricans*)	Jay W. de Beaubien, Kaaiwi Point, Kona, May 31, 1982	1,376	0	624	140
8	Sixgilled shark (*Hexanchus griseus*)	Clemens Rump, Ascension Island, Nov 21, 2002	1,298	0	588	760
9	Great hammerhead shark (*Sphyrna mokarran*)	Bucky Dennis, Boca Grande, Florida, USA, May 23, 2006	1,280	0	580	598
10	Shortfin mako shark (*Isurus oxyrinchus*)	Luke Sweeney, Chatham, Massachusetts, USA, Jul 21, 2001	1,221	0	553	840

Source: International Game Fish Association

Land Mammals

THE 10 **SLOWEST MAMMALS**

	MAMMAL / SCIENTIFIC NAME	AVERAGE SPEED* MPH	KM/H
1	Three-toed sloth (*Bradypus variegatus*)	0.06–0.19	0.1–0.3
2	Short-tailed (giant mole) shrew (*Blarina brevicauda*)	1.4	2.2
3	= Pine vole (*Microtus pinetorum*)	2.6	4.2
	= Red-backed vole (*Clethrionomys gapperi*)	2.6	4.2
5	Opossum (order *Didelphimorphia*)	2.7	4.4
6	Deer mouse (order *Peromyscus*)	2.8	4.5
7	Woodland jumping mouse (*Napaeozapus insignis*)	3.3	5.3
8	Meadow jumping mouse (*Zapus hudsonius*)	3.4	5.5
9	Meadow mouse or meadow vole (*Microtus pennsylvanicus*)	4.1	6.6
10	White-footed mouse (*Peromyscus leucopus*)	4.2	6.8

* Of those species for which data available

TOP 10 **LAND ANIMALS WITH THE BIGGEST BRAINS**

	ANIMAL SPECIES	AVERAGE BRAIN WEIGHT LB	OZ	G
1	Elephant	13	4	6,000
2	Adult human	3	0	1,350
3	Camel	1	11	762
4	Giraffe	1	8	680
5	Hippopotamus	1	4	582
6	Horse	1	3	532
7	Gorilla	1	1	500
8	Polar bear	1	1	498
9	Cow	0	15	445
10	Chimpanzee	0	15	420

Brain power
Elephant brain (background) in comparison with the brain of an adult human (red) and a chimpanzee (blue).

TOP 10 **SLEEPIEST MAMMALS**

ANIMAL / SCIENTIFIC NAME / AVERAGE HOURS OF SLEEP PER DAY

 1 = Lion (*Panthera leo*) 20

= Three-toed sloth (*Bradypus variegatus*) 20

 3 Little brown bat (*Myotis lucifugus*) 19.9

 4 Big brown bat (*Eptesicus fuscus*) 19.7

 5 = Opossum (*Didelphis virginiana*) 19.4

= Water opossum (Yapok) (*Chironectes minimus*) 19.4

 7 Giant armadillo (*Priodontes maximus*) 18.1

 8 Koala (*Phascolarctos cinereus*) up to 18

 9 Nine-banded armadillo (*Dasypus novemcinctus*) 17.4

10 Southern owl monkey (*Aotus azarai*) 17.0

The list excludes periods of hibernation, which can last up to several months among creatures such as the ground squirrel, marmot, and brown bear. Marsupials such as the pygmy possum may remain dormant for a year.

Weighty weight
The lengthy gestation of an African elephant is 380 days longer than the average for a human.

TOP 10 **FASTEST MAMMALS**

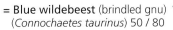

MAMMAL / SCIENTIFIC NAME / MAX. RECORDED SPEED* MPH / KM/H

Cheetah (*Acinonyx jubatus*) 71 / 114

Pronghorn antelope (*Antilocapra americana*) 57 / 95

= Blue wildebeest (brindled gnu) (*Connochaetes taurinus*) 50 / 80
= Lion (*Panthera leo*) 50 / 80
= Springbok (*Antidorcas marsupialis*) 50 / 80

= Brown hare (*Lepus capensis*) 48 / 77
= Red fox (*Vulpes vulpes*) 48 / 77

= Grant's gazelle (*Gazella granti*) 47 / 76
= Thomson's gazelle (*Gazella thomsonii*) 47 / 76

Horse (*Equus caballus*) 45 / 72

* Of those species for which data available

TOP 10 **MAMMALS WITH THE LONGEST GESTATION PERIODS**

MAMMAL / SCIENTIFIC NAME	AVERAGE GESTATION (DAYS)
1 African elephant (*Loxodonta africana*)	660
2 Asiatic elephant (*Elephas maximus*)	600
3 White rhinoceros (*Ceratotherium simum*)	490
4 Walrus (*Odobenus rosmarus*)	480
5 = Black rhinoceros (*Diceros bicornis*)	450
= Giraffe (*Giraffa camelopardalis*)	450
7 Bactrian camel (dromedary) (*Camelus bactrianus*)	410
8 Tapir (*Tapirus*)	400
9 Arabian camel (dromedary) (*Camelus dromedarius*)	390
10 Grant's zebra (*Equus quagga*)	365

Fastest feline
The cheetah is capable of accelerating faster than most sportscars, and holds the world record speed for a land animal over short distances.

Creepy Crawlies

Long story
For over a century naturalists have sought to confirm the existence of giant anacondas, so far without success.

TOP 10 **LONGEST SNAKES**

SNAKE / SCIENTIFIC NAME	MAX. LENGTH	
	FT	M
1 Reticulated (royal) python (*Python reticulatus*)	32	10.0
2 Anaconda (*Eunectes murinus*)	28	8.5
3 Indian python (*Python molurus molurus*)	25	7.6
4 Diamond python (*Morelia spilota spilota*)	21	6.4
5 King cobra (*Opiophagus hannah*)	19	5.8
6 Boa constrictor (*Boa constrictor*)	16	4.9
7 Bushmaster (*Lachesis muta*)	12	3.7
8 Giant brown snake (*Oxyuranus scutellatus*)	11	3.4
9 Diamondback rattlesnake (*Crotalus atrox*)	9	2.7
10 Indigo or gopher snake (*Drymarchon corais*)	8	2.4

US president and hunting enthusiast Theodore Roosevelt offered $1,000 as a reward for an anaconda of more than 30 ft (9 m). The prize now stands at $50,000, but remains unclaimed. The four largest snakes are all constrictors; the king cobra is the longest venomous snake.

THE 10 **DEADLIEST SNAKES**

SNAKE / SCIENTIFIC NAME	EST. LETHAL DOSE FOR HUMANS (MG)	AVERAGE VENOM PER BITE (MG)	POTENTIAL HUMANS KILLED PER BITE
1 Coastal taipan (*Oxyuranus scutellatus*)	1	120	120
2 Common krait (*Bungarus caeruleus*)	0.5	42	84
3 Philippine cobra (*Naja naja philippinensis*)	2	120	60
4 = King cobra (*Ophiophagus hannah*)	20	1,000	50
= Russell's viper (*Daboia russelli*)	3	150	50
6 Black mamba (*Dendroaspis polyepis*)	3	135	45
7 Yellow-jawed tommygoff (*Bothrops asper*)	25	1,000	40
8 = Multibanded krait (*Bungarus multicinctus*)	0.8	28	35
= Tiger snake (*Notechis scutatus*)	1	35	35
10 Jararacussu (*Bothrops jarararcussu*)	25	800	32

Source: Russell E. Gough

This list takes account of the various factors that determine the relative danger posed by poisonous snakes, including the strength of the venom (and hence the estimated lethal dose for an adult), and the typical amount injected per bite.

Along came a spider
The Heteropoda maxima *huntsman spiders of Laos have a legspan of up to 1 ft (30 cm).*

TOP 10 **MOST COMMON INSECTS** *

SPECIES / SCIENTIFIC NAME	APPROX. NO. OF KNOWN SPECIES
1 Beetles (*Coleoptera*)	400,000
2 Ants, bees and wasps (*Hymenoptera*)	250,000
3 Butterflies and moths (*Lepidoptera*)	190,000
4 True flies (*Diptera*)	120,000
5 True bugs (*Hemiptera*)	100,000
6 Crickets, grasshoppers and locusts (*Orthoptera*)	20,000
7 Caddisflies (*Trichoptera*)	12,627
8 Dragonflies and damselflies (*Odonata*)	5,600
9 Lice (*Phthiraptera/Psocoptera*)	5,000
10 Lacewings (*Neuroptera*)	4,700

* By number of known species

Triton's trumpet trumps
The Triton's trumpet sea snail is among the biggest marine snails. The largest land gastropod, the giant Ghana snail, measures barely half its size.

TOP 10 **LARGEST SNAILS**

SNAIL / SCIENTIFIC NAME	LENGTH IN	MM
1 Australian trumpet (*Syrinx aruanus*)	30.3	770
2 Horse conch (*Pleuroploc filamentosa*)	22.8	580
3 = Baler shell (*Voluta amphora*)	18.8	480
= Triton's trumpet (*Charonia tritonis*)	18.8	480
5 Beck's volute (*Voluta becki*)	18.5	470
6 Umbilicate volute (*Voluta umbilicalis*)	16.5	420
7 Madagascar helmet (*Cassis madagascariensis*)	16.1	409
8 Spider conch (*Lambis truncata*)	15.7	400
9 Knobbly trumpet (*Charonia nodifera*)	15.3	390
10 Goliath conch (*Strombus goliath*)	14.9	380

TOP 10 **LARGEST SPIDERS**

SPECIES	LEGSPAN IN	MM
1 Huntsman spider (*Heteropoda maxima*)	11.8	300
2 Brazilian salmon pink (*Lasiodora parahybana*)	10.6	270
3 Brazilian giant tawny red (*Grammostola mollicoma*)	10.2	260
4 = Goliath tarantula or bird-eating spider (*Theraphosa blondi*)	10.0	254
= Wolf spider (*Cupiennius sallei*)	10.0	254
6 = Purple bloom bird-eating (*Xenesthis immanis*)	9.1	230
= Xenesthis monstrosa	9.1	230
8 Hercules baboon (*Hysterocrates hercules*)	8.0	203
9 Hysterocrates sp.	7.0	178
10 Tegenaria parietin	5.5	140

It should be noted that although these represent the average legspans of the world's largest spiders, their body size is often considerably smaller: that of the *Lasiodora*, found in Brazil, is around 3.6 in (92 mm), while that of the *Tegenaris parietina*, the largest spider found in Britain, may measure as little as 0.7 in (18 mm).

Birdlife

TOP 10 **HEAVIEST FLIGHTED BIRDS***

BIRD / SCIENTIFIC NAME	WEIGHT		
	LB	OZ	KG
1 Mute swan (*Cygnus olor*)	49	6	22.50
2 Kori bustard (*Ardeotis kori*)	41	8	19.00
3 = Andean condor (*Vultur gryphus*)	33	1	15.00
= Great white pelican (*Pelecanus onocrotalus*)	33	1	15.00
5 Eurasian black vulture (*Aegypius monachus*)	27	5	12.50
6 Sarus crane (*Grus antigone*)	26	9	12.24
7 Himalayan griffon (vulture) (*Gyps himalayensis*)	26	5	12.00
8 Wandering albatross (*Diomedea exulans*)	24	9	11.30
9 Steller's sea eagle (*Haliaeetus pelagicus*)	19	8	9.00
10 Marabou stork (*Leptoptilos crumeniferus*)	19	6	8.90

* By species

Source: Chris Mead

Biggest Bird

Aepyornis maximus, the so-called elephant bird, was the largest known bird. It was flightless and stood some 10 ft (3 m) tall, and weighed about 1,000 lb (454 kg). Its eggs, the biggest on record, measured 12 in (30 cm) in length and had a volume equivalent to more than seven ostrich eggs or 180 chicken's eggs. It lived only on the island of Madagascar and probably became extinct sometime during the seventeenth century.

Heavyweight champion
Exceptionally large specimens of the mute swan establish it as the heaviest of all flighted birds, with a wingspan of more than 6 ft 7 in (2 m).

TOP 10 **FASTEST BIRDS IN FLIGHT**

BIRD / SCIENTIFIC NAME	MAX. RECORDED FLYING SPEED	
	MPH	KM/H
1 Common eider (*Somateria mollissima*)	47	76
2 Bewick's swan (*Cygnus columbianus*)	44	72
3 = Barnacle goose (*Branta leucopsis*)	42	68
= Common crane (*Grus grus*)	42	68
5 Mallard (*Anas platyrhynchos*)	40	65
6 = Red-throated loon (*Gavia stellata*)	38	61
= Wood pigeon (*Columba palumbus*)	38	61
8 Oystercatcher (*Haematopus ostralegus*)	36	58
9 = Ring-necked pheasant (*Phasianus colchichus*)	33	54
= White-fronted goose (*Anser albifrons*)	33	54

Source: Chris Mead

TOP 10 **MOST COMMON CHRISTMAS BIRDS IN THE USA***

BIRD	SAMPLE
1 European starling	371,437
2 American crow	250,642
3 Mallard	227,869
4 Canada goose	204,373
5 Dark-eyed junco	147,384
6 Bohemian waxwing	146,750
7 Black-capped chickadee	140,971
8 House sparrow	137,371
9 Rock pigeon	127,371
10 Glaucus-winged gull	119,326

* Based on the 106th Christmas Bird Count

Winged wonder
The wandering albatross has a wingspan equal to the height of two 6-ft (2-m) humans.

TOP 10 **BIRDS WITH THE LARGEST WINGSPANS**

BIRD* / SCIENTIFIC NAME	MAX. WINGSPAN IN	CM
1 Wandering albatross# (*Diomedea exulans*)	146	370
2 Great white pelican (*Pelecanus onocrotalus*)	141	360
3 Andean condor (*Vultur gryphus*)	126	320
4 Himalayan griffon (vulture) (*Gyps himalayensis*)	122	310
5 Eurasian black vulture (*Aegypius monachus*)	116	295
6 Marabou stork (*Leptoptilos crumeniferus*)	113	287
7 Lammergeier (*Gypaetus barbatus*)	111	282
8 Sarus crane (*Grus antigone*)	110	280
9 Kori bustard (*Ardeotis kori*)	106	270
10 Steller's sea eagle (*Haliaeetus pelagicus*)	104	265

* By species
# Royal albatross, a close relative, is the same size

Source: Chris Mead

The measurements given are, as far as can be ascertained, for wingtip to wingtip for live birds measured in a natural position—much larger wingspans have been claimed for many species, but dead specimens may easily be stretched by 15 to 20 percent.

TOP 10 **LONGEST-LIVED RINGED WILD BIRDS**

BIRD / SCIENTIFIC NAME	AGE* YEARS	MONTHS
1 Royal albatross (*Diomedea epomophora*)	50	0
2 Fulmar (*Fulmarus glacialis*)	40	11
3 Manx shearwater (*Puffinus puffinus*)	37	0
4 Gannet (*Morus bassanus*)	36	4
5 Oystercatcher (*Haematopus ostralegus*)	36	0
6 White (Fairy) tern (*Gygis alba*)	35	11
7 Common eider (*Somateria mollissima*)	35	0
8 Lesser Black-backed gull (*Larus fuscus*)	34	10
9 Pink-footed goose (*Anser brachyrhynchus*)	34	2
10 Great frigate bird (*Fregata minor*)	33	9

* Elapsed time between marking and report

Source: Chris Mead

Only by ringing can the true age of a wild bird be reliably monitored. Hard rings, likely to last as long as the bird, started to be used over 50 years ago. Land-based songbirds do not live as long as the slow-breeding seabirds. In general, big birds live longer than small ones, so the tiny Fairy tern (*Sterna nereis*) and Storm petrel (*Hydrobates pelagicus*), at 31 years 11 months, are particularly noteworthy. Records of birds in captivity are even more impressive.

Cats & Dogs

TOP 10 PEDIGREE CAT BREEDS IN THE USA

1. Persian
2. Maine coon
3. Exotic
4. Siamese
5. Ragdoll
6. Abyssinian
7. Birman
8. American shorthair
9. Oriental
10. Sphynx

Source: The Cat Fanciers' Association

TOP 10 CAT NAMES IN THE USA*

1. Tigger
2. Tiger
3. Max
4. Smokey
5. Sam
6. Kitty
7. Sassy
8. Shadow
9. Simba
10. Patch

* Based on a survey of the most popular names on pet identification tags

TOP 10 BESTSELLING BRANDS OF CAT FOOD

BRAND / MANUFACTURER / % BRAND SHARE BY VALUE

1	Whiskas (Mars)	14.4
2	Friskies (Nestlé)	12.4
3	Iams (Procter & Gamble)	5.6
4	Felix (Nestlé)	4.6
5	Hill's Science Diet (Colgate-Palmolive)	4.4
6	Kitekat (Mars)	4.3
7 =	Cat Chow (Nestlé)	2.9
=	Sheba (Mars)	2.9
9	Fancy Feast (Nestlé)	1.9
10 =	Meow Mix (Meow Mix)	1.8
= 9	Lives (Del Monte Foods)	1.8

Source: Euromonitor International

The world market for prepared cat food grew by 10.4 percent in the period 2000–05. An estimated 5.1 million tons, worth a total of $16.2 billion, were sold globally in 2005.

Left: Top cat
The increasingly popular Maine coon is one of the largest of all domestic cats. Its name derives from the myth that they are the offspring of a cat and a raccoon.

TOP 10 DOGS' NAMES IN THE USA

2007		1987
Max	1	Lady
Jake	2	King
Buddy	3	Duke
Maggie	4	Peppy
Bear	5	Prince
Molly	6	Pepper
Bailey	7	Snoopy
Shadow	8	Princess
Sam	9	Heidi
Lady	10	Sam

Surveys of names appearing on dog licenses in 1987 and pet identification tags in 2007 both produced lists that demonstrate the trend for dogs' names to become increasingly humanized. The earlier list also exposed a number of bizarre dogs' names, including Beowulf, Bikini, Rembrandt, and Twit.

TOP 10 PEDIGREE DOG BREEDS IN THE USA

BREED / NO. REGISTERED BY AMERICAN KENNEL CLUB 2006

1 Labrador retriever 123,760
2 Yorkshire terrier 48,346
3 German shepherd 43,575
4 Golden retriever 42,962
5 Beagle 39,484
6 Dachshund 36,033
7 Boxer 35,388
8 Poodle 29,939
9 Shih Tzu 27,282
10 Miniature schnauzer 22,920

Source: The American Kennel Club

TOP 10 BESTSELLING BRANDS OF DOG FOOD

BRAND / MANUFACTURER / % BRAND SHARE BY VALUE

1 Pedigree (Mars) 13.2
2 Hill's Science Diet (Colgate-Palmolive) 5.7
3 Iams (Procter & Gamble) 4.7
4 Dog Chow (Nestlé) 4.0
5 Friskies (Nestlé) 2.7
6 Pal (Mars) 2.3
7 Eukanuba (Procter & Gamble) 2.2
8 Alpo (Nestlé) 2.1
9 Royal Canin (Mars) 2.0
10 Cesar (Mars) 1.8

The world market for dog food grew by 17.7 percent in the period 2000–05. Globally, some 12.4 million tons, worth $25.9 billion, were sold in 2005.

Source: Euromonitor International

Livestock

TOP 10 **TYPES OF LIVESTOCK**

ANIMAL / WORLD STOCKS

1 animal represents approx. 500,000,000

1 Chickens 16,365,353,100 **2** Cattle 1,364,950,514 **3** Sheep 1,059,810,132 **4** Ducks 1,032,257,000 **5** Pigs 943,762,330

Source (all livestock lists): Food and Agriculture Organization of the United Nations (latest available year)

TOP 10 **CHICKEN COUNTRIES**

	COUNTRY	CHICKENS
1	China	4,214,748,000
2	USA	1,970,000,000
3	Indonesia	1,149,374,000
4	Brazil	1,100,000,000
5	= India	425,000,000
	= Mexico	425,000,000
7	Russia	328,338,000
8	Iran	290,000,000
9	Japan	284,926,000
10	Turkey	277,533,000
	World total	*16,365,353,100*

TOP 10 **CATTLE COUNTRIES**

	COUNTRY	CATTLE
1	Brazil	204,512,736
2	India	185,500,000
3	China	112,536,523
4	USA	94,888,000
5	Argentina	50,768,000
6	Sudan	38,325,000
7	Ethiopia	38,102,688
8	Mexico	31,700,000
9	Australia	27,460,000
10	Colombia	24,950,000
	World total	*1,364,950,514*

TOP 10 **SHEEP COUNTRIES**

	COUNTRY	SHEEP
1	China	157,330,215
2	Australia	101,300,000
3	India	62,500,000
4	Iran	54,000,000
5	Sudan	48,000,000
6	New Zealand	39,271,000
7	UK	35,848,000
8	Turkey	25,431,000
9	South Africa	25,360,000
10	Pakistan	24,700,000
	USA	*6,105,000*
	World total	*1,059,810,132*

Cash cows
Brazil's ranking as the worlds No. 1 cattle country has been achieved at huge cost, as forests have been cleared to create pastureland.

6 Goats 790,028,397   **7** Rabbits 526,412,890   **8** Geese 295,127,500   **9** Turkeys 276,552,000   **10** Buffaloes 171,954,765

TOP 10 **PIG COUNTRIES**

COUNTRY	PIGS
1 China	472,895,791
2 USA	60,443,700
3 Brazil	33,085,300
4 Germany	26,495,000
5 Vietnam	26,143,728
6 Spain	24,894,956
7 Poland	16,987,900
8 Russia	15,979,833
9 France	15,004,320
10 Mexico	14,625,199
World total	*943,762,330*

TOP 10 **TURKEY COUNTRIES**

COUNTRY	TURKEYS
1 USA	88,000,000
2 France	33,648,000
3 Chile	25,700,000
4 Italy	25,000,000
5 Brazil	16,200,000
6 Germany	9,000,000
7 UK	8,300,000
8 Portugal	7,000,000
9 Slovakia	5,800,000
10 Canada	5,520,000
World total	*276,552,000*

TOP 10 **DUCK COUNTRIES**

COUNTRY	DUCKS
1 China	710,361,000
2 Vietnam	59,000,000
3 India	33,000,000
4 Indonesia	32,572,000
5 France	22,870,000
6 Ukraine	20,000,000
7 Malaysia	16,000,000
8 Thailand	15,649,000
9 Bangladesh	11,700,000
10 Philippines	10,211,000
USA	*6,900,000*
World total	*1,032,257,000*

Ducks in a row
*A major item on the national menu, two of
every three of the world's ducks are in China.*

Living off the Land

TOP 10 FRUIT CROPS

CROP / ANNUAL PRODUCTION (TONS)

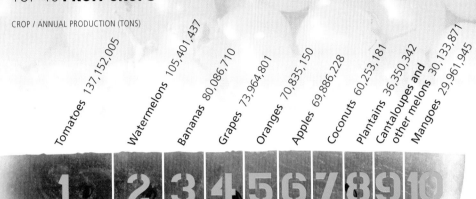

1. Tomatoes 137,152,005
2. Watermelons 105,401,437
3. Bananas 80,086,710
4. Grapes 73,964,801
5. Oranges 70,835,150
6. Apples 69,886,228
7. Coconuts 60,253,181
8. Plantains 36,350,342
9. Cantaloupes and other melons 30,133,871
10. Mangoes 29,961,945

The status of the tomato is controversial: botanically, it is a fruit, but, based on its use in cooking, for legal and import duty purposes certain countries consider it a vegetable.

TOP 10 BANANA-PRODUCING COUNTRIES

COUNTRY / ANNUAL PRODUCTION (TONS)

1. India 18,540,876
2. Brazil 7,257,136
3. China 6,884,926
4. Ecuador 6,655,840
5. Philippines 6,207,335
6. Indonesia 5,373,149
7. Costa Rica 2,447,131
8. Mexico 2,314,853
9. Thailand 2,204,623
10. Burundi 1,763,698

USA 8,245
World total 80,086,710

TOP 10 VEGETABLE CROPS

CROP / ANNUAL PRODUCTION (TONS)

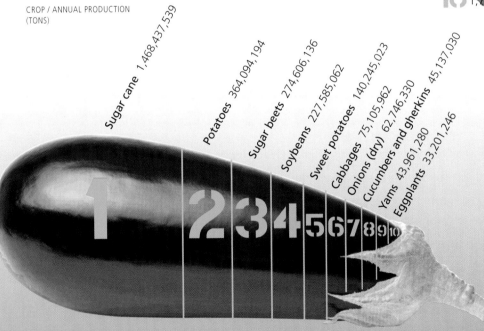

1. Sugar cane 1,468,437,539
2. Potatoes 364,094,194
3. Sugar beets 274,606,136
4. Soybeans 227,585,062
5. Sweet potatoes 140,245,023
6. Cabbages 75,105,962
7. Onions (dry) 62,746,330
8. Cucumbers and gherkins 45,137,030
9. Yams 43,961,280
10. Eggplants 33,201,246

TOP 10 CEREAL CROPS

CROP / ANNUAL PRODUCTION (TONS)

1. Maize 798,722,647
2. Wheat 697,316,315
3. Rice (paddy) 668,296,012
4. Barley 169,909,127
5. Sorghum 64,717,745
6. Millet 30,609,248
7. Oats 28,721,593
8. Rye 19,457,602
9. Triticale (wheat/rye hybrid) 15,293,952
10. Mixed grain 5,974,813

Source (all lists this page): Food and Agriculture Organization of the United Nations (latest available year)

TOP 10 **SUNFLOWER SEED-PRODUCING COUNTRIES**

	COUNTRY	ANNUAL PRODUCTION (TONS)
1	Russia	5,291,877
2	Argentina	3,417,165
3	Ukraine	3,362,160
4	China	1,929,045
5	Romania	1,717,195
6	France	1,611,036
7	India	1,349,228
8	Hungary	1,307,540
9	Bulgaria	1,189,209
10	USA	1,024,808
	World total	29,064,150

Source: Food and Agriculture Organization of the United Nations (latest available year)

Bearing fruit
Of all countries, the USA has undergone the greatest increase in organic acreage as, despite high costs and low yields, the demand for organically grown crops such as strawberries escalates.

TOP 10 **ORGANIC FARMING COUNTRIES**

	COUNTRY	TOTAL ORGANIC FARMING LAND ACRES	HECTARES
1	Australia	29,158,390	11,800,000
2	Argentina	7,658,839	3,099,427
3	China	5,683,415	2,300,000
4	USA	4,003,968	1,620,351
5	Italy	2,636,862	1,067,102
6	Brazil	2,080,624	842,000
7	Spain	1,995,543	807,569
8	Germany	1,995,141	807,406
9	Uruguay	1,875,527	759,000
10	UK	1,531,685	619,852
	World total	75,510,798	30,558,183

Source: International Federation of Organic Agriculture Movements, *The World of Organic Agriculture*, 2007

Starting some 70 years ago as a reaction to the use of artificial fertilizers, and for long a minority movement, organic farming has gained such momentum and widespread public support in recent years that the world total area of land devoted to organic production is now, at 117,985 sq miles (305,582 sq km), greater than the size of Italy.

TOP 10 **ORGANIC CROPS***

	CROP	TOTAL ORGANIC FARMING LAND ACRES	HECTARES
1	Olives	875,938	354,480
2	Coffee	765,000	309,585
3	Fruits and nuts	417,096	168,793
4	Grapes	256,166	103,667
5	Tropical fruits	244,164	98,810
6	Cocoa	189,594	76,726
7	Citrus fruit	82,800	33,508
8	Tea	76,059	30,780
9	Sugar cane	26,302	10,644
10	Medicinal and aromatic plants	4,310	1,744
	Special crops (oil palm, hops, etc.)	*50,180*	*20,307*
	Other permanent crops	*455,580*	*188,414*

* Permanent crops only

Source: International Federation of Organic Agriculture Movements, *The World of Organic Agriculture*, 2007

In addition to these permanent crops, which occupy a total of 3,443,643 acres (1,393,595 hectares), some 3,571,809 acres (1,445,462 hectares) worldwide are devoted to cereal production.

Trees & Forests

TOP 10 **DEFORESTING COUNTRIES***

COUNTRY / ANNUAL FOREST LOSS (2000–05) SQ MILES/SQ KM

1 AXE REPRESENTS APPROX. 386 SQ MILES (1,000 SQ KM)

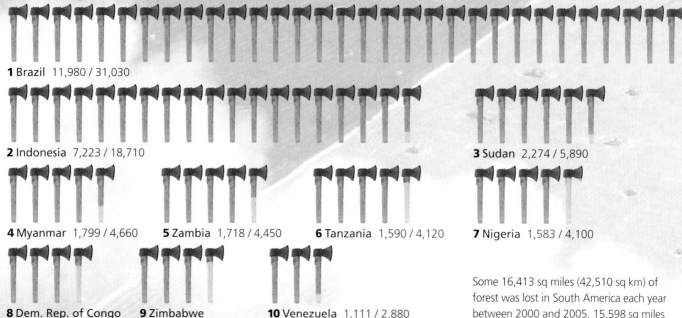

1 Brazil 11,980 / 31,030

2 Indonesia 7,223 / 18,710

3 Sudan 2,274 / 5,890

4 Myanmar 1,799 / 4,660   **5** Zambia 1,718 / 4,450   **6** Tanzania 1,590 / 4,120   **7** Nigeria 1,583 / 4,100

8 Dem. Rep. of Congo
1,231 / 3,190

9 Zimbabwe
1,208 / 3,130

10 Venezuela 1,111 / 2,880

World total 28,251 / 73,170

* Countries for which data available

Source: Food and Agriculture Organization of
the United Nations, *Global Forest Resources
Assessment 2005*

Some 16,413 sq miles (42,510 sq km) of
forest was lost in South America each year
between 2000 and 2005, 15,598 sq miles
(40,400 sq km) in Africa, and 14,826 sq
miles (38,400 sq km) in Asia. The total
global loss during the period was 169,506
sq miles (439,020 sq km), an area equivalent
to more than three times that of the UK.

TOP 10 **REFORESTING COUNTRIES***

COUNTRY / ANNUAL FOREST GAIN (2000–05) SQ MILES/SQ KM

1 TREE REPRESENTS APPROX. 386 SQ MILES (1,000 SQ KM)

1 China 15,629 / 40,480   **2** Spain 1,142 / 2,960   **3** Vietnam 930 / 2,410   **4** USA 613 / 1,590   **5** Italy 409 / 1,060

6 Chile
220 / 570

7 Cuba
216 / 560

8 Bulgaria
193 / 500

9 France
158 / 410

10 Portugal
154 / 400

* Countries for which data available

Source: Food and Agriculture
Organization of the United Nations,
*Global Forest Resources Assessment
2005*

TOP 10 COUNTRIES WITH THE LARGEST AREAS OF TROPICAL FOREST

	COUNTRY	SQ MILES	AREA SQ KM
1	Brazil	1,163,222	3,012,730
2	Dem. Rep. of Congo	521,512	1,350,710
3	Indonesia	343,029	887,440
4	Peru	292,032	756,360
5	Bolivia	265,012	686,380
6	Venezuela	214,730	556,150
7	Columbia	205,352	531,860
8	Mexico	176,700	457,650
9	India	171,622	444,500
10	Angola	145,035	375,640
	World total	*5,434,964*	*14,076,490*

Source: Food and Agriculture Organization of the United Nations, *State of the World's Forests, 2005*

Brazilian rainforest
Despite losing an area the size of Belgium every year, Brazil retains the world's greatest area of rainforest.

TOP 10 COUNTRIES WITH THE LARGEST AREAS OF FOREST

	COUNTRY	SQ MILES	% OF TOTAL	SQ KM
1	Russia	3,122,756	47.9	8,087,900
2	Brazil	1,844,402	57.2	4,776,980
3	Canada	1,197,434	33.6	3,101,340
4	USA	1,170,233	33.1	3,030,890
5	China	761,741	21.2	1,972,900
6	Australia	631,964	21.3	1,636,780
7	Dem. Rep. of Congo	515,871	58.9	1,336,100
8	Indonesia	341,681	48.8	884,950
9	Peru	265,414	53.7	687,420
10	India	261,395	22.8	677,010
	World total	*15,258,855*	*30.3*	*39,520,250*

Source: Food and Agriculture Organization of the United Nations, *Global Forest Resources Assessment 2005*

TOP 10 MOST COMMON TREES IN THE USA

	TREE	SCIENTIFIC NAME
1	Silver maple	*Acer saccharinum*
2	Black cherry	*Prunus serotina*
3	Box elder	*Acer negundo*
4	Eastern cottonwood	*Populus deltoides*
5	Black willow	*Salix nigra*
6	Northern red oak	*Quercus rubra*
7	Flowering dogwood	*Cornus florida*
8	Black oak	*Quercus kelloggii*
9	Ponderosa pine	*Pinus ponderosa*
10	Coast Douglas fir	*Pseudotsuga menziesii*

Source: American Forests

Hardwood trees native to the eastern and southern states prevail in this list, while the Ponderosa pine and Douglas fir are softwoods most typical of the northwest coast forests.

THE HUMAN WORLD

The Amazing Human Body

TOP 10 **MOST COMMON ELEMENTS IN THE HUMAN BODY**

	ELEMENT	SYMBOL	AVERAGE ADULT* TOTAL OZ	AVERAGE ADULT* TOTAL G
1	Oxygen#	O	1,721	48,800
2	Carbon	C	649	18,400
3	Hydrogen#	H	282	8,000
4	Nitrogen	N	73	2,080
5	Calcium	Ca	39.5	1,120
6	Phosphorus	P	31.0	880
7	= Potassium	K	5.6	160
	= Sulfur	S	5.6	160
9	Sodium	Na	4.0	112
10	Chlorine	Cl	3.4	96

* 80 kg male
\# Mostly combined as water

The Top 10 elements account for more than 99 percent of the total, the balance comprising minute quantities of metallic elements including iron—enough (0.17 oz/4.8 g) to make a 6-in (15-cm) nail—as well as zinc, tin, and aluminum.

TOP 10 **LONGEST BONES IN THE HUMAN BODY**

	BONE	AVERAGE LENGTH IN	AVERAGE LENGTH CM
1	Femur (thighbone—upper leg)	19.88	50.50
2	Tibia (shinbone—inner lower leg)	16.94	43.03
3	Fibula (outer lower leg)	15.94	40.50
4	Humerus (upper arm)	14.35	36.46
5	Ulna (inner lower arm)	11.10	28.20
6	Radius (outer lower arm)	10.40	26.42
7	7th rib	9.45	24.00
8	8th rib	9.06	23.00
9	Innominate bone (hipbone—half pelvis)	7.28	18.50
10	Sternum (breastbone)	6.69	17.00

These are average dimensions of the bones of an adult male measured from their extremities (ribs are curved and the pelvis measurement is taken diagonally). The same bones in the female skeleton are usually six to 13 percent smaller, with the exception of the sternum, which is virtually identical.

TOP 10 **LARGEST HUMAN ORGANS**

	ORGAN		AVERAGE WEIGHT OZ	AVERAGE WEIGHT G
1	Skin		384.0	10,886
2	Liver		55.0	1,560
3	Brain	male	49.7	1,408
		female	44.6	1,263
4	Lungs	right	20.5	580
		left	18.0	510
		total	38.5	1,090
5	Heart	male	11.1	315
		female	9.3	265
6	Kidneys	right	4.9	140
		left	5.3	150
		total	10.2	290
7	Spleen		6.0	170
8	Pancreas		3.5	98
9	Thyroid		1.2	35
10	Prostate	male only	0.7	20

This list is based on average immediate post-mortem weights, as recorded during a 10-year period. Various instances of organs far in excess of the average have been recorded, including male brains of over 4.4 lb (2 kg). According to some definitions, the skin may be considered an organ, and since it can constitute 16 percent of a body's total weight, or 384 oz (10,886 g) in a person weighing 150 lb (68 kg), it heads the Top 10.

Great Brain

The brain of Albert Einstein was removed during his autopsy on April 18, 1955 by pathologist Thomas Stoltz Harvey. Far from being larger than the brain of the average male, it was on the small side, at 43 oz (1,230 g). Harvey cut it into 240 sections, keeping the largest part himself and distributing others to researchers to attempt to uncover the source of Einstein's remarkable brainpower.

THE 10 **WORLD'S HEAVIEST PEOPLE**

NAME / DATES*	MAX. WEIGHT LB	KG
1 Carol Yager (1960–94)	1,600	726
2 Jon Brower Minnoch (1941–83)	1,400	635
3 Manuel Uribe Garza (b. 1965), Mexico	1,234	560
4 Rosalie Bradford (1943–2006)	1,200	544
5 Walter Hudson (1944–91)	1,197	543
6 Francis John Lang aka Michael Walker (b. 1934)	1,187	538
7 Johnny Alee (1853–87)	1,132	513
8 Michael Hebranko (b. 1953)	1,100	499
9 Patrick Deuel (b. 1962)	1,072	486
10 Robert Earl Hughes (1926–58)	1,069	485

* All USA unless otherwise stated

Precise weights of certain people were exaggerated for commercial reasons or never verified, while some were so huge that they could not be moved, or broke the scales, but these are the main contenders for the list of "world's heaviest," based on records of their peak weights. Some later dieted and reduced their weights—in the case of Rosalie Bradford, down from her 1987 peak to 283 lb (128 kg) in 1994.

Robert Earl Hughes
Although relegated by even heavier people, Hughes' chest measurement of 10 ft 4 in (3.15 m) remains an unbroken record.

THE 10 **LATEST PEOPLE TO HOLD THE RECORD AS "WORLD'S OLDEST"**

NAME / COUNTRY	AGE YRS	MTHS	DAYS	BORN	DIED
1 Edna (Scott) Parker, USA	114	10	11	Apr 20, 1893	*
2 Yone Minagawa, Japan	114	7	10	Jan 4, 1893	Aug 13, 2007
3 Emma Fanchon (Faust) Tillman, USA	114	2	7	Nov 22, 1892	Jan 28, 2007
4 Emiliano Mercado Del Toro, Puerto Rico#	115	5	4	Aug 21, 1891	Jan 24, 2007
5 Elizabeth (Jones) Bolden, USA	116	3	27	Aug 15, 1890	Dec 11, 2006
6 María Esther (Heredia Lecaro) Capovilla, Ecuador	116	11	14	Sep 14, 1889	Aug 27, 2006
7 Ramona Trinidad (Iglesias y Jordan de) Soler, Puerto Rico	114	8	29	Sep 1, 1889	May 29, 2004
8 Mitoyo Kawate, Japan	114	5	30	May 15, 1889	Nov 13, 2003
9 Kamato Hongo, Japan	116	1	16	Sep 16, 1887	Oct 31, 2003
10 Maud (Davis) Farris-Luse, USA	115	1	26	Jan 21, 1887	Mar 18, 2002

* Alive as at May 8, 2008
# Male—all others female

This list is based on the longevity of the successive holders of the record as "world's oldest" among people for whom there is undisputed evidence of their birth date. None of those in the past decade has come within five years of the record 122-year 5-month 15-day lifespan of Jeanne Calment (France), who lived from February 21, 1875 to August 4, 1997.

TOP 10 DISEASE BURDENS

	DISEASE	% OF DALYS*
1	HIV/AIDS	7.4
2	Coronary heart disease	6.8
3	Stroke	5.0
4	Depression	4.8
5	Road-traffic injuries	4.3
6	Tuberculosis	4.2
7	Alcohol abuse	3.4
8	Violence	3.3
9	Obstructive pulmonary disease	3.1
10	Hearing loss	2.7

* Among men aged over 15

Source: World Health Organization

DALYs—Disability-adjusted Life Years, expressed here as world averages—are potential healthy years of life that are lost as a result of contracting diseases or through injury or other disability. This is used as a measure of the "burden of disease" that affects not only the individual sufferer but also has an effect on the cost of the provision of health services and consequent loss to a country's economy.

TOP 10 VITAMIN AND DIETARY SUPPLEMENT CONSUMERS

COUNTRY	$ PER CAPITA PER ANNUM (2007)
1 Norway	95.61
2 Japan	92.96
3 Singapore	85.10
4 Taiwan	62.61
5 USA	57.02
6 South Korea	41.31
7 Australia	40.15
8 Belgium	31.84
9 Italy	28.35
10 New Zealand	26.79

Source: Euromonitor International

TOP 10 COUNTRIES SPENDING THE MOST ON HEALTHCARE

	COUNTRY	HEALTH SPENDING PER CAPITA IN 2004 ($)
1	USA	6,096
2	Luxembourg	5,904
3	Switzerland	5,572
4	Norway	5,405
5	Monaco	5,330
6	Iceland	4,413
7	Denmark	3,897
8	Austria	3,683
9	Sweden	3,532
10	Germany	3,521

Source: World Health Organization, *World Health Statistics 2007*

THE 10 **MOST COMMON PHOBIAS**

OBJECT OF PHOBIA	MEDICAL TERM
1 Open spaces	Agoraphobia, cenophobia, or kenophobia
2 Driving	No medical term; can be a symptom of agoraphobia
3 Vomiting	Emetophobia or emitophobia
4 Confined spaces	Claustrophobia, cleisiophobia, cleithrophobia, or clithrophobia
5 Insects	Entemophobia
6 Illness	Nosemophobia
7 Animals	Zoophobia
8 Flying	Aerophobia or aviatophobia
9 Blushing	Erythrophobia
10 Heights	Acrophobia, altophobia, hypsophobia, or hypsiphobia

Source: National Phobics Society

A phobia is a morbid fear that is out of proportion to the object of the fear. Many people would admit to having these phobias to some degree, as well as others, such as snakes (ophiophobia), injections (trypanophobia), or ghosts (phasmophobia), but most do not become obsessive or allow such fears to rule their lives. Perhaps surprisingly, the Top 10 does not remain static and new phobias arise, for example the recently noted "nonophobia," the fear of being out of cellphone contact, as well as certain more unusual or rare ones, such as:

Beards	Pogonophobia
Chins	Geniophobia
Eggshells	No medical term
Everything	Pantophobia, panophobia, panphobia, or pamphobia
Going to bed	Clinophobia
Opening one's eyes	Optophobia
Gravity	Barophobia
Hair	Chaetophobia
Mirrors	Eisoptrophobia
Money	Chrometophobia
Satellites plunging to Earth	Keraunothnetophobia
Slime	Blennophobia or myxophobia
String	Linonophobia
Teeth	Odontophobia
The number 13	Terdekaphobia, tridecaphobia, triakaidekaphobia, or triskaidekaphobia

Lost in space
Agoraphobia—literally "fear of the marketplace"—is a phobia where individuals dread having a panic attack and being unable to escape, and so avoid open spaces and public places.

THE 10 **MOST COMMON FATAL DISEASES**

CAUSE	APPROX. ANNUAL DEATHS
1 Ischaemic heart disease	7,208,000
2 Cancers	7,121,000
3 Cerebrovascular disease	5,509,000
4 Lower respiratory infections	3,884,000
5 HIV/AIDS	2,777,000
6 Chronic obstructive pulmonary disease	2,748,000
7 Perinatal conditions	2,462,000
8 Diarrhoeal diseases	1,798,000
9 Tuberculosis	1,566,000
10 Malaria	1,272,000
Top 10 total	*36,345,000*
World total	*57,029,000*

Source: World Health Organization, *World Health Report 2004*

Living Standards

THE 10 **MOST OBESE COUNTRIES**

% OF OBESE ADULTS*

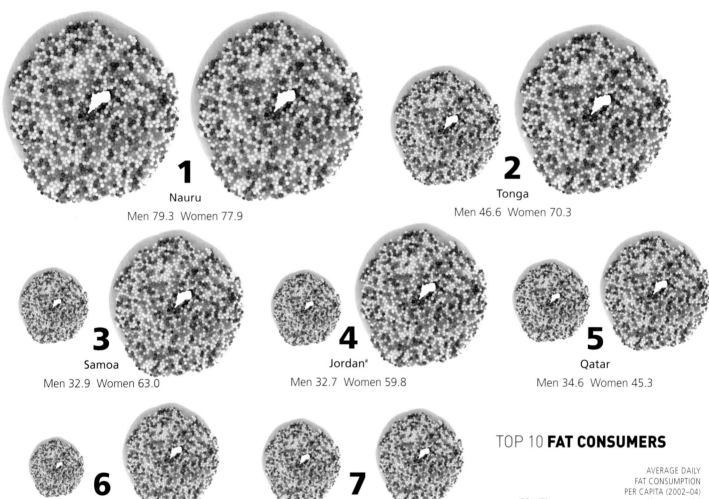

1 Nauru
Men 79.3 Women 77.9

2 Tonga
Men 46.6 Women 70.3

3 Samoa
Men 32.9 Women 63.0

4 Jordan#
Men 32.7 Women 59.8

5 Qatar
Men 34.6 Women 45.3

6 Saudi Arabia
Men 26.4 Women 44.0

7 Lebanon
Men 36.3 Women 38.3

8 Paraguay
Men 22.9 Women 35.7

9 Albania#
Men 22.8 Women 35.6

USA   *31.1*   *33.2*

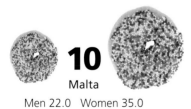

10 Malta
Men 22.0 Women 35.0

* Ranked by percentage of obese women (those
with a BMI greater than 30) in those countries
and latest year for which data available
Urban population only

Source: International Obesity Task Force (IOTF)

TOP 10 **FAT CONSUMERS**

	COUNTRY	AVERAGE DAILY FAT CONSUMPTION PER CAPITA (2002–04)	
		G	OZ
1	France	157	5.53
2	Austria	154	5.43
3	= Belgium	149	5.25
	= Italy	149	5.25
	= Spain	149	5.25
	= Switzerland	149	5.25
7	USA	144	5.07
8	= Canada	141	4.97
	= Hungary	141	4.97
10	= Greece	140	4.93
	= Norway	140	4.93

Source: Food and Agriculture Organization of
the United Nations

THE 10 LEAST FAT CONSUMERS

	COUNTRY	AVERAGE DAILY FAT CONSUMPTION PER CAPITA (2002–04)	
		OZ	G
1	Burundi	0.38	11
2	Rwanda	0.56	16
3	Ethiopia	0.74	21
4	= Bangladesh	0.88	25
	= Dem. Rep. of Congo	0.88	25
6	= Laos	0.98	28
	= Madagascar	0.98	28
8	Zambia	0.98	29
9	Eritrea	1.05	30
10	Mozambique	1.09	31

Source: Food and Agriculture Organization of the United Nations

THE 10 MOST DEVELOPED COUNTRIES

	COUNTRY	HUMAN DEVELOPMENT INDEX
1	= Iceland	0.968
	= Norway	0.968
3	Australia	0.962
4	Canada	0.961
5	Ireland	0.959
6	Sweden	0.956
7	Switzerland	0.955
8	= Japan	0.953
	= Netherlands	0.953
10	= Finland	0.952
	= France	0.952
	USA	0.951

Source: United Nations, *Human Development Report 2007/2008*

HDI rankings are based on a range of factors, including life expectancy, income, education level and living standards. The maximum possible HDI would be 1.00. Although not all member countries are included (some are omitted through lack of reliable data), the figures are widely used by economists, aid organizations, and other agencies as a comparative measure of quality of life.

THE 10 LEAST DEVELOPED COUNTRIES

	COUNTRY	HUMAN DEVELOPMENT INDEX
1	Sierra Leone	0.336
2	Burkina Faso	0.370
3	= Niger	0.374
	= Guinea-Bissau	0.374
5	Mali	0.380
6	= Central African Republic	0.384
	= Mozambique	0.384
8	Chad	0.388
9	Ethiopia	0.406
10	Dem. Rep. of Congo	0.411

Source: United Nations, *Human Development Report 2007/2008*

THE 10 COUNTRIES WITH THE MOST DEATHS FROM HEART DISEASE

	COUNTRY	TOTAL DEATHS	AGE-STANDARDIZED DEATH RATE PER 100,000
1	Turkmenistan	11,670	461
2	Moldova	18,558	423
3	Ukraine	335,609	418
4	Azerbaijan	22,301	410
5	Belarus	59,422	396
6	= Uzbekistan	55,692	386
	= Kazakhstan	51,947	386
8	Afghanistan	33,157	354
9	Russia	711,570	343
10	Tajikistan	11,447	339
	USA	514,449	105

Source: World Health Organization

THE 10 LEAST CALORIE-CONSUMING COUNTRIES

	COUNTRY	AVERAGE DAILY CALORIE CONSUMPTION PER CAPITA (2002–04)
1	Eritrea	1,500
2	Dem. Rep. of Congo	1,590
3	Burundi	1,660
4	Comoros	1,770
5	Ethiopia	1,850
6	Takikistan	1,900
7	Sierra Leone	1,910
8	Liberia	1,930
9	Zambia	1,950
10	= Central African Republic	1,960
	= Tanzania	1,960

Source: Food and Agriculture Organization of the United Nations

TOP 10 PROTEIN CONSUMERS

	COUNTRY	AVERAGE DAILY PROTEIN CONSUMPTION PER CAPITA (2002–04)	
		OZ	G
1	Israel	4.79	136
2	Iceland	4.73	134
3	USA	4.69	133
4	= Ireland	4.44	126
	= Malta	4.44	126
6	= Portugal	4.41	125
	= France	4.41	125
	= Greece	4.41	125
	= Italy	4.41	125
	= Lithuania	4.41	125

Source: Food and Agriculture Organization of the United Nations

Births, Marriages, & Deaths

	COUNTRY	MARRIAGES PER 1,000 PER ANNUM*
1	Barbados	13.1
2	Vietnam	12.1
3	Ethiopia	10.2
4	Seychelles	9.9
5	Jordan	9.7
6	Iran	8.9
7 =	Algeria	8.8
=	Mauritius	8.8
=	USA	8.8
10	Jamaica	8.3

* In 2005 or latest year in those countries for which data available

Source: United Nations

Mass wedding
Jordan, one of the countries with a high marriage rate, offers group weddings, sometimes of hundreds of couples, to enable cost-sharing.

THE 10 **COUNTRIES WITH THE LOWEST MARRIAGE RATE**

	COUNTRY	MARRIAGES PER 1,000 PER ANNUM*
1 =	Colombia	1.7
2 =	Dominican Republic	2.8
=	Saint Lucia	2.8
=	Venezuela	2.8
5 =	Andorra	2.9
=	Peru	2.9
7	United Arab Emirates	3.1
8 =	Argentina	3.2
=	Slovenia	3.2
10	Panama	3.3

* In 2005 or latest year in those countries for which data available

Source: United Nations

THE 10 **COUNTRIES WITH THE LOWEST BIRTH RATE**

	COUNTRY	EST. BIRTH RATE (LIVE BIRTHS PER 1,000, 2009)
1	Japan	7.64
2	Andorra	8.04
3 =	Germany	8.18
=	Italy	8.18
5	Austria	8.65
6	Singapore	8.82
7	Czech Republic	8.83
8	Bosnia and Herzegovina	8.85
9	Slovenia	8.97
10 =	Lithuania	9.11
=	Monaco	9.11
	USA	14.20

Source: US Census Bureau, International Data Base

Although not independent countries, several places record similarly low rates, among them Hong Kong (7.42) and Guernsey (8.46).

TOP 10 **COUNTRIES WITH THE HIGHEST BIRTH RATE**

	COUNTRY	EST. BIRTH RATE (LIVE BIRTHS PER 1,000, 2009)
1	Mali	49.15
2	Niger	49.08
3	Uganda	47.84
4	Afghanistan	45.46
5	Sierra Leone	44.71
6	Burkina Faso	44.58
7	Angola	43.69
8	Somalia	43.68
9	Liberia	42.25
10	Yemen	42.14
	World average	19.80

Source: US Census Bureau, International Data Base

The countries with the highest birth rates—often also those with the highest fertility rates—are among the poorest in the world.

TOP 10 COUNTRIES WITH THE HIGHEST LIFE EXPECTANCY

2009

	COUNTRY	LIFE EXPECTANCY AT BIRTH
1	Andorra	83.54
2	Japan	82.12
3	Singapore	81.98
4	San Marino	81.97
5	France	80.98
6	Sweden	80.86
7 =	Australia	80.85
=	Switzerland	80.85
9	Iceland	80.67
10	Canada	80.58
	USA	75.42

1989

	COUNTRY	LIFE EXPECTANCY AT BIRTH
1	San Marino	79.24
2	Japan	79.00
3	Hong Kong	78.30
4	Iceland	78.17
5	Switzerland	77.89
6	Sweden	77.65
7	Spain	77.30
8	Canada	77.10
9	Greece	77.01
10	Liechtenstein	76.89
	USA	71.70

Source: US Census Bureau, International Data Base

THE 10 COUNTRIES WITH THE LOWEST DEATH RATE

	COUNTRY	EST. DEATH RATE (DEATHS PER 1,000, 2009)
1	United Arab Emirates	2.11
2	Kuwait	2.35
3	Saudi Arabia	2.50
4	Jordan	2.75
5	Brunei	3.29
6	Libya	3.45
7	Oman	3.71
8	Solomon Islands	3.78
9	Ecuador	4.21
10 =	Bahrain	4.37
=	Nicaragua	4.37
	USA	8.28

Source: US Census Bureau, International Data Base

The crude death rate is derived by dividing the total number of deaths in a given year by the total population and multiplying by 1,000. However, because countries with young populations thus appear to have low death rates and older populations high rates, statisticians also use age-standardized death rates, which factor in the age structure to produce a more accurate assessment.

TOP 10 COUNTRIES WITH THE HIGHEST DEATH RATE

	COUNTRY	EST. DEATH RATE (DEATHS PER 1,000, 2009)
1	Swaziland	30.83
2	Angola	24.08
3	South Africa	22.77
4	Lesotho	22.20
5	Sierra Leone	21.91
6	Zimbabwe	21.64
7	Zambia	21.34
8	Liberia	20.73
9	Mozambique	20.07
10	Niger	19.94
	World average	8.30

Source: US Census Bureau, International Data Base

Names to Conjure With

TOP 10 FIRST NAMES FOR TWINS IN THE USA

NAME / NO.

1 Jacob, Joshua — 67

2 Matthew, Michael — 54

3 Daniel, David — 52

4 = Ella, Emma — 38

4 = Isaac, Isaiah — 38

6 Madison, Morgan — 36

7 = Landon, Logan — 35

7 = Taylor, Tyler — 35

9 Brandon, Bryan — 34

10 Christian, Christopher — 33

* Born in 2006

TOP 10 US PATRONYMS

NAME / ORIGIN / % OF ALL US NAMES

1 JOHNSON ("son of John") 0.810

2 WILLIAMS ("son of William") 0.699

3 JONES ("son of John") 0.621

4 DAVIS/DAVIES ("son of David") 0.480

5 WILSON ("son of Will") 0.339

6 ANDERSON ("son of Andrew") 0.311

7 THOMAS ("son of Thomas") 0.311

8 JACKSON ("son of Jack") 0.310

9 HARRIS ("son of Harry") 0.275

10 MARTIN ("son of Martin") 0.273

Source: US Census Bureau

Patronyms are names recalling a father or other ancestor. Up to one-third of all US surnames may be patronymic in origin. Several US presidents have borne such names, including Andrew Johnson, Lyndon Johnson, Woodrow Wilson, William Henry and Benjamin Harrison, Thomas Jefferson, and James Madison.

TOP 10 SURNAMES IN THE USA

	NAME	APPROX. NO.
1	Smith	2,515,000
2	Johnson	2,025,000
3	Williams	1,747,500
4 =	Brown	1,552,500
=	Jones	1,552,500
6	Davis	1,200,000
7	Miller	1,060,000
8	Wilson	847,500
9	Moore	780,000
10 =	Anderson	777,500
=	Taylor	777,500
=	Thomas	777,500

The Top 10 (or, in view of those in equal 10th place, 12) US surnames together make up over six percent of the entire US population—in other words, one American in every 16 bears one of these names. Extending the list, some 28 different names comprise 10 percent of the entire population.

TOP 10 **FIRST NAMES IN THE USA**

2007

BOYS		GIRLS
Jacob	1	Emily
Michael	2	Emma
Joshua	3	Madison
Ethan	4	Isabella
Matthew	5	Ava
Daniel	6	Abigail
Christopher	7	Olivia
Andrew	8	Hannah
Anthony	9	Sophia
William	10	Samantha

1987

BOYS		GIRLS
Michael	1	Jessica
Christopher	2	Ashley
Matthew	3	Amanda
Joshua	4	Jennifer
David	5	Sarah
Andrew	6	Stephanie
Daniel	7	Brittany
James	8	Nicole
Justin	9	Heather
Robert	10	Elizabeth

TOP 10 **GIRLS' AND BOYS' NAMES IN THE USA 100 YEARS AGO**

GIRLS		BOYS
Mary	1	John
Helen	2	William
Margaret	3	James
Ruth	4	George
Dorothy	5	Robert
Anna	6	Joseph
Elizabeth	7	Charles
Mildred	8	Frank
Marie	9	Edward
Alice	10	Thomas

TOP 10 **SURNAMES IN CHINA**

1 Li
2 Wáng
3 Zhang
4 Liú
5 Chén
6 Yáng
7 Huáng
8 Zhào
9 Zhou
10 Wú

Source: Chinese
Academy of Sciences

This ranking is based on a 2006 survey of 296 million Chinese inhabitants in 1,110 counties and cities. The survey recorded a total of 4,100 different surnames, but it has been estimated that there are more than 100 million people with the surnames in the first three in the list, with the Top 10 reckoned to be used by much as 40 percent of the entire Chinese population of 1.3 billion.

Rulers & Royals

TOP 10 **IN LINE TO THE BRITISH THRONE**

HRH The Prince of Wales
(Prince Charles Philip Arthur George)
b. November 14, 1948,
then his elder son:

HRH Prince William of Wales
(Prince William Arthur Philip Louis)
b. June 21, 1982,
then his younger brother:

HRH Prince Henry ("Harry") of Wales
(Prince Henry Charles Albert David)
b. September 15, 1984,
then his uncle:

HRH The Duke of York
(Prince Andrew Albert Christian Edward)
b. February 19, 1960,
then his elder daughter:

HRH Princess Beatrice of York
(Princess Beatrice Elizabeth Mary)
b. August 8, 1988,
then her younger sister:

HRH Princess Eugenie of York
(Princess Eugenie Victoria Helena)
b. March 23, 1990,
then her uncle:

HRH Prince Edward
(Prince Edward Antony Richard Louis)
b. March 10, 1964,
then his son:

Viscount Severn
(James Alexander Philip Theo Windsor)
b. December 17, 2007,
then his sister:

Lady Louise Windsor
(Louise Alice Elizabeth Mary Mountbatten Windsor)
b. November 8, 2003
then her aunt:

HRH The Princess Royal
(Princess Anne Elizabeth Alice Louise)
b. August 15, 1950

Right: Consigned to history
Mohammad Reza Pahlavi ruled as shah of Iran after his father was deposed in 1941. He was himself deposed and the monarchy abolished on February 11, 1979, as the Iranian Revolution resulted in Ayatollah Khomeini coming to power. The shah died in exile a year later.

TOP 10 **MONARCHIES WITH THE MOST SUBJECTS** *

	COUNTRY	MONARCH (ACCESSION)	POPULATION (2009)
1	Britain#	Elizabeth II (1952)	130,906,870
2	Japan	Akihito (1989)	127,078,679
3	Thailand	Bhumibol Adulyadej (1946)	65,905,410
4	Spain	Juan Carlos I (1975)	40,525,002
5	Morocco	Mohammed VI (1999)	34,787,968
6	Nepal	Gyanendra Bir Bikram Shah Dev (2001)	30,138,172
7	Saudi Arabia	Abdullah (2005)	28,701,335
8	Malaysia	Mizan Zainal Abidin (2006)	25,700,294
9	Netherlands	Beatrix (1980)	16,715,999
10	Cambodia	Norodom Sihamoni (1999)	14,494,293

* By population
\# Total of British Commonwealth realms with monarch as head of state

Source: US Census Bureau

A total of 45 countries (including 16 belonging to the British Commonwealth) have monarchies, the Top 10 alone with some 515 million subjects. With a population of 32,920, Monaco is the world's smallest monarchy.

THE 10 **LATEST COUNTRIES TO ABOLISH MONARCHIES**

COUNTRY / MONARCHY ABOLISHED

1 **Iran** 1979
2 **Laos** 1975
3 **Ethiopia*** 1974
4 **Afghanistan** 1973
5 **Greece**# 1973
6 **Cambodia**† 1970
7 **Libya** 1969
8 **Maldives** 1968
9 **Burundi** 1966
10 **Zanzibar**§ 1964

* Emperor deposed 1974
\# King exiled 1967
† Restored 1993
§ Joined with Tanganyika to form Tanzania

This list excludes countries that detached from British rule and became republics.

Revolving monarchy
The 2006 coronation of Mizan Zainal Abidin, the 13th Malaysian ruler since the country's independence in 1957, with Sultanah Nur Zahirah. Malaysia has a revolving monarchy, with a new Yang di-Pertuan, often translated as "king," serving a five-year term.

THE 10 **LATEST MONARCHS TO ASCEND THE THRONE**

	TITLE / NAME	COUNTRY	ACCESSION
1	King Jigme Khesar Namgyal Wangchuck	Bhutan	Dec 15, 2006
2	Sultan Mizan Zainal Abidin	Malaysia	Dec 13, 2006
3	Emir Sabah al-Ahmad al-Saba	Kuwait	Jan 29, 2006
4	King George Tupou V	Tonga	Sep 11, 2006
5	Emir Sabah Al-Ahmad Al-Jaber Al-Sabah	Kuwait	Jan 29, 2006
6	Emir Mohammed bin Rashid Al Maktoum	Dubai	Jan 4, 2006
7	King Abdullah	Saudi Arabia	Aug 1, 2005
8	Prince Albert II	Monaco	Apr 6, 2005
9	Emir Khalifa bin Zayed Al Nahayan	Abu Dhabi	Nov 3, 2004
10	King Norodom Sihamoni	Cambodia	Oct 14, 2004

TOP 10 **LONGEST-SERVING PRESIDENTS TODAY**

	PRESIDENT	COUNTRY	TOOK OFFICE
1	El Hadj Omar Bongo	Gabon	Dec 2, 1967
2	Colonel Mu'ammar Gaddafi*	Libya	Sep 1, 1969
3	Ali Abdullah Saleh	Yemen	Jul 17, 1978
4	Maumoon Abdul Gayoom	Maldives	Nov 11, 1978
5	Teodoro Obiang Nguema Mbasogo	Equatorial Guinea	Aug 3, 1979
6	José Eduardo dos Santos	Angola	Sep 21, 1979
7	Hosni Mubarak	Egypt	Oct 6, 1981
8	Paul Biya	Cameroon	Nov 7, 1982
9	Lansana Conté	Guinea	Apr 3, 1984
10	Yoweri Museveni	Uganda	Jan 29, 1986

* Since a reorganization in 1979, Colonel Gaddafi has held no formal position, but continues to rule under the ceremonial title of "Leader and Guide of the Revolution"

All the presidents in this list have been in power for more than 22—some for more than 40—years. Fidel Castro became prime minister of Cuba in 1959, president in 1976, and retired on February 24, 2008.

Mr President

TOP 10 LONGEST-LIVED US PRESIDENTS

	PRESIDENT	BORN	DIED	LIFESPAN YRS	MTHS	DAYS
1	Gerald Ford	Jul 14, 1913	Dec 26, 2006	93	5	13
2	Ronald Reagan	Feb 6, 1911	Jun 5, 2004	93	4	0
3	John Adams	Oct 30, 1735	Jul 4, 1826	90	8	5
4	Herbert Hoover	Aug 10, 1874	Oct 20, 1964	90	2	11
5	Harry S. Truman	May 8, 1884	Dec 26, 1972	88	7	19
6	James Madison	Mar 16, 1751	Jun 28, 1836	85	3	13
7	Thomas Jefferson	Apr 13, 1743	Jul 4, 1826	83	2	22
8	George H. W. Bush	Jun 12, 1924	*	82	6	21
9	Jimmy Carter	Oct 1, 1924	*	82	3	1
10	Richard Nixon	Jan 9, 1913	Apr 22, 1994	81	3	14

* Still alive, age at January 1, 2008

Political stature
Lyndon B. Johnson was only fractionally shorter than Lincoln—whose height has been claimed to have resulted from his suffering from an endocrine deficiency.

THE 10 LAST US PRESIDENTS AND VICE-PRESIDENTS TO DIE IN OFFICE

NAME / PRESIDENT/VICE-PRESIDENT / DEATH DATE

1 John F. Kennedy* (P)
Nov 22, 1963

2 Franklin D. Roosevelt (P)
Apr 12, 1945

3 Warren G. Harding (P)
Aug 2, 1923

4 James S. Sherman (V-P)
Oct 30, 1912

5 William McKinley* (P)
Sep 14, 1901

6 Garret A. Hobart (V-P)
Nov 21, 1899

7 Thomas A. Hendricks (V-P)
Nov 25, 1885

8 James A. Garfield* (P)
Sep 19, 1881

9 Henry Wilson (V-P)
Nov 10, 1875

10 Abraham Lincoln* (P)
Apr 15, 1865

* Assassinated

John Fitzgerald Kennedy was the 15th and last US president or vice-president to die in office, and the fourth to die by an assassin's bullet. Prior to Lincoln, two presidents and three vice-presidents had died in office.

TOP 10 TALLEST US PRESIDENTS

	PRESIDENT	HEIGHT FT	IN	M
1	Abraham Lincoln	6	3.75	1.92
2	Lyndon B. Johnson	6	3.5	1.91
3	Thomas Jefferson	6	2.5	1.89
4	= Chester A. Arthur	6	2	1.88
	= George H. W. Bush	6	2	1.88
	= Franklin D. Roosevelt	6	2	1.88
7	= Bill Clinton	6	1.5	1.87
	= George Washington	6	1.5	1.87
9	= Andrew Jackson	6	1	1.85
	= Ronald Reagan	6	1	1.85

It is often claimed that the taller candidate has always won US presidential elections, but statistically this is only marginally true.

TOP 10 **MOST POPULAR US PRESIDENTS**

	PRESIDENT	SURVEY DATE	HIGHEST APPROVAL RATING (%)*
1	George W. Bush	Sep 21–22, 2001	90
2	George H. W. Bush	Feb 28, 1991	89
3	Harry S. Truman	May/Jun 1945	87
4	Franklin D. Roosevelt	Jan 1942	84
5	John F. Kennedy	Apr 28, 1961	83
6	Dwight D. Eisenhower	Dec 14, 1956	79
7	Lyndon B. Johnson	Dec 5, 1963	78
8	Jimmy Carter	Mar 18, 1977	75
9	Gerald Ford	Aug 16, 1974	71
10	Bill Clinton	30–1 Feb 1, 1998	69

* Identical or inferior ratings recorded on other occasions during presidency

Source: The Gallup Organization

The Gallup Organization began surveying approval ratings of US presidents in October 1938. Since then, the only president not to make the Top 10 is Richard Nixon, whose highest approval rating was 67 percent. George W. Bush's highest ratings were achieved shortly after the events of 9/11. In response to the continuing presence of US troops in Iraq and Afghanistan, the state of the US economy and other factors, he has recorded the biggest ever differential between approval ratings, a total of 73 percentage points. The one president to not make the least popular list is John F. Kennedy, whose highest disapproval was 30 percent in September 1963, the survey compiled two months before his assassination.

THE 10 **LEAST POPULAR US PRESIDENTS**

	PRESIDENT	SURVEY DATE	LOWEST APPROVAL RATING (%)*
1	George W. Bush	Feb 15–19, 2008	19
2	Harry S. Truman	Sep 9–14, 1952	22
3	Richard Nixon	Jul 12–15, 1974	24
4	Jimmy Carter	Jun 29–Jul 2, 1979	28
5	George H. W. Bush	Jul 31–Aug 2, 1992	29
6	=Ronald W. Reagan	Jan 1, 1983	35
	=Lyndon B. Johnson	Aug 7, 1968	35
8	=Gerald Ford	Mar 31, 1975	37
	=Bill Clinton	May 27, 1994	37
10	Dwight D. Eisenhower	Jul 1960	49

* Identical or better ratings recorded on other occasions during presidency

Source: The Gallup Organization

Rise and fall
George W. Bush's approval rating has swung between two extremes, reflecting the highs and lows of his two terms in office.

To the Ends of the Earth

THE 10 **FIRST EUROPEAN EXPLORERS TO LAND IN THE AMERICAS**

EXPLORER* / COUNTRY	TERRITORY	LANDED
1 Christopher Columbus, Italy	West Indies	Oct 12, 1492
2 John Cabot, Italy/England	Nova Scotia/ Newfoundland	Jun 24, 1497
3 Alonso de Ojeda, Spain	Brazil	1499
4 Vicente Yáñez Pinzón, Spain	Amazon	Jan 26, 1500
5 Pedro Alvarez Cabral, Portugal	Brazil	Apr 23, 1500
6 Gaspar Corte-Real, Portugal	Labrador	late 1500
7 Rodrigo de Bastidas, Spain	Central America	Mar 1501
8 Vasco Nuñez de Balboa, Spain	Panama	Sep 25, 1513
9 Juan Ponce de León, Spain	Florida	Apr 8, 1513
10 Juan Díaz de Solís, Spain	Río de la Plata	Jan 1, 1516

* Expedition leader only listed

After his pioneering voyage of 1492, Columbus made three subsequent journeys to the West Indies and South America. Although Ojeda (or Hojeda) was the leader of the 1499 expedition, Amerigo Vespucci, after whom America is named, was also on the voyage.

THE 10 **FIRST MOUNTAINEERS TO CLIMB EVEREST**

MOUNTAINEER / COUNTRY	DATE
1 Edmund Hillary, New Zealand	May 29, 1953
2 Tenzing Norgay, Nepal	May 29, 1953
3 Jürg Marmet, Switzerland	May 23, 1956
4 Ernst Schmied, Switzerland	May 23, 1956
5 Hans-Rudolf von Gunten, Switzerland	May 24, 1956
6 Adolf Reist, Switzerland	May 24, 1956
7 Wang Fu-chou, China	May 25, 1960
8 Chu Ying-hua, China	May 25, 1960
9 Konbu, China	May 25, 1960
10 = Nawang Gombu, India	May 1, 1963
= James Whittaker, USA	May 1, 1963

Nawang Gombu and James Whittaker are 10th equal because, neither wishing to deny the other the privilege of being first, they ascended the last steps to the summit side by side. Up to the end of 2007 there were 3,679 successful ascents of Everest—40 of them on a single day, May 10, 1993—but some 210 have died in the attempt, the bodies of many remaining on the mountain.

TOP 10 **FASTEST CROSS-CHANNEL SWIMS**

SWIMMER / COUNTRY / YEAR / TIME (HR:MIN)

1 Petar Stoychev, Bulgaria
Aug 24, 2007 / 6:58

2 Christof Wandratsch, Germany
Aug 1, 2005 / 7:04

3 Yuri Kudinov, Russia
Aug 24, 2007 / 7:06

4 Chad Hundeby, USA
Sep 27, 1994 / 7:17

5 Christof Wandratsch, Germany
Aug 20, 2003 / 7:20

THE 10 **FIRST PEOPLE TO REACH THE SOUTH POLE**

NAME / COUNTRY	DATE
1 = Roald Amundsen* (Norway; 1872–1928)	Dec 14, 1911
= Olav Olavson Bjaaland (Norway; 1873–1961)	Dec 14, 1911
= Helmer Julius Hanssen (Norway; 1870–1956)	Dec 14, 1911
= Sverre Helge Hassel (Norway; 1876–1928)	Dec 14, 1911
= Oscar Wisting (Norway; 1871–1936)	Dec 14, 1911
6 = Robert Falcon Scott* (Britain; 1868–1912)	Jan 17, 1912
= Henry Robinson Bowers (Britain; 1883–1912)	Jan 17, 1912
= Edgar Evans (Britain; 1876–1912)	Jan 17, 1912
= Lawrence Edward Grace Oates (Britain; 1880–1912)	Jan 17, 1912
= Edward Adrian Wilson (Britain; 1872–1912)	Jan 17, 1912

* Expedition leader

Just 33 days separate the first two expeditions to reach the South Pole. Scott's British Antarctic Expedition was organized with its avowed goal "to reach the South Pole and to secure for the British Empire the honor of this achievement." Meanwhile, Norwegian explorer Roald Amundsen also set out on an expedition to the Pole. When Scott eventually reached his goal, he discovered that the Norwegians had beaten him. Demoralized, Scott's team began the arduous return journey, but plagued by illness, hunger, bad weather, and exhaustion, the entire expedition died just as Amundsen's triumph was being reported to the world.

THE 10 **FIRST PEOPLE CLAIMED TO HAVE REACHED THE NORTH POLE**

NAME / COUNTRY	DATE
1 = Frederick Albert Cook, USA	Apr 21, 1908
= Ahwelah, Inuit	Apr 21, 1908
= Etukishook, Inuit	Apr 21, 1908
4 = Robert Edwin Peary, USA	Apr 6, 1909
= Matthew Alexander Henson, USA	Apr 6, 1909
= Ooqueah, Inuit	Apr 6, 1909
= Ootah, Inuit	Apr 6, 1909
= Egingwah, Inuit	Apr 6, 1909
= Seegloo, Inuit	Apr 6, 1909
10 = Pavel Afanaseyevich Geordiyenko, USSR	Apr 23, 1948
= Mikhail Yemel'yenovich Ostrekin, USSR	Apr 23, 1948
= Pavel Kononovich Sen'ko, USSR	Apr 23, 1948
= Mikhail Mikhaylovich Somov, USSR	Apr 23, 1948

Cook's claim to have reached the North Pole is not generally accepted. Doubts also remain as to the validity of Peary's team's claim, which has never been officially corroborated. The first undisputed "conquest," that of the 1948 Soviet team, was achieved by landing in an aircraft, rather than overland.

* Fastest woman swimmer

6 Petar Stoychev,
Bulgaria
Aug 22, 2006 / 7:21

7 David Meca,
Spain
Aug 29, 2005 / 7:22

8 Yvetta Hlavácová*,
Czech Republic
Aug 5, 2006 / 7:25

9 Penny Lee Dean,
USA
Jul 29, 1978 / 7:40

10 Tamara Bruce,
Australia
Sep 2, 1994 / 7:53

Nobel Prizes

THE 10 **LATEST WINNERS OF THE NOBEL PEACE PRIZE**

YEAR / WINNER / COUNTRY

2007
Intergovernmental
Panel on Climate
Change and Al Gore Jr
USA

2006
Muhammad Yunus
and Grameen Bank
Bangladesh

2005
International Atomic
Energy Agency and
Mohamed El Baradei
Egypt

2004
Wangari Maathai
Kenya

2003
Shirin Ebadi
Iran

2002
Jimmy Carter
USA

2001
United Nations and
Kofi Annan, Ghana

2000
Kim Dae-jung
South Korea

1999
Médecins Sans
Frontières

1998
John Hume and
David Trimble, UK

TOP 10 **YOUNGEST NOBEL PRIZE WINNERS**

WINNER / COUNTRY / DATE OF BIRTH	AWARD	YRS	AGE* MTHS	DAYS
1 William Lawrence Bragg (UK) Mar 31, 1890	Physics 1915	25	8	10
2 Werner Karl Heisenberg (Germany) Dec 5, 1901	Physics 1932	31	0	5
3 Tsung-dao Lee (China) Nov 24, 1926	Physics 1957	31	0	16
4 Carl David Anderson (USA) Sept 3, 1905	Physics 1936	31	3	7
5 Paul Adrien Maurice Dirac (UK) Aug 8, 1902	Physics 1933	31	4	2
6 Frederick Grant Banting (Canada) Nov 14, 1891	Medicine 1923	32	0	26
7 Rudolf Ludwig Mössbauer (West Germany) Jan 31, 1929	Physics 1961	32	10	10
8 Maidread Corrigan (UK) Jan 27, 1944	Peace 1976	32	10	13
9 Joshua Lederberg (USA) May 23, 1925	Medicine 1958	33	6	17
10 Betty Williams (UK) May 22, 1943	Peace 1976	33	6	18

* At date of award ceremony; prizes are awarded annually on
December 10, Alfred Nobel's birthday

TOP 10 **OLDEST NOBEL PRIZE WINNERS**

WINNER / COUNTRY / DATE OF BIRTH	AWARD	YRS	AGE* MTHS	DAYS
1 Leonid Hurwicz (USA) Aug 21, 1917	Economics 2007	90	3	28
2 Raymond Davis, Jr. (USA) Oct 14, 1914	Physics 2002	88	1	26
3 Doris Lessing (UK) Oct 22, 1919	Literature 2007	88	1	18
4 Vitaly L. Ginzburg (Russia) Oct 4, 1916	Physics 2003	87	2	6
5 Peyton Rous (USA) Oct 5, 1879	Medicine 1966	87	2	5
6 Joseph Rotblat (UK) Nov 4, 1908	Peace 1995	87	1	6
7 Karl von Frisch (Germany) Nov 20, 1886	Medicine 1973	87	0	20
8 Ferdinand Buisson (France) Dec 20, 1841	Peace 1927	85	11	20
9 John B. Fenn (USA) Jun 15, 1917	Chemistry 2002	85	5	25
10 Thomas S. Schelling (USA) Apr 14, 1921	Economics 2005	84	7	26

* At date of award ceremony; prizes are awarded annually on
December 10, Alfred Nobel's birthday

THE 10 **LATEST WINNERS OF THE NOBEL PRIZE FOR LITERATURE**

YEAR / WINNER / COUNTRY

2007 Doris Lessing, UK

2006 Orhan Pamuk, Turkey

2005 Harold Pinter, UK

2004 Elfriede Jelinek, Austria

2003 J. M. Coetzee, South Africa

2002 Imre Kertész, Hungary

2001 Sir V. S. Naipaul, UK

2000 Gao Xingjian, China

1999 Günter Grass, Germany

1998 José Saramago, Portugal

Doris Lessing
British writer Doris Lessing is the most recent of the 11 women to be awarded the Nobel Prize for Literature, and the oldest of all 34 female Nobel laureates.

TOP 10 **LANGUAGES OF NOBEL PRIZE FOR LITERATURE WINNERS**

	LANGUAGE	% OF TOTAL*	NO.
1	English	25.47	27
2	French	12.26	13
3	German	11.32	12
4	Spanish	9.43	10
5	= Italian	5.67	6
	= Swedish	5.67	6
7	Russian	4.72	5
8	Polish	3.77	4
9	= Danish	2.83	3
	= Norwegian	2.83	3

* Of 106 Nobel Prizes awarded 1901–2007

THE 10 **LATEST WOMEN TO WIN A NOBEL PRIZE**

	WINNER	COUNTRY	PRIZE	YEAR
1	Doris Lessing (b. 1919)	UK	Literature	2007
2	= Linda B. Buck (b. 1947)	USA	Medicine	2004
	= Elfriede Jelinek (b. 1946)	Austria	Literature	2004
	= Wangari Maathai (b. 1940)	Kenya	Peace	2004
5	Shirin Ebadi (b. 1947)	Iran	Peace	2003
6	Jody Williams (b. 1950)	USA	Peace	1997
7	Wislawa Szymborska (b. 1923)	Poland	Literature	1996
8	Christiane Nüsslein-Volhard (b. 1942)	Germany	Medicine	1995
9	Toni Morrison (b. 1931)	USA	Literature	1993
10	Rigoberta Menchú Tum (b. 1959)	Guatemala	Peace	1992

A total of 34 women have won Nobel Prizes since 1901, 12 of them for Peace, 11 for Literature, three for Physiology or Medicine, three for Chemistry, and two for Physics. The total includes Marie Curie, who won twice: for Physics (1903) and Chemistry (1911). No woman has ever won the Nobel Prize for Economics.

Criminal Records

THE 10 COUNTRIES WITH THE HIGHEST REPORTED CRIME RATES

COUNTRY / REPORTED CRIMES PER 100,000 POPULATION

Iceland
21,211.97

Sweden
13,836.67

UK
11,014.38

Finland
10,005.65

Belgium
9,421.74

Denmark
9,137.07

Netherlands
8,813.57

Austria
6,863.95

South Africa
5,918.73

Luxembourg
5,866.22

USA *4,118.76*

Source: United Nations Office on Drugs and Crime, *Eighth United Nations Survey of Crime Trends and Operations of Criminal Justice Systems*, 2006

An appearance in this list does not necessarily confirm these as the most crime-ridden countries, since the rate of reporting relates closely to such factors as confidence in local law-enforcement authorities. However, a rate of approximately 1,000 per 100,000 may be considered average, so those in the Top 10 are well above it.

TOP 10 TYPES OF PROPERTY STOLEN IN THE USA (BY VALUE)

	TYPE OF PROPERTY	VALUE OF PROPERTY STOLEN ($)
1	Locally stolen motor vehicles	6,891,284,744
2	Jewelry and precious metals	1,215,235,529
3	Currency, notes, etc	1,108,666,932
4	Televisions, radios, stereos, etc.	867,735,960
5	Office equipment	601,742,665
6	Household goods	280,613,770
7	Clothing and furs	250,515,900
8	Consumable goods	125,561,212
9	Firearms	103,559,485
10	Livestock	19,787,860
	Miscellaneous (unspecified)	*3,475,581,316*
	Total	*14,940,285,373*

Source: US Justice Department/FBI, *Crime in the United States 2006*

THE 10 MOST COMMON CRIMES IN THE USA

	CRIME	NO. RECORDED (2006)
1	Property crime	9,080,788
2	Larceny-theft	5,971,647
3	Burglary	1,990,468
4	Violent crime	1,308,436
5	Motor vehicle theft	1,118,673
6	Aggravated assault	789,793
7	Robbery	422,375
8	Forcible rape	80,414
9	Arson	66,065
10	Murder and nonnegligent manslaughter	15,854
	Total	*20,844,513*

Source: US Justice Depertment/FBI, *Crime in the United States 2006*

WANTED

Donald Eugene Webb

After the killing of a police officer in 1980, Donald Eugene Webb (born July 14, 1931) became the 375th person and longest resident on the FBI's "Most Wanted" list.

THE 10 **CRIMINALS LONGEST ON THE FBI'S "10 MOST WANTED" LIST**

FUGITIVE (FBI NO.) / CRIME	ADDED TO LIST	REMOVED FROM LIST	PERIOD ON LIST		
			YRS	MTHS	DAYS
1 Donald Eugene Webb (375) Alleged cop killer	May 4, 1981	Mar 31, 2007	25	10	27
2 Victor Manuel Gerena (386) Armed robbery	May 14, 1984	*	23	10	25
3 Charles Lee Heron (265) Murder	Feb 9, 1968	Jun 18, 1986	18	4	9
4 Frederick J. Tenuto (14) Murder	May 14, 1950	Mar 9, 1964	13	9	14
5 Katherine Ann Power (315) Bank robbery	Oct 17, 1970	Jun 15, 1984	13	7	29
6 Glen Stewart Godwin (447) Murder	Dec 7, 1996	*	11	4	1
7 Arthur Lee Washington Jr (427) Attempted murder	Oct 18, 1989	Dec 27, 2000	11	2	19
8 David Daniel Keegan (78) Murder, robbery	Jun 21, 1954	Dec 13, 1963	9	5	22
9 James Eddie Diggs (36) Alleged murder	Aug 27, 1952	Dec 14, 1961	9	3	17
10 Eugene Francis Newman (97) Car theft, burglary	May 28, 1956	Jun 11, 1965	9	0	14

* Still at large, periods as at April 8, 2008

The United States' Federal Bureau of Investigation officially launched its celebrated "10 Most Wanted" list on March 14, 1950. Since then almost 500 criminals have figured on it, the most notable in recent years being No. 456, Osama Bin Laden, who has been included since June 7, 1999. Names appear until individuals are captured, die, or charges are dropped. On January 8, 1969 bank robber and double cop murderer Billie Austin Bryant appeared on the list for the record shortest time—just two hours—before he was arrested.

Murder Most Foul

THE 10 **COUNTRIES WITH THE HIGHEST MURDER RATES**

COUNTRY / MURDERS PER 100,000 POPULATION*

1 Venezuela 42.0

2 South Africa 39.5

3 Colombia 39.3

4 Jamaica 31.6

5 El Salvador 31.5

6 Brazil 27.0

7 Guatemala 25.5

8 Russia 19.8

9 Ecuador 18.3

10 Kazakhstan 16.3

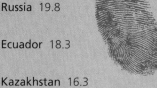

* In latest year for which figures available

THE 10 **MOST COMMON MURDER WEAPONS AND METHODS IN THE USA**

WEAPON/METHOD	VICTIMS (2006)
1 Firearms, (of which: handguns 7,795, type not stated 1,465, shotguns 481, rifles 436)	10,177
2 Knives or cutting instruments	1,822
3 "Personal weapons" (hands, feet, fists, etc.)	830
4 Blunt objects (hammers, clubs, etc.)	607
5 Strangulation	135
6 Fire	115
7 Asphyxiation	96
8 Narcotics	42
9 Drowning	12
10 Poison	11
Other/weapons not stated	*1,128*
Total	*14,990*

Source: FBI Uniform Crime Reports

THE 10 **WORST YEARS FOR MURDER IN THE USA**

YEAR	MURDER RATE PER 100,000 POPULATION	TOTAL*
1 **1991**	9.8	24,703
2 **1993**	9.5	24,526
3 **1992**	9.3	23,760
4 **1990**	9.4	23,438
5 **1994**	9.0	23,326
6 **1980**	10.2	23,040
7 **1981**	9.8	22,520
8 **1989**	8.7	21,500
9 **1979**	9.7	21,460
10 **1982**	9.1	21,010

* Includes non-negligent manslaughter victims; victims of September 11, 2001 terrorist attacks are excluded

Source: Bureau of Justice Statistics

Murders in the USA first exceeded 2,000 in 1910 and increased rapidly as a result of gang warfare during the Prohibition era, topping 10,000 in 1930. The total rose to over 20,000 for the first time in 1974.

PERPETRATOR / LOCATION / DATE / CIRCUMSTANCES   NO. KILLED

57

1   Woo Bum Kong, SangNamdo, South Korea, Apr 28, 1982
Off-duty policeman Woo Bum Kong (or Wou BomKon), 27, went
on a drunken rampage with rifles and hand grenades, killing 57
and injuring 38 before blowing himself up with a grenade.

35

2   Martin Bryant, Port Arthur, Tasmania, Australia, Apr 28, 1996
Bryant, a 28-year-old Hobart resident, used a rifle in a horrific
spree that began in a restaurant and ended with a siege in a
guesthouse, in which he held hostages. He set it on fire before
being captured by police.

32

3   Seung-Hui Cho, Virginia Tech, Blacksburg,
Virginia, USA, Apr 16, 2007
South Korean-born Cho used handguns to kill 27 fellow students
and five faculty members of Virginia Tech before turning a gun on
himself in America's worst school shooting.

29

4= Baruch Kappel Goldstein, Hebron, occupied West Bank,
Israel, February 25, 1994
Goldstein, a 42-year-old US immigrant doctor, carried out a gun
massacre of Palestinians at prayer at the Tomb of the Patriarchs
before being beaten to death by the crowd.

4= Matsuo Toi, Tsuyama, Japan, May 21, 1938
Twenty-one-year old Toi used a rifle and swords to kill 29 of his
neighbors before committing suicide.

28

6   Campo Elias Delgado, Bogota, Colombia, Dec 4, 1986
Delgado, a Vietnamese war veteran and electronics engineer,
stabbed two and shot a further 26 people before being killed
by police.

22

7= George Jo Hennard, Killeen, Texas, USA, Oct 16, 1991
Hennard drove his pickup truck through the window of Luby's
Cafeteria and, in 11 minutes, killed 22 with semiautomatic pistols
before shooting himself.

7= James Oliver Huberty, San Ysidro, California, USA,
Jul 18, 1984
Huberty, aged 41, opened fire in a McDonald's restaurant, killing
21 before being shot dead by a SWAT marksman. A further 19
were wounded, including a victim who died the following day.

17

9= Thomas Hamilton, Dunblane, Stirling, UK, Mar 13, 1996
Hamilton, 43, shot 16 children and a teacher in Dunblane Primary
School before killing himself in the UK's worst shooting incident—
as a result of which firearm laws were tightened in the UK.

9= Robert Steinhäuser, Erfurt, Germany, Apr 26, 2000
Former student Steinhäuser returned to Johann Gutenberg
Secondary School and killed 14 teachers, two students,
and a police officer with a handgun before shooting himself.

* By individuals, excluding terrorist and military actions;
totals exclude perpetrator

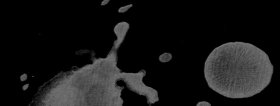

Punishment

THE 10 FEDERAL PRISONS IN THE USA WITH THE HIGHEST OCCUPANCY

INSTITUTION / LOCATION	CURRENT OCCUPANCY*
1 Big Spring Correctional Institution#, Texas	2,858
2 California City Correctional Institution#, California	2,601
3 Brooklyn Metropolitan Detention Center, New York	2,550
4 Reeves Correctional Institution#, Texas	2,192
5 Fort Dix Federal Correctional Institution, New Jersey	2,176
6 Atlanta US Penitentiary, Georgia	1,975
7 Forest City Federal Correctional Institution, Arkansas	1,946
8 Coleman Federal Correctional Institution (low security), Florida	1,945
9 Elkton Federal Correctional Institution, Ohio	1,922
10 Seagonville Federal Correctional Institution, Texas	1,899

* As at October 11, 2007
\# Privately managed prison

Source: Federal Bureau of Prisons

THE 10 STATES WITH THE MOST EXECUTIONS*

	STATE	1608–1976	EXECUTIONS SINCE 1976
1	Texas	755	405
2	Virginia	1,277	98
3	Oklahoma	132	86
4	Missouri	285	66
5	Florida	314	64
6	North Carolina	784	43
7	Georgia	950	41
8	Alabama	708	38
9	South Carolina	641	37
10 =	Arkansas	478	27
=	Louisiana	632	27

* To May 8, 2008

Source: Death Penalty Information Center

A total of 1,058 people have been executed in the United Stated since 1976, when the death penalty was reintroduced after a 10-year moratorium. During this period, 17 states and Washington, D.C., have not carried out any executions.

THE 10 FIRST COUNTRIES TO ABOLISH CAPITAL PUNISHMENT

COUNTRY / ABOLISHED	
1 Russia	1826
2 Venezuela	1863
3 San Marino	1865
4 Portugal	1867
5 Costa Rica	1877
6 Brazil	1889
7 Panama	1903
8 Norway	1905
9 Ecuador	1906
10 Uruguay	1907

Some countries abolished capital punishment in peacetime only, or for all crimes except treason, later extending it totally. Some countries officially retain capital punishment, but have effectively abolished it: the last execution in Liechtenstein, for example, took place in 1785. Among countries to abolish the death penalty recently are the Philippines in 2006, Albania and Rwanda in 2007, and Uzbekistan in 2008.

THE 10 US STATES WITH THE MOST PRISONERS ON DEATH ROW

STATE	PRISONERS UNDER DEATH SENTENCE*
1 California	669
2 Florida	388
3 Texas	370
4 Pennsylvania	228
5 Alabama	201
6 Ohio	186
7 North Carolina	166
8 Arizona	114
9 Georgia	107
10 Tennessee	96
Total	3,263

* As at February 2008

Source: Death Penalty Information Center

Prison numbers

Inmates at a Russian correctional labour settlement. Russia has the world's third largest prison population, but is second only to the United States for its incarceration rate as a percentage of the population.

THE 10 **COUNTRIES WITH THE HIGHEST PRISON POPULATIONS**

	COUNTRY	PRISONERS PER 100,000 OF POPULATION	TOTAL PRISONERS*
1	USA	751	2,258,983
2	China	119	1,565,771
3	Russia	632	892,330
4	Brazil	219	419,551
5	India	32	358,368
6	Mexico	198	217,436
7	South Africa	348	165,987
8	Thailand	253	165,316
9	Iran	222	158,351
10	Ukraine	325	149,690

* As at date of most recent data

Source: International Centre for Prison Studies

Girl gang

A female chain gang in the USA: women represent over nine percent of the total prison population—12.9 percent of local jail inmates and 7.2 of state and federal prisoners.

World Wars

THE 10 **LARGEST ARMED FORCES OF WORLD WAR I**

SOLDIER = 1,000,000 / COUNTRY   PERSONNEL*

	COUNTRY	PERSONNEL*
1	Russia	12,000,000
2	Germany	11,000,000
3	British Empire	8,904,467
4	France	8,410,000
5	Austria-Hungary	7,800,000
6	Italy	5,615,000
7	USA	4,355,000
8	Turkey	2,850,000
9	Bulgaria	1,200,000
10	Japan	800,000

Total at peak strength

Russia's armed forces were relatively small in relation to the country's population—some six percent, compared with 17 percent in Germany. Several other European nations had forces that were similarly substantial in relation to their populations: Serbia's army was equivalent to 14 percent of its population. In total, more than 65,000,000 combatants were involved in fighting some of the costliest battles—in terms of numbers killed—that the world has ever known.

THE 10 **LARGEST ARMED FORCES OF WORLD WAR II**

1 SOLDIER = 1,000,000 / COUNTRY   PERSONNEL*

	COUNTRY	PERSONNEL*
1	USSR	12,500,000
2	USA	12,364,000
3	Germany	10,000,000
4	Japan	6,095,000
5	France	5,700,000
6	UK	4,683,000
7	Italy	4,500,000
8	China	3,800,000
9	India	2,150,000
10	Poland	1,000,000

* Total at peak strength

Allowing for deaths and casualties, the total forces mobilized during the course of the war is, of course, greater than the peak strength figures: that of the USSR, for example, has been put as high as 20,000,000, the USA 16,354,000, Germany 17,900,000 , Japan 9,100,000 , and the UK 5,896,000. In contrast, the forces of a number of Central and South American countries that did not declare war until a late stage were numbered in the low thousands.

THE 10 **COUNTRIES SUFFERING THE GREATEST MILITARY LOSSES IN WORLD WAR I**

	COUNTRY	KILLED
1	Germany	1,773,700
2	Russia	1,700,000
3	France	1,357,800
4	Austria-Hungary	1,200,000
5	British Empire*	908,371
6	Italy	650,000
7	Romania	335,706
8	Turkey	325,000
9	USA	116,516
10	Bulgaria	87,500

* Including Australia, Canada, India, New Zealand, South Africa, etc.

THE 10 **COUNTRIES SUFFERING THE GREATEST MILITARY LOSSES IN WORLD WAR II**

	COUNTRY	KILLED
1	USSR	13,600,000*
2	Germany	3,300,000
3	China	1,324,516
4	Japan	1,140,429
5	British Empire* (UK 264,000)	357,116
6	Romania	350,000
7	Poland	320,000
8	Yugoslavia	305,000
9	USA	292,131
10	Italy	279,800
	Total	*21,268,992*

* Total, of which 7.8 million battlefield deaths
\# Including Australia, Canada, India, New

TOP 10 BRITISH AND COMMONWEALTH AIR ACES OF WORLD WAR II

	PILOT	COUNTRY	KILLS CLAIMED
1	Sqd. Ldr. Marmaduke Thomas St. John Pattle	South Africa	50.67
2	Gp. Capt. James Edgar "Johnny" Johnson	UK	36.92
3	Wng Cdr Brendan Eamonn Fergus "Paddy" Finucane	Ireland	32.00
4	William "Cherry" Vale	UK	31.50
5	Flt. Lt. George Frederick Beurling	Canada	31.33
6	Gp. Capt. Adolph Gysbert "Sailor" Malan	South Africa	29.50
7	Wng. Cdr. John Randall Daniel "Bob" Braham	UK	29.00
8	Wng. Cdr. Clive Robert Caldwell	Australia	28.50
9	Sqd. Ldr. James Harry "Ginger" Lacey	UK	28.00
10	Wng. Cdr. Colin Falkland Gray	New Zealand	27.70

TOP 10 LUFTWAFFE ACES OF WORLD WAR II

	PILOT	KILLS CLAIMED
1	Major Eric Hartmann	352
2	Major Gerhard Barkhorn	301
3	Major Günther Rall	275
4	Oberleutnant Otto Kittel	267
5	Major Walther Nowotny	258
6	Major Wilhelm Batz	237
7	Major Erich Rudorffer	222
8	Oberst. Heinz Bär	220
9	Oberst. Hermann Graf	212
10	Major Heinrich Ehrler	209

Kills that are expressed as fractions refer to those that were shared with others, the number of fighters involved and the extent of each pilot's participation determining the proportion allocated to him. "Probable" victories are excluded.

Scramble!
British and Commonwealth fighter pilots take to the skies. Many air aces' combat victories were achieved in the Battle of Britain, during the summer of 1940.

Right: Eric Hartmann
Although the Luftwaffe's apparently high claims have been dismissed by some military historians as inflated for propaganda purposes, few have questioned the so-called "Blond Knight" Eric Hartmann's achievement, however, and his victories over Soviet aircraft so outraged the USSR that after the war he was arrested and sentenced to 25 years in a Russian labor camp. He was released in 1955, returned to serve in the West German air force, and died on September 20, 1993.

The Military Balance

TOP 10 **LARGEST ARMED FORCES**

	COUNTRY	ARMY	ESTIMATED ACTIVE FORCES		TOTAL
			NAVY	AIR	
1	China	1,600,000	255,000	250,000	2,105,000
2	USA	593,327	341,588	336,081	1,498,157*
3	India	1,100,000	55,000	125,000	1,288,000#
4	North Korea	950,000	46,000	110,000	1,106,000
5	Russia	360,000	142,000	195,000	1,027,000†
6	South Korea	560,000	63,000	64,000	687,000
7	Pakistan	550,000	24,000	45,000	619,000
8	Iran	350,000	18,000	52,000	545,000§
9	Turkey	402,000	48,600	60,000	510,600
10	Egypt	340,000	18,500	30,000	468,500‡

* Includes 186,661 Marine Corps and 40,500 Coast Guard
\# Includes 8,000 Coast Guard
† Includes 80,000 Strategic Deterrent Forces and 250,000 Command and Support
§ Includes 125,000 Islamic Revolutionary Guard Corps
‡ Includes 80,000 Air Defence Command

Source: The International Institute for Strategic Studies, *The Military Balance 2008*

Several countries also have substantial reserves on standby: South Korea's has been estimated at some 4.5 million plus 3.5 Paramilitary, Vietnam's at five million and China's 800,000. North Korea has the highest number of troops in relation to its population—47.85 per 1,000.

Korean People's Army
Despite its precarious economy, North Korea is the world's most militarized country, with one in five of its adult population in the armed forces, the highest military/civilian ratio.

TOP 10 **COUNTRIES WITH THE MOST SUBMARINES**

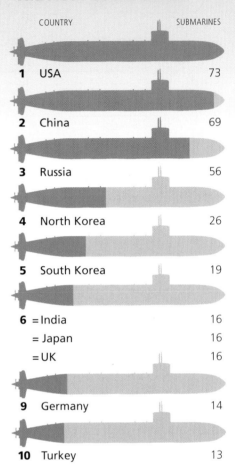

	COUNTRY	SUBMARINES
1	USA	73
2	China	69
3	Russia	56
4	North Korea	26
5	South Korea	19
6	= India	16
	= Japan	16
	= UK	16
9	Germany	14
10	Turkey	13

TOP 10 **ARMS IMPORTERS**

COUNTRY (1 CRATE = $1 MILLION)	IMPORTS 2006 ($)
1 China	11,677,000,000
2 India	8,526,000,000
3 Greece	5,263,000,000
4 UK	3,395,000,000
5 Turkey	3,298,000,000
6 Egypt	3,103,000,000
7 South Korea	2,755,000,000
8 United Arab Emirates	2,581,000,000
9 Australia	2,177,000,000
10 Pakistan	2,018,000,000
USA	*1,760,000,000*

Source: Stockholm International Peace Research Institute

TOP 10 **ARMS MANUFACTURERS**

COMPANY / COUNTRY	SALES 2006 ($)
1 Boeing (USA)	28,050,000,000
2 Northrop Grumman (USA)	27,590,000,000
3 Lockheed Martin (USA)	26,460,000,000
4 BAE Systems (UK)	23,230,000,000
5 Raytheon (USA)	19,800,000,000
6 General Dynamics (USA)	16,570,000,000
7 Finmeccanica (Italy)	9,800,000,000
8 EADS (Europe)	9,580,000,000
9 L-3 Communications (USA)	8,970,000,000
10 Thales (France)	8,940,000,000

TOP 10 **MILITARY EXPENDITURE COUNTRIES**

COUNTRY	MILITARY EXPENDITURE 2006 ($) PER CAPITA	TOTAL
1 USA	1,756	528,700,000,000
2 UK	990	59,200,000,000
3 France	875	53,100,000,000
4 China	37	49,500,000,000
5 Japan	341	43,700,000,000
6 Germany	447	37,000,000,000
7 Russia	244	34,700,000,000
8 Italy	514	29,900,000,000
9 Saudi Arabia	1,152	29,000,000,000
10 India	21	23,900,000,000
Top 10	–	*888,700,000,000*
World total	–	*1,158,000,000,000*

Source: SIPRI

World Religions

TOP 10 RELIGIOUS BELIEFS

	RELIGION	FOLLOWERS
1	Christianity	2,159,141,594
2	Islam	1,345,175,832
3	Hinduism	859,893,462
4	Buddhism	380,567,154
5	Chinese folk-religions	380,486,297
6	Ethnic religions	258,307,065
7	New religions	104,923,020
8	Sikhism	22,199,953
9	Judaism	14,678,791
10	Spiritists	13,176,576

Source: World Christian Database

These authoritative estimates imply that almost one-third of the world's population are nominally (self-declared), if not practicing, Christians, and one-fifth followers of Islam. Mainstream religions have seen a decline in formal attendance, while it is reckoned that more than 14 percent of the world population profess no religious beliefs of any kind.

Time for prayer
A Bedouin Arab in the Negev Desert, Israel, faces Mecca to perform salah – the ritual of prayer that Muslims practice five times daily.

TOP 10 LARGEST CHRISTIAN POPULATIONS

	COUNTRY	CHRISTIANS
1	USA	244,520,177
2	Brazil	170,208,945
3	Russia	113,269,039
4	China	109,815,781
5	Mexico	102,594,161
6	Philippines	74,170,629
7	India	64,514,845
8	Nigeria	59,960,048
9	Germany	59,382,852
10	Dem. Rep. of Congo	54,882,976
	World	*2,159,141,594*

Source: World Christian Database

TOP 10 LARGEST MUSLIM POPULATIONS

	COUNTRY	MUSLIMS
1	Pakistan	151,428,138
2	India	150,951,110
3	Bangladesh	125,614,365
4	Indonesia	124,903,322
5	Turkey	71,285,299
6	Iran	68,339,642
7	Egypt	62,948,005
8	Nigeria	58,053,739
9	Algeria	31,831,159
10	Morocco	30,965,312
	USA	*4,760,437*
	World	*1,345,175,832*

Source: World Christian Database

TOP 10 COUNTRIES WITH MOST ATHEISTS AND NONRELIGIOUS PEOPLE

	COUNTRY	ATHEISTS	NONRELIGIOUS	TOTAL
1	China	106,975,051	540,062,607	647,037,658
2	USA	1,160,293	33,742,215	34,902,508
3	Germany	1,971,964	17,162,813	19,134,777
4	Japan	3,675,370	13,032,785	16,708,155
5	Vietnam	5,781,497	10,653,043	16,434,540
6	North Korea	3,503,650	12,523,632	16,027,282
7	India	1,771,096	13,729,435	15,500,531
8	Russia	2,197,538	10,375,595	12,573,133
9	France	2,387,472	9,617,460	12,004,932
10	Italy	2,083,530	7,404,434	9,487,964
	World	*148,028,092*	*764,002,046*	*912,030,138*

Source: World Christian Database

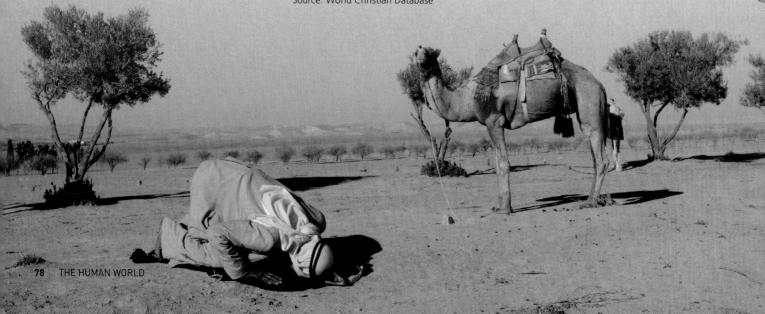

TOP 10 **LARGEST JEWISH POPULATIONS**

	COUNTRY	JEWS
1	USA	5,729,147
2	Israel	4,867,198
3	France	604,955
4	Argentina	512,671
5	Canada	418,285
6	Brazil	383,837
7	UK	279,602
8	Germany	225,063
9	Russia	186,935
10	Ukraine	*180,726*
	World	*14,678,791*

Source: World Christian Database

Almost every country in the world has Jewish communities. While not an independent country, the Gaza Strip and West Bank are reckoned to contain 437,638 Jews.

TOP 10 **LARGEST HINDU POPULATIONS**

	COUNTRY	HINDUS
1	India	803,533,560
2	Nepal	19,329,934
3	Bangladesh	13,661,586
4	Indonesia	7,112,335
5	Sri Lanka	2,342,834
6	Pakistan	2,055,274
7	Malaysia	1,588,790
8	USA	1,330,446
9	South Africa	1,128,942
10	Myanmar	861,787
	World	*859,893,462*

Source: World Christian Database

Hindus comprise 73 percent of the population of India and 71 percent of Nepal, but only 10 percent of that of Bangladesh.

TOP 10 **LARGEST BUDDHIST POPULATIONS**

	COUNTRY	BUDDHISTS
1	China	117,016,597
2	Japan	71,533,450
3	Thailand	53,394,844
4	Vietnam	40,821,035
5	Myanmar	37,419,764
6	Sri Lanka	14,302,328
7	Cambodia	11,999,857
8	India	7,576,063
9	South Korea	7,225,875
10	Malaysia	5,970,800
	USA	*2,795,460*
	World	*380,567,154*

Source: World Christian Database

Indian religion
The elephant deity Ganesh is at the center of a Hindu festival in Mumbai, India.

TOWN & COUNTRY

Countries Large & Small

TOP 10 **LARGEST LANDLOCKED COUNTRIES**

COUNTRY / NEIGHBOURS	SQ MILES	AREA SQ KM
1 Kazakhstan China, Kyrgyzstan, Russia, Turkmenistan, Uzbekistan	1,049,156	2,717,300
2 Mongolia China, Russia	603,908	1,564,116
3 Niger Algeria, Benin, Burkina Faso, Chad, Libya, Mali, Nigeria	489,075	1,266,699
4 Chad Cameroon, Central African Republic, Libya, Niger, Nigeria, Sudan	486,180	1,259,201
5 Mali Algeria, Burkina Faso, Côte d'Ivoire, Guinea, Mauritania, Niger, Senegal	471,044	1,219,999
6 Ethiopia Djibouti, Eritrea, Kenya, Somalia, Sudan	435,186	1,127,127
7 Bolivia Argentina, Brazil, Chile, Paraguay, Peru	424,164	1,098,580
8 Zambia Angola, Dem. Rep. of Congo, Malawi, Mozambique, Namibia, Tanzania, Zimbabwe	290,585	752,614
9 Afghanistan China, Iran, Pakistan, Tajikistan, Turkmenistan, Uzbekistan	250,001	647,500
10 Central African Republic Cameroon, Chad, Congo, Dem. Rep. of Congo, Sudan	240,535	622,984

There are 43 landlocked countries in the world. Kazakhstan and Turkmenistan both have coasts on the Caspian Sea—which is itself landlocked.

One steppe beyond
Mongolia, the world's least densely populated country, is second in size only to Kazakhstan among the world's landlocked countries. The economies of such territories often suffer through their lack of coastal access for trade.

TOP 10 **LARGEST COUNTRIES**

COUNTRY	SQ MILES	AREA SQ KM	% OF WORLD TOTAL
1 Russia	6,592,772	17,075,200	11.5
2 Canada	3,855,103	9,984,670	6.7
3 USA	3,718,712	9,631,420	6.5
4 China	3,705,407	9,596,960	6.4
5 Brazil	3,286,488	8,511,965	5.7
6 Australia	2,967,910	7,686,850	5.2
7 India	1,269,346	3,287,590	2.2
8 Argentina	1,068,302	2,766,890	2.1
9 Kazakhstan	1,049,156	2,717,300	1.9
10 Sudan	967,499	2,505,810	1.7
World total	*57,506,062*	*148,940,000*	*100.0*

Source: CIA, *The World Factbook 2007*

This list is based on the total area of a country within its borders, including offshore islands, inland water such as lakes and rivers, and reservoirs. It may thus differ from versions in which these are excluded. Antarctica has an approximate area of 5,096,549 sq miles (13,200,000 sq km), but is discounted as it is not considered a country. The countries in the Top 10 collectively comprise 50 percent of the total Earth's surface.

Landlocked Doubles
Two countries in the world are doubly landlocked—completely surrounded by other landlocked countries: Uzbekistan (surrounded by Afghanistan, Kazakhstan, Kyrgyzstan, Tajikistan, and Turkmenistan) and Liechtenstein (Austria and Switzerland), the third smallest landlocked country after Vatican City (0.17 sq miles/0.44 sq km) and San Marino (23.63 sq miles/)61.20 sq km, both of which are surrounded by Italy.

TOP 10 **COUNTRIES WITH THE LONGEST SINGLE COUNTRY BORDER**

	COUNTRY / BORDERED BY	BORDER MILES	KM
1	Canada (USA)	5,530	8,893
2	Portugal (Spain)	754	1,214
3	Lesotho (South Africa)	565	909
4	The Gambia (Senegal)	460	740
5	Brunei (Malaysia)	237	381
6	= Dominican Republic (Haiti)	220	360
	= Ireland (UK: Northern Ireland)	220	360
8	South Korea (North Korea)	148	238
9	East Timor (Indonesia)	142	228
10	Denmark (Germany)	42	68

Canada coastline
Including all its islands, the coastline of Canada is more than six times as long as the distance round the Earth at the Equator.

TOP 10 **COUNTRIES WITH THE LONGEST COASTLINES**

	COUNTRY	TOTAL COASTLINE LENGTH MILES	KM
1	Canada	125,566	202,080
2	Indonesia	33,999	54,716
3	Russia	23,396	37,653
4	Philippines	22,559	36,289
5	Japan	18,486	29,751
6	Australia	16,007	25,760
7	Norway	15,626	25,148
8	USA	12,380	19,924
9	New Zealand	9,404	15,134
10	China	9,010	14,500

Source: CIA, *The World Factbook 2007*

THE 10 **SMALLEST COUNTRIES**

	COUNTRY	AREA SQ MILES	SQ KM
1	Vatican City	0.17	0.44
2	Monaco	0.75	1.95
3	Nauru	8.18	21.20
4	Tuvalu	9.89	25.63
5	San Marino	23.63	61.20
6	Liechtenstein	61.77	160.00
7	Marshall Islands	70.05	181.43
8	Saint Kitts and Nevis	104.01	269.40
9	Maldives	115.05	298.00
10	Malta	121.66	315.10

There are some 25 "microstates"—independent countries with a land area of less than 386 sq miles (1,000 sq km).

Countries—Population

TOP 10 **MOST DENSELY POPULATED COUNTRIES**

	COUNTRY	AREA (SQ KM)	POPULATION (2009 EST.)	POPULATION PER SQ KM
1	Monaco	1.95	32,920	16,460.0
2	Singapore	683	4,657,542	6,819.2
3	Vatican City	0.44	932	2,118.2
4	Maldives	300	389,434	1,298.1
5	Malta	316	405,165	1,282.2
6	Bangladesh	133,910	156,654,645	1,169.9
7	Bahrain	665	727,785	1,094.4
8	Nauru	21	14,014	667.3
9	Barbados	431	282,967	656.5
10	Mauritius	2,030	1,284,264	632.6
	USA	*9,161,923*	*306,499,395*	*33.5*
	World	*130,772,591*	*6,757,062,760*	*51.7*

Source: US Census Bureau, International Data Base

TOP 10 **LEAST DENSELY POPULATED COUNTRIES**

	COUNTRY	AREA (SQ KM)	POPULATION (2009 EST.)	POPULATION PER SQ KM
1	Mongolia	1,564,116	3,041,142	1.94
2	Namibia	825,418	2,071,015	2.50
3	Australia	7,617,930	20,764,417	2.73
4	Suriname	161,470	481,267	2.98
5	Iceland	100,250	306,694	3.06
6	Botswana	585,370	1,868,330	3.19
7	Mauritania	1,030,400	3,462,063	3.36
8	Libya	1,759,540	6,310,434	3.59
9	Canada	9,093,507	33,966,667	3.74
10	Guyana	196,850	772,298	3.92

Source: US Census Bureau, International Data Base

In contrast to those countries that have population densities in the hundreds (and, in some instances, thousands) per sq km, these sparsely populated countries of the world generally present environmental disadvantages that make human habitation challenging, with large tracts of mountain, desert, or dense forest, or extreme climates. Although not a country, Greenland, with an area of 2,166,086 sq km and a population of 56,307, has a density of just 0.03 people per sq km.

Crowded islands
Although some of its islands are virtually uninhabited, the Maldives has one of the world's highest birth rates and average population densities.

TOP 10 **LEAST POPULATED COUNTRIES**

COUNTRY	POPULATION (2009 EST.)
1 Vatican City	932
2 Tuvalu	12,378
3 Nauru	14,014
4 Palau	21,331
5 San Marino	30,324
6 Monaco	32,920
7 Liechtenstein	34,741
8 Saint Kitts and Nevis	39,941
9 Marshall Islands	64,522
10 Antigua and Barbuda	70,194

Source: US Census Bureau, International Data Base

The most recent and unusually precise official census statistics, published by Vatican City in 2007, revealed that the resident population comprised the pope and 57 cardinals, 293 clergy members of pontifical representations, 62 other clergy, 101 members of the Swiss Guard, and 43 lay persons with unspecified functions.

TOP 10 **MOST POPULATED COUNTRIES**

COUNTRY	POPULATION (2009 EST.)
1 China	1,338,612,968
2 India	1,166,079,217
3 USA	306,499,395
4 Indonesia	240,271,522
5 Brazil	193,767,441
6 Pakistan	170,790,583
7 Bangladesh	156,654,645
8 Nigeria	141,617,030
9 Russia	140,041,247
10 Japan	127,078,679
World	*6,757,062,760*

Source: US Census Bureau, International Data Base

In 2009, the population of Nigeria will overtake that of Russia, which has experienced progressive decline. Mexico (111,211,789), is the only other country with a population of more than 100 million.

Youngest country
Precisely half the population of Uganda is aged under 15, imposing a considerable economic and social burden on the country.

TOP 10 **COUNTRIES WITH THE YOUNGEST POPULATIONS**

COUNTRY	% UNDER 15 (2009 EST.)
1 Uganda	50.0
2 Mali	48.3
3 Dem. Rep. of Congo	47.3
4 Niger	46.9
5 São Tomé and Príncipe	46.8
6 Chad	46.7
7 Burkina Faso	46.4
8 = Burundi	46.2
= Yemen	46.2
10 Congo	46.0
USA	*20.1*
World average	*26.9*

TOP 10 **COUNTRIES WITH THE OLDEST POPULATIONS**

COUNTRY	% OVER 65 (2009 EST.)
1 Monaco	22.9
2 Japan	22.2
3 = Germany	20.3
= Italy	20.3
5 Greece	19.2
6 Sweden	18.8
7 Spain	18.1
8 Bulgaria	17.7
9 = Belgium	17.6
= Portugal	17.6
USA	*12.9*
World	*7.7*

Source: US Census Bureau, International Data Base

With lower death rates and a higher life expectancy than elsewhere, nine of these 10 countries are in Europe. On average, 18 percent of people in Western Europe are over 65 and five percent over 80.

Population Projections

The only way is up
Its dense population has compelled Singapore to build upward: it has 38 skyscrapers higher than 500 ft (152 m).

TOP 10 **MOST DENSELY POPULATED COUNTRIES IN 2050**

	COUNTRY	AREA (SQ KM)	EST. POPULATION (2050)	EST. POPULATION PER SQ KM
1	Monaco	1.95	32,964	16,482.0
2	Singapore	683	4,635,110	6,786.4
3	Maldives	300	815,031	2,716.8
4	Bangladesh	133,910	279,955,405	2,090.6
5	Bahrain	665	973,412	1,463.8
6	Malta	316	395,639	1,344.7
7	Nauru	21	22,696	1,252.0
8	Rwanda	24,948	25,128,735	1,007.2
9	Burundi	25,650	22,852,556	890.9
10	Comoros	2,170	1,837,671	846.9
	USA	*9,161,923*	*420,080,587*	*45.9*
	World	*130,772,591*	*9,401,550,854*	*71.9*

Source: US Census Bureau, International Data Base

THE 10 **LEAST DENSELY POPULATED COUNTRIES IN 2050**

	COUNTRY	AREA (SQ KM)	EST. POPULATION (2050)	EST. POPULATION PER SQ KM
1	Namibia	825,418	1,795,852	2.2
2	Mongolia	1,564,116	4,340,496	2.8
3	Guyana	196,850	597,806	3.0
4	Australia	7,617,930	24,175,783	3.2
5	Iceland	100,250	350,922	3.5
6	Suriname	161,470	617,249	3.8
7	Botswana	585,370	2,385,685	4.1
8	Canada	9,093,507	41,429,579	4.6
9	Kazakhstan	2,669,800	15,099,700	5.7
10	Libya	1,759,540	10,817,176	6.1

Source: US Census Bureau, International Data Base

Russia, with a vast area (16,995,800 sq km) and projected 2050 population of 109,187,353, falls just short of the Top 10. While not an independent country, Greenland (410,449 sq km; projected 2050 population 56,644) will have just 0.14 people per sq km.

TOP 10 **FASTEST-GROWING COUNTRIES**

COUNTRY / POPULATION INCREASE 2006–50   RED FIGURES REPRESENT % GROWTH

Source: Population Reference Bureau, *2006 World Population Data Sheet*

1 Uganda
371

2= Niger
248
= Malawi
248

4 Burundi
229

5 Guinea-Bissau
225

6 East Timor
224

7 Liberia
217

8= Yemen
214
= Chad
214

10 Mali
202

World 41

TOP 10 **MOST POPULATED COUNTRIES IN 2025**

	COUNTRY	EST. POPULATION (2025)
1	China	1,453,123,817
2	India	1,448,821,234
3	USA	349,666,199
4	Indonesia	278,502,882
5	Pakistan	218,495,756
6	Brazil	217,825,222
7	Nigeria	206,165,946
8	Bangladesh	204,538,715
9	Mexico	130,198,692
10	Russia	128,180,396
	Top 10 total	*4,635,518,859*
	World	*7,958,508,362*

Source: US Census Bureau, International Data Base

In a single generation, from 2000 to 2025, Nigeria's population is forecast to increase by almost 75 percent, elevating it from tenth to sixth place in this list, while Mexico makes leaps into the Top 10, ousting Japan.

TOP 10 **MOST POPULATED COUNTRIES IN 2050**

	COUNTRY	EST. POPULATION (2050)
1	India	1,807,878,574
2	China	1,424,161,948
3	USA	420,080,587
4	Nigeria	356,523,597
5	Indonesia	313,020,847
6	Bangladesh	279,955,405
7	Pakistan	277,554,980
8	Brazil	228,426,737
9	Dem. Rep. of Congo	203,039,557
10	Mexico	47,907,650
	Top 10 total	*5,358,549,882*
	World	*9,401,505,490*

Source: US Census Bureau, International Data Base

Estimates of national populations in 2050 present a striking change as longtime world leader China is markedly eclipsed by India, a reversal that is projected to take place around the year 2026.

Slowing the tide
Since the introduction 30 years ago of a one-child policy, China's runaway population growth has been curbed and is projected to decline as India's goes into overdrive and overtakes it to become the world's most populous country.

THE 10 **LEAST POPULATED COUNTRIES IN 2050**

	COUNTRY	EST. POPULATION (2050)
1	Tuvalu	20,018
2	Nauru	22,696
3	Palau	26,300
4	Monaco	32,964
5	San Marino	35,335
6	Liechtenstein	35,776
7	Saint Kitts and Nevis	52,348
8	Dominica	64,772
9	Andorra	69,129
10	Antigua and Barbuda	69,259

Source: US Census Bureau, International Data Base

Cities

TOP 10 **MOST URBANIZED COUNTRIES**

	COUNTRY	% OF POPULATION LIVING IN URBAN AREAS (2005)
1	= Singapore	100.0
	= Monaco	100.0
	= Nauru	100.0
	= Vatican	100.0
5	Kuwait	98.3
6	Belgium	97.2
7	Bahrain	96.5
8	Qatar	95.4
9	Malta	95.3
10	Venezuela	93.4
	USA	*80.8*
	World	*48.6*

Source: United Nations, *Human Development Report 2007–2008*

THE 10 **LEAST URBANIZED COUNTRIES**

	COUNTRY	% OF POPULATION LIVING IN URBAN AREAS (2005)
1	Burundi	10.0
2	Bhutan	11.1
3	Trinidad & Tobago	12.2
4	Papua New Guinea	13.4
5	Uganda	14.5
6	Sri Lanka	15.1
7	Nepal	15.8
8	Ethiopia	16.0
9	Niger	16.8
10	Solomon Islands	17.0

Source: United Nations, *Human Development Report 2007–2008*

2007   NOW & THEN   1987

TOP 10 **LARGEST CITIES**

2007

	CITY / COUNTRY	POPULATION
1	Tokyo, Japan	33,600,000
2	Seoul, South Korea	23,400,000
3	Mexico City, Mexico	22,400,000
4	New York, USA	21,900,000
5	Mumbai (Bombay), India	21,600,000
6	Delhi, India	21,500,000
7	São Paulo, Brazil	20,600,000
8	Los Angeles, USA	18,000,000
9	Shanghai, China	17,500,000
10	Osaka, Japan	16,700,000

1987

	CITY / COUNTRY	POPULATION
1	Tokyo, Japan	23,322,000
2	New York, USA	15,827,000
3	Mexico City, Mexico	14,474,000
4	São Paulo, Brazil	13,427,000
5	Shanghai, China	12,396,000
6	Los Angeles, USA	10,445,000
7	Osaka, Japan	10,351,000
8	Buenos Aires, Argentina	10,269,000
9	Bombay, India	9,898,000
10	Calcutta, India	9,882,000

Source: Th. Brinkhoff: The Principal Agglomerations of the World, http://www.citypopulation.de, 2007-09-30

The populations listed are those of the urban agglomerations—the central cities and surrounding continuous built-up suburban areas, regardless of administrative boundaries. Specific definitions of agglomerations usually identify them as those with a density of over 1,000 people per sq mile (400 people per sq km). In the 20 years from 1987 to 2007, the total population of the cities in each Top 10 went up from 130,291,000 to 217,200,000.

Megacity
Tokyo's population grew by 44 percent between 1987 and 2007 and is now greater than that of Canada.

TOP 10 **LARGEST CAPITAL CITIES**

CITY / COUNTRY	EST. POPULATION (2007)
1 Tokyo (including Yokohama and Kawasaki), Japan	33,600,000
2 Seoul (including Bucheon, Goyang, Incheon, Seongnam and Suweon), South Korea	23,400,000
3 Mexico City (including Nezahualcóyotl, Ecatepec and Naucalpan), Mexico	22,400,000
4 Delhi (including Faridabad and Ghaziabad), India	21,500,000
5 Cairo (including Al-Jizah and Shubra al-Khaymah), Egypt	16,100,000
6 Manila (including Kalookan and Quezon City), Philippines	15,600,000
7 Jakarta (including Bekasi, Bogor, Depok and Tangerang), Indonesia	15,100,000
8 Buenos Aires (including San Justo and La Plata), Argentina	13,600,000
9 Moscow, Russia	13,500,000
10 Beijing, China	12,800,000

Source: Th. Brinkhoff: The Principal Agglomerations of the World, http://www.citypopulation.de, 2007-09-30

On top of the world
Founded as a silver-mining town, the elevated city of Potosí, Bolivia, dates to the mid-sixteenth century. It was once home to the country's National Mint and is a UNESCO World Heritage Site.

TOP 10 **HIGHEST TOWNS AND CITIES**

CITY / COUNTRY	HEIGHT FT	HEIGHT M
1 La Rinconada, Peru	16,732	5,100
2 Wenzhuan, Tibet, China	16,730	5,099
3 El Alto*, Bolivia	13,615	4,150
4 Potosí, Bolivia	13,419	4,090
5 Oruro, Bolivia	12,146	3,702
6 Lhasa#, Tibet, China	12,087	3,684
7 Apartaderos, Venezuela	11,502	3,505
8 Cusco, Peru	11,024	3,360
9 Huancayo, Peru	10,732	3,271
10 Alma, Colorado, USA	10,361	3,158

* A suburb of La Paz; the main city—the world's highest capital—is at 11,916 ft (3,632 m)
# Former capital of independent Tibet

Place Names

	FORMER NAME	CURRENT NAME	YEAR CHANGED	AREA SQ MILES	AREA SQ KM
1	Zaïre	Dem. Rep. of Congo	1997	905,567	2,345,410
2	Dutch East Indies	Indonesia	1945	741,100	1,919,440
3	Persia	Iran	1935	636,296	1,648,000
4	Tanganyika/Zanzibar	Tanzania	1964	364,900	945,087
5	South West Africa	Namibia	1990	318,695	825,418
6	Northern Rhodesia	Zambia	1964	290,586	752,614
7	Burma	Myanmar	1989	261,970	678,500
8	Ubanghi Shari	Central African Republic	1960	240,535	622,984
9	Bechuanaland	Botswana	1966	231,804	600,370
10	Siam	Thailand	1939	198,457	514,000

Source: CIA, *The World Factbook 2008*

Although not a country, Greenland (836,331 sq miles/2,166,086 sq km) has been officially known as Kalaallit Nunaat since 1979.

TOP 10 **MOST COMMON STREET NAMES IN THE USA**

STREET / TOTAL

1 Second Street 10,866
2 Third Street 10,131
3 First Street 9,898
4 Fourth Street 9,190
5 Park Street 8,926
6 Fifth Street 8,186
7 Main Street 7,664
8 Sixth Street 7,283
9 Oak Street 6,946
10 Seventh Street 6,377

Source: US Census Bureau

First is not first, because many streets that would be so designated are instead called Main. Washington is the highest-ranked street name derived from a personal name, with 4,974 examples.

TOP 10 MOST COMMON PLACE NAMES IN THE USA

	NAME	STATES* / PLACES
1	MIDWAY	39 / 211
2	FAIRVIEW	40 / 202
3	OAK GROVE	31 / 160
4	FIVE POINTS	28 / 147
5 =	PLEASANT HILL	29 / 119
=	RIVERSIDE	46 / 119
7	MOUNT PLEASANT	32 / 115
8	BETHEL	34 / 110
9	CENTERVILLE	43 / 108
10	NEW HOPE	25 / 105

* No. of states with at least one example

Source: US Geological Survey Geographical Names Information System (GNIS)

Fairview figures prominently in certain states—there are 27 in Tennessee alone. It is also one of the most common cemetery names in the USA, with no fewer than 59 examples; there are also 81 cemeteries called Riverside and 43 called Oak Grove.

TOP 10 **LONGEST PLACE NAMES***

NAME	LETTERS

1 Krung Thep Mahanakhon Amon Rattanakosin Mahinthara Ayuthaya Mahadilok Phop Noppharat Ratchathani Burirom Udomratchaniwet Mahasathan Amon Piman Awatan Sathit Sakkathattiya Witsanukam Prasit — **168**

It means "The city of angels, the great city, the eternal jewel city, the impregnable city of God Indra, the grand capital of the world endowed with nine precious gems, the happy city, abounding in an enormous Royal Palace that resembles the heavenly abode where reigns the reincarnated god, a city given by Indra and built by Vishnukarn." When the poetic name of Bangkok, capital of Thailand, is used, it is usually abbreviated to "Krung Thep" (city of angels).

2 Taumatawhakatangihangakoauauotamateaturipukakapiki-maungahoronukupokaiwhenuakitanatahu — **85**

This is the longer version (the other has a mere 83 letters) of the Maori name of a hill in New Zealand. It translates as "The place where Tamatea, the man with the big knees, who slid, climbed and swallowed mountains, known as land-eater, played on the flute to his loved one."

3 Gorsafawddachaidraigddanheddogleddollônpenrhyn-areurdraethceredigion — **67**

A name contrived by the Fairbourne Steam Railway, Gwynedd, North Wales, for publicity purposes and in order to outdo its rival, No. 4. It means "The Mawddach station and its dragon teeth at the Northern Penrhyn Road on the golden beach of Cardigan Bay."

4 Llanfairpwllgwyngyllgogerychwyrndrobwllllantysilio-gogogoch — **58**

It means "St Mary's Church in the hollow of the white hazel near to the rapid whirlpool of the church of St Tysilio near the Red Cave." Questions have been raised about its authenticity, since its official name comprises only the first 20 letters, and the full name appears to have been invented as a hoax.

5 El Pueblo de Nuestra Señora la Reina de los Ángeles de la Porciúncula — **57**

The site of a Franciscan mission and the full Spanish name of Los Angeles; it means "The town of Our Lady the Queen of the Angels of the Little Portion." Nowadays it is customarily known by its initial letters, "LA," making it also one of the shortest-named cities in the world.

6 Chargoggagoggmanchaugagoggchaubunagungamaug — **43**

America's longest place name, a lake near Webster, Massachusetts. Its Indian name, loosely translated, is claimed to mean "You fish on your side, I'll fish on mine, and no one fishes in the middle." It is said to be pronounced "Char-gogg-a-gogg (pause) man-chaugg-a-gog (pause) chau-bun-a-gung-amaug." It is, however, an invented extension of its real name (Chabunagungamaug, or "boundary fishing place"), devised in the 1920s by Larry Daly, the editor of the *Webster Times.*

7 = Lower North Branch Little Southwest Miramichi — **40**

Canada's longest place name—a short river in New Brunswick.

= Villa Real de la Santa Fé de San Francisco de Asis — **40**

The full Spanish name of Santa Fe, New Mexico, translates as, "Royal city of the holy faith of St. Francis of Assisi."

9 Te Whakatakanga-o-te-ngarehu-o-te-ahi-a-Tamatea — **38**

The Maori name of Hammer Springs, New Zealand; like the second name in this list, it refers to a legend of Tamatea, explaining how the springs were warmed by "the falling of the cinders of the fire of Tamatea."

10 Meallan Liath Coire Mhic Dhubhghaill — **32**

The longest multiple name in Scotland, a place near Aultanrynie, Highland, alternatively spelled Meallan Liath Coire Mhic Dhughaill (30 letters).

* Including single-word, hyphenated, and multiple names

United States

THE 10 FIRST US STATES

	STATE	ENTERED UNION
1	Delaware	Dec 7, 1787
2	Pennsylvania	Dec 12, 1787
3	New Jersey	Dec 18, 1787
4	Georgia	Jan 2, 1788
5	Connecticut	Jan 9, 1788
6	Massachusetts	Feb 6, 1788
7	Maryland	Apr 28, 1788
8	South Carolina	May 23, 1788
9	New Hampshire	Jun 21, 1788
10	Virginia	Jun 25, 1788

THE 10 LAST US STATES

	STATE	ENTERED UNION
1	Hawaii	Aug 21, 1959
2	Alaska	Jan 3, 1959
3	Arizona	Feb 14, 1912
4	New Mexico	Jan 6, 1912
5	Oklahoma	Nov 16, 1907
6	Utah	Jan 4, 1896
7	Wyoming	Jul 10, 1890
8	Idaho	Jul 3, 1890
9	Washington	Nov 18, 1889
10	Montana	Nov 8, 1889

THE 10 LEAST POPULATED STATES

	STATE	POPULATION (2006)
1	Wyoming	515,004
2	Vermont	623,908
3	North Dakota	635,867
4	Alaska	670,053
5	South Dakota	781,919
6	Delaware	853,476
7	Montana	944,632
8	Rhode Island	1,067,610
9	Hawaii	1,285,498
10	New Hampshire	1,314,895

Source: US Census Bureau

TOP 10 MOST POPULATED STATES

	STATE	POPULATION (2006)
1	California	36,457,549
2	Texas	23,507,783
3	New York	19,306,183
4	Florida	18,089,888
5	Illinois	12,831,970
6	Pennsylvania	12,440,621
7	Ohio	11,478,006
8	Michigan	10,095,643
9	Georgia	9,363,941
10	North Carolina	8,856,505

American extremes
Alaska, the penultimate state to join the Union, is also the largest, comprising more than 16 percent of the entire area of the USA. In total contrast, Rhode Island measures just 37 miles (60 km) by 48 miles (77 km), but has a tidal shoreline totaling 384 miles (618 km).

THE 10 LEAST DENSELY POPULATED US STATES

	STATE	POPULATION DENSITY (2005)	
		SQ MILES	SQ KM
1	Alaska	1.2	0.46
2	Wyoming	5.2	2.00
3	Montana	6.4	2.47
4	North Dakota	9.2	3.55
5	South Dakota	10.2	3.93
6	New Mexico	15.9	6.13
7	Idaho	17.3	6.67
8	Nevada	22.0	8.49
9	Nebraska	22.9	8.84
10	Utah	30.1	11.62

Source: US Census Bureau

THE 10 MOST DENSELY POPULATED US STATES

	STATE	POPULATION DENSITY (2005)	
		SQ MILES	SQ KM
1	New Jersey	1,175.3	453.79
2	Rhode Island	1,029.9	396.74
3	Massachusetts	816.2	315.13
4	Connecticut	724.5	279.73
5	Maryland	573.0	221.23
6	Delaware	431.8	166.71
7	New York	407.8	157.45
8	Florida	329.9	127.37
9	Ohio	280.0	108.10
10	Pennsylvania	277.3	107.06
	US average	*83.8*	*32.35*

Source: US Census Bureau

TOP 10 **LARGEST US STATES**

STATE	LAND AREA* SQ MILES	SQ KM
1 Alaska	571,951	1,481,347
2 Texas	261,797	678,051
3 California	155,959	403,933
4 Montana	145,552	376,979
5 New Mexico	121,356	314,309
6 Arizona	113,635	294,312
7 Nevada	109,826	284,448
8 Colorado	103,718	268,627
9 Wyoming	97,100	251,489
10 Oregon	95,997	248,631
Total (all states)	*3,537,438*	*9,161,923*

* Excluding water

The total land area of the United States has grown progressively: in 1800 it was 867,980 sq miles (2,248,058 sq km), and by 1900 it had grown to 2,974,159 sq miles (7,703,036 sq km).

TOP 10 **SMALLEST US STATES**

STATE	LAND AREA* SQ MILES	SQ KM
1 Rhode Island	1,045	2,706
2 Delaware	1,955	5,063
3 Connecticut	4,845	12,548
4 Hawaii	6,423	16,635
5 New Jersey	7,419	19,215
6 Massachusetts	7,838	20,300
7 New Hampshire	8,969	23,229
8 Vermont	9,249	23,955
9 Maryland	9,775	25,317
10 West Virginia	24,087	62,385

* Excluding water

Smallest state Rhode Island has the longest official name, "State of Rhode Island and Providence Plantations." A total of 547 Rhode Islands—which also includes some 500 sq miles (1,295 sq km) of inland water—could be fitted into the land area of Alaska.

Reaching for the Sky

TOP 10 **CITIES WITH MOST SKYSCRAPERS***

	CITY / LOCATION	SKYSCRAPERS
1	Hong Kong, China	199
2	New York City, USA	190
3	Chicago, USA	90
4	Shanghai, China	71
5	Tokyo, Japan	69
6	Singapore City, Singapore	38
7	Dubai, UAR	35
8	Shenzen, China	31
9	Houston, USA	29
10	Seoul, South Korea	27

* Completed habitable buildings of more than 500 ft (152 m)

Inspired by spires
Its recent surge in high-rise building has resulted in Hong Kong, with more skyscrapers and the greatest density of tall buildings in the world, seizing New York's longstanding world lead.

TOP 10 **TALLEST HABITABLE BUILDINGS IN THE USA***

	BUILDING / LOCATION	YEAR COMPLETED	STOREYS	ROOF HEIGHT FT	M
1	Sears Tower, Chicago, IL with spires	1973	110	442.3 527.3	1,451 1,730
2	Empire State Building, New York, NY with spire	1931	102	381.0 448.7	1,250 1,472
3	Trump International IL Hotel & Tower, Chicago,	2008	92	365.9 415.1	1,171 1,362
4	Aon Center, Chicago, IL	1973	83	346.3	1,136
5	John Hancock Centre, Chicago, IL with spires	1969	100	343.5 457.2	1,127 1,500
6	Waterview Tower, Chicago, IL	2009	90	318.2	1,044
7	US Bank Tower, Los Angeles, CA	1989	73	310.3	1,018
8	JPMorgan Chase Tower, Houston, TX	1982	75	305.4	1,002
9	Wells Fargo Plaza, Houston, TX	1983	71	302.4	992
10	Comcast Center, Philadelphia, PA	2008	57	297.2	975

* Excluding communications masts and towers, chimneys, and church spires

TOP 10 **TALLEST CHURCHES**

	CHURCH / LOCATION / YEAR COMPLETED	HEIGHT* FT	M
1	Sagrada Família, Barcelona, Spain, 2026#	558	170.0
2	Ulm Cathedral, Ulm, Germany, 1890	530	161.5
3	Our Lady of Peace Basilica, Yamoussoukro, Côte d'Ivoire, 1990	518	158.0
4	Cologne Cathedral, Cologne, Germany, 1880	516	157.4
5	Notre-Dame Cathedral, Rouen, France, 1876	495	151.0
6	St Nicholas, Hamburg, Germany, 1847	483	147.3
7	Notre Dame Cathedral, Strasbourg, France, 1439	472	144.0
8	St Peter's, Rome, Italy, 1626	454	138.0
9	St Stephen's Cathedral, Vienna, Austria, 1570	449	137.0
10	Neuer Dom, Linz, Austria, 1924	440	134.1

* To tip of spire
# Under construction—scheduled completion date

The Chicago Methodist Temple (completed 1924) is 568 ft (173 m) high, but is sited atop a 25-storey, 328-ft (100-m) building.

TOP 10 **TALLEST HABITABLE BUILDINGS**

2009

BUILDING / LOCATION / YEAR COMPLETED	STOREYS	ROOF HEIGHT FT	M
1 Burj Dubai, Dubai, UAR 2008*	162	2,110	643.2
2 Shanghai World Financial Center, Shanghai, China 2008*	101	1,614	492.0
3 Abraj Al Bait Hotel Tower, Mecca, Saudi Arabia 2008*	76	1,591	485.0
4 Greenland Square Zifeng Tower, Nanjing, China 2008*	69	1,476	450.0
5 Taipei 101, Taipei, Taiwan 2004	101	1,474	449.2
6 Sears Tower, Chicago, USA 1973	110	1,451	442.3
7 Guangzhou Twin Towers, Guangzhou, China 2009*	103	1,435	437.5
8 Jin Mao Tower, Shanghai, China 1998	88	1,380	420.5
9 Princess Tower, Dubai, UAE 2009*	107	1,358	414.0
10 Al Hamra Tower, Kuwait 2008*	77	1,352	412.0

* Under construction—scheduled completion date

1989

BUILDING / LOCATION / YEAR COMPLETED	STOREYS	ROOF HEIGHT FT	M
1 Sears Tower, Chicago, USA 1973	110	1,451	442.3
2 1 World Trade Center, New York, USA* 1972	110	1,368	417.0
3 2 World Trade Center, New York, USA* 1973	110	1,363	415.4
4 Empire State Building, New York, USA 1931	102	1,250	381.0
5 Aon Center, Chicago, USA 1973	83	1,136	346.3
6 John Hancock Center, Chicago, USA 1969	100	1,127	343.5
7 US Bank Tower, Los Angeles 1989	73	1,018	310.3
8 J. P. Morgan Chase Tower, Houston, USA 1982	75	1,002	305.0
9 Wells Fargo Plaza, Houston, USA 1983	71	992	302.4
10 First Canadian Place, Toronto, Canada 1975	72	978	298.1

* Destroyed in 9/11 terrorist attacks

Below: Top tower
Completed in 2008, the Burj Dubai (Dubai Tower) is the world's tallest structure of any kind ever built.

Right: High wire
The Sears Tower, Chicago, during construction. Once the world's tallest building, it has since been overtaken by Middle- and Far-Eastern skyscrapers.

Bridges

TOP 10 LONGEST BRIDGES IN THE USA

BRIDGE / LOCATION	YEAR COMPLETED	LENGTH OF MAIN SPAN FT	M
1 Verrazano Narrows, New York	1964	4,260	1,298
2 Golden Gate, San Francisco, California	1937	4,200	1,280
3 Mackinac Straits, Michigan	1957	3,800	1,158
4 George Washington, New York	1931/62*	3,500	1,067
5 Tacoma Narrows II, Washington	1950	2,800	853
6 Al Zampa Memorial (New Carquinez), Carquinez, California	2003	2,388	728
7 Transbay, San Francisco, California#	1936	2,310	704
8 Bronx-Whitestone, New York	1939	2,300	701
9 Delaware Memorial, Wilmington, Delaware#	1951/68	2,150	655
10 Walt Whitman, Philadelphia, Pennsylvania	1957	2,000	610

* Lower deck added
# Twin spans

All 10 listed here are suspension bridges.

TOP 10 LONGEST CANTILEVER BRIDGES

BRIDGE / LOCATION	YEAR COMPLETED	LONGEST SPAN FT	M
1 Pont de Québec, Canada	1917	1,800	549
2 Firth of Forth, Scotland	1890	1,710	521
3 Minato Ohashi, Osaka, Japan	1974	1,673	510
4 Commodore John Barry, New Jersey/Pennsylvania, USA	1974	1,622	494
5 =Greater New Orleans 1*, Louisiana, USA	1958	1,575	480
=Greater New Orleans 2*, Louisiana, USA	1988	1,575	480
7 Howrah, Calcutta, India	1943	1,500	457
8 Veterans Memorial, Gramercy, Louisiana, USA	1995	1,460	445
9 Transbay, San Francisco, USA	1936	1,400	427
10 Horace Wilkinson, Baton Rouge, Louisiana, USA	1969	1,235	376

* Jointly known as Crescent City Connection

TOP 10 LONGEST CABLE-STAYED BRIDGES

BRIDGE / LOCATION

1 Sutong, Changshu-Nantong, China

2 Stonecutters, Hong Kong

3 Tatara, Onomichi-Imabari, Japan

4 Pont de Normandie, Le Havre, France

5 Incheon-Yeongjong, South Korea

6 Third Nanjing Yangtze Bridge, Nanjing, China

7 Suramdu, Madura Strait, Indonesia

8 Second Nanjing Yangtze Bridge, Nanjing, China

9 Baishazhou, Wuhan, China

10 Minjiang, Qinghzhou China

TOP 10 **LONGEST STEEL ARCH BRIDGES**

	BRIDGE / LOCATION	YEAR COMPLETED	LONGEST SPAN FT	M
1	Chaotianmen, Chongqing, China	2008	1,811	552
2	New River Gorge, Fayetteville, West Virginia, USA	1977	1,699	518
3	Kill van Kull, Bayonne, New Jersey/ Staten Island, New York, USA	1931	1,654	504
4	Sydney Harbour, Australia	1932	1,650	503
5	Caiyuanba, Chongqing, China	2007	1,378	420
6	Fremont, Portland, Oregon, USA	1973	1,253	382
7	Port Mann, Vancouver, Canada	1964	1,201	366
8 =	Cold Spring Canyon, Santa Barbara, California, USA	1963	1,148	350
=	Nanning Yonghe, Nanning, China	2004	1,148	350
10	Bridge of the Americas, Balboa, Panama	1962	1,129	344

This list includes only exclusively steel structures. The Lupu Bridge, Shanghai, China, completed in 2003, and at 1,804 ft (550 m) then the world's longest arch construction, combines steel and concrete.

Bridge of size
The longest exclusively steel arch bridge in the world, the Chaotianmen Bridge features a six-lane highway on its upper deck, a four-lane road and light railroad on the lower, and pedestrian walkways on both.

YEAR COMPLETED	LENGTH OF MAIN SPAN FT	M
2008	3,570	1,088
2008	3,339	1,018
1999	2,920	890
1994	2,808	856
2009	2,625	800
2005	2,126	648
2008	2,067	630
2001	2,060	628
2000	2,027	618
1999	1,985	605

TOP 10 **LONGEST SUSPENSION BRIDGES**

	BRIDGE / LOCATION	YEAR COMPLETED	LENGTH OF MAIN SPAN FT	M
1	Akashi-Kaikyo, Kobe-Naruto, Japan	1998	6,532	1,991
2	Xihoumen, China	2007	5,413	1,650
3	Great Belt, Denmark	1997	5,328	1,624
4	Ryungyang, China	2005	4,888	1,490
5	Humber Estuary, UK	1980	4,625	1,410
6	Jiangyin, China	1998	4,543	1,385
7	Tsing Ma, Hong Kong, China	1997	4,518	1,377
8	Verrazano Narrows, New York, USA	1964	4,260	1,298
9 =	Golden Gate, San Francisco, USA	1937	4,200	1,280
=	Yangluo, China	2007	4,200	1,280

The planned Messina Strait Bridge between Sicily and Calabria, Italy, would have had the longest center span of any bridge at 10,827 ft (3,300 m), but the project was canceled on October 11, 2006.

Tunnels

TOP 10 LONGEST CANAL TUNNELS

TUNNEL / CANAL / LOCATION	YEAR COMPLETED	LENGTH FT	M
1 Le Rôve, Canal de Marseille au Rhône, France	1927	23,359	7,120
2 Bony ("Le Grand Souterrain"), Canal de St Quentin, France	1810	18,625	5,677
3 Standedge, Huddersfield Narrow, UK	1811	17,093	5,210
4 Mauvages, Canal de la Marne et Rhin, France	1853	16,305	4,970
5 Balesmes, Canal Marne à la Saône, France	1883	15,813	4,820
6 Ruyaulcourt, Canal du Nord, France	1923	14,763	4,500
7 Strood*, Thames and Medway, UK	1924	11,837	3,608
8 Lapal, Birmingham, UK	1798	11,712	3,570
9 Sapperton, Thames and Severn, UK	1789	11,443	3,488
10 Pouilly-en-Auxois, Canal de Bourgogne, France	1832	10,935	3,333

* Later converted to a rail tunnel

Begun in 1911, work on the Rôve tunnel, cut through the Chaîne de l'Estaque, was put on hold during World War I and finally completed in 1927. Although out of service since June 16, 1963, it remains the longest and largest canal tunnel in the world, once capable of accommodating oceangoing ships. It is 72 ft (22 m) wide and 50.5 ft (15.4 m) high, with a bore area of 3,444 sq ft (320 sq m), or about six times the size of a double-track rail tunnel. A total volume of 88,286,674 cu ft (2,500,000 cu m) of rock was extracted.

TOP 10 LONGEST SUBSEA TUNNELS

TUNNEL / LOCATION	YEAR COMPLETED	LENGTH FT	M
1 Seikan, Japan	1988	176,673	53,850
2 Channel Tunnel, France/England	1994	165,518	50,450
3 Shin-Kanmon, Japan	1975	61,286	18,680
4 Tokyo Bay Aqualine Expressway*, Japan	1997	31,440	9,583
5 Great Belt Fixed Link (Eastern Tunnel), Denmark	1997	26,325	8,024
6 Bømlafjord*, Norway	2000	26,020	7,931
7 Eiksund*, Norway	2008	25,581	7,797
8 Oslofjord*, Norway	2000	24,245	7,390
9 Severn, UK	1886	22,992	7,008
10 Magerøysund*, Norway	1999	22,556	6,875

* Road; others rail

The need to connect the Japanese islands of Honshu, Kyushu, and Hokkaido has resulted in a wave of undersea tunnel building in recent years, with the Seikan the most ambitious project of all. Connecting Honshu and Hokkaido, 14.4 miles (23.3 km) of the tunnel is 328 ft (100 m) below the seabed. The Channel Tunnel was first proposed in 1802 and test borings undertaken in 1876, but it was over 100 years before technology made it feasible. Its overall length is shorter than the Seikan Tunnel, but the undersea portion is longer, at 23.6 miles (38.0 km).

TOP 10 LONGEST WATER-SUPPLY TUNNELS

TUNNEL / LOCATION	YEAR COMPLETED	LENGTH MILES	KM
1 Delaware Aqueduct, New York, USA	1945	105.0	169.0
2 Päijänne, Finland	1982	74.6	120.0
3 Orange-Fish, South Africa	1975	51.4	82.8
4 Bolmen, Sweden	1987	51.0	82.0
5 Thames Water Ring Main, London, UK	1994	49.7	80.0
6 West Delaware, New York, USA	1960	44.0	70.8
7 Zelivka, Czech Republic	1972	32.2	51.9
8 Central outfall, Mexico City	1975	31.1	50.0
9 Thames Lee, UK	1960	18.8	30.3
10 Shandaken, USA	1923	18.1	29.1

TOP 10 **LONGEST ROAD TUNNELS**

TUNNEL / LOCATION	YEAR COMPLETED	LENGTH FT	M
1 Lærdal, Norway	2000	80,413	24,510
2 Zhongnanshan, China	2007	59,186	18,040
3 St Gotthard, Switzerland	1980	55,505	16,918
4 Arlberg, Austria	1978	45,850	13,972
5 Hsuehshan, Taiwan	2006	42,323	12,900
6 Fréjus, France/Italy	1980	42,306	12,895
7 Mont-Blanc, France/Italy	1965	38,094	11,611
8 Gudvangen, Norway	1991	37,493	11,428
9 Folgefonn, Norway	2001	36,417	11,100
10 Kan-Etsu II (southbound), Japan	1991	36,122	11,010

Nos. 1, 3, 4, and 7 have all held the record as "world's longest road tunnel." Previous record-holders include the 19,206-ft (5,854-m) Grand San Bernardo (Italy-Switzerland; 1964); the 16,841-ft (5,133-m) Alfonos XIII or Viella (Spain; 1948); and the 10,620-ft (3,237-m) Queensway (Mersey) Tunnel (connecting Liverpool and Birkenhead, UK; 1934). The 13,780-ft (4,200-m) Ted Williams/ Interstate 190 Extension tunnel, Boston, Massachusetts (1995–2003) is the USA's longest road tunnel, while the 13,727-ft (4,184-m) Anton Anderson Memorial Tunnel, Alaska, is America's longest combined rail and road tunnel. The Eisenhower-Johnson Memorial Tunnel, Colorado, is, at 11,158 ft (3,401 m), the highest road tunnel in the world.

Breakthrough!
Workers celebrate as two sections of the world-beating Gotthard AlpTransit are connected in 2006—with 12 more years of work ahead of them.

TOP 10 **LONGEST RAIL TUNNELS**

TUNNEL / LOCATION	YEAR COMPLETED	LENGTH FT	M
1 Gotthard AlpTransit, Switzerland	2018*	187,244	57,072
2 Seikan, Japan	1988	176,673	53,850
3 Channel Tunnel, France/England	1994	165,518	50,450
4 Moscow Metro (Serpukhovsko-Timiryazevskaya line), Russia	1983	127,625	38,900
5 Lötschberg Base, Switzerland	2007	113,442	34,577
6 Guadarrama, Spain	2007	97,100	28,377
7 London Underground (East Finchley/Morden, Northern Line), UK	1939	91,339	27,840
8 Hakkoda, Japan	2010*	86,795	26,455
9 Iwate-Ichinohe, Japan	2002	84,678	25,810
10 Pajares Base, Spain	2011*	80,928	24,667

* Under construction—scheduled completion date

The world's longest rail tunnel, the Gotthard AlpTransit, Switzerland, was proposed as early as 1947 and given the go-ahead in 1998 after a referendum of the Swiss electorate. When completed, trains will travel through it at 155 mph (250 km/h).

CULTURE & LEARNING

Language

TOP 10 **LONGEST WORDS IN THE OXFORD ENGLISH DICTIONARY**

	WORD (EARLIEST RECORDED USE) / MEANING	LETTERS
1	Supercalifragilisticexpialidocious (1964) Wonderful, from song of this title in the film *Mary Poppins*.	34
2	Floccinaucinihilipilification (1741) The action or habit of estimating as worthless	29
3	Honorificabilitudinitatibus (1599) Honorableness	27
4	Antidisestablishmentarians (1900) Those opposed to the disestablishment of the Church of England	26
5	Overintellectualization (1922) Excessive intellectualization	23
6	= Incircumscriptibleness (1550) Incapable of being circumscribed	22
	= Omnirepresentativeness (1842) The quality of being representative of all forms or kinds	22
	= Reinstitutionalization (1978) Institutionalize again	22
9	Undercharacterization (1968) To depict or play with insufficient characterization or subtlety	21
10	Lithochromatographic* (1843) Color printing technique using stone	20

* One of several examples of 20-letter words

These are strictly nonmedical terms or names of chemical compounds, which can achieve colossal lengths. It thus excludes words such as the 45-letter pneumonoultramicroscopicsilico-volcanoconiosis (1935), which the OED admits occurs "only as an instance of a very long word," along with others invented by writers with inclusion in reference books in mind.

TOP 10 **ONLINE LANGUAGES**

	LANGUAGE	% OF ALL INTERNET USERS	INTERNET USERS*
1	English	30.1	379,529,347
2	Chinese (Mandarin)	14.7	184,901,513
3	Spanish	9.0	113,463,158
4	Japanese	6.9	87,540,000
5	French	5.1	63,761,141
6	German	4.9	61,912,361
7	Portuguese	4.0	50,828,760
8	Arabic	3.7	46,359,140
9	Korean	2.7	34,430,000
10	Italian	2.6	33,143,152
	Top 10 languages	83.7	1,055,868,572
	Rest of world languages	16.3	206,164,125
	World total	100.0	1,262,032,697

* As at November 30, 2007

Source: www.internetworldstats.com

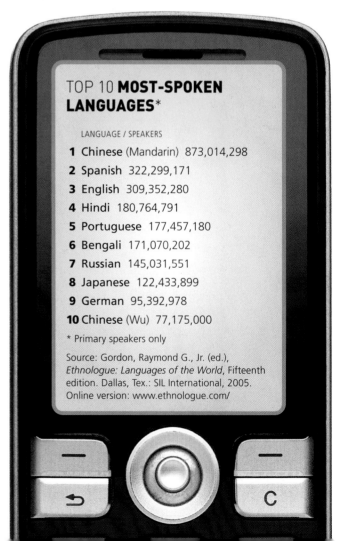

TOP 10 **MOST-SPOKEN LANGUAGES***

LANGUAGE / SPEAKERS

1 Chinese (Mandarin) 873,014,298
2 Spanish 322,299,171
3 English 309,352,280
4 Hindi 180,764,791
5 Portuguese 177,457,180
6 Bengali 171,070,202
7 Russian 145,031,551
8 Japanese 122,433,899
9 German 95,392,978
10 Chinese (Wu) 77,175,000

* Primary speakers only

Source: Gordon, Raymond G., Jr. (ed.), *Ethnologue: Languages of the World*, Fifteenth edition. Dallas, Tex.: SIL International, 2005. Online version: www.ethnologue.com/

Chinese whispers
Mandarin is the most commonly spoken language across China, but another five languages in China have more than 20 million speakers, in addition to numerous minor languages and mutually unintelligible dialects.

The Ultimate Polyglot

New Zealand-born Harold Williams (1876–1928) is considered one of the greatest linguists of all time. He was able to speak 58 different languages and many dialects, ranging from Ancient Greek and Swahili to Basque and various Polynesian tongues. As the foreign editor of the *London Times*, he was the only person capable of addressing all the members of the League of Nations (the forerunner of the United Nations) in their own language.

TOP 10 **COUNTRIES WITH THE MOST ENGLISH-LANGUAGE SPEAKERS**

	COUNTRY	APPROX. NO. OF SPEAKERS*
1	USA	215,423,557
2	UK	58,190,000
3	Canada	20,000,000
4	Australia	14,987,000
5	Ireland	3,750,000
6	= New Zealand	3,700,000
	= South Africa	3,700,000
8	Jamaica#	2,600,000
9	Trinidad and Tobago#	1,145,000
10	Guyana#	650,000

* People for whom English is their mother tongue
\# Includes English Creole

The Top 10 represents the countries with the greatest numbers of inhabitants who speak English as their mother tongue.

TOP 10 **COUNTRIES WITH THE MOST SPANISH-LANGUAGE SPEAKERS**

	COUNTRY	APPROX. NO. OF NATIVE SPEAKERS
1	Mexico	106,255,000
2	Colombia	45,600,000
3	Spain	44,400,000
4	Argentina	41,248,000
5	USA	31,000,000
6	Venezuela	26,021,000
7	Peru	23,191,000
8	Chile	15,795,000
9	Cuba	11,285,000
10	Ecuador	10,946,000

As a result of colonization in parts of Africa, the Americas and Asia, a total of 21 countries speak Spanish as their principal language, making it the second most spoken after Mandarin Chinese and the third most used language on the Internet.

Education

Primary colors
An art class in Indonesia. After India and China, the country has more children in primary school than any other.

TOP 10 **LARGEST UNIVERSITIES**

UNIVERSITY / LOCATION	APPROX. ENROLMENT
1 Allama Iqbal Open University, Islamabad, Pakistan	1,806,214
2 Indira Gandhi National Open University, New Delhi, India	1,500,000
3 Islamic Azad University, Tehran, Iran	1,300,000
4 Anadolu University, Eski ehir, Turkey	884,081
5 Bangladesh Open University, Gazipur, Bangladesh	600,000
6 Dr Babasaheb Ambedkar Open University, Andhra Pradesh, India	450,000
7 State University of New York, New York, USA	418,000
8 California State University, California, USA	417,000
9 Universitas Terbuka, Jakarta, Indonesia	350,000
10 Universidad de Buenos Aires, Buenos Aires, Argentina	316,050

TOP 10 **COUNTRIES WITH MOST PRIMARY SCHOOL PUPILS**

COUNTRY	PRIMARY SCHOOL PUPILS (2005)
1 India	140,012,901
2 China	112,739,964
3 Indonesia	29,149,746
4 USA	24,454,602
5 Nigeria	22,267,407
6 Brazil	18,968,584
7 Bangladesh	17,953,300
8 Pakistan	17,257,947
9 Mexico	14,700,005
10 Philippines	13,083,744
Top 10 total	*410,588,200*
World total	*688,784,276*

Source: UNESCO, *Global Education Digest 2007*

TOP 10 **COUNTRIES WITH MOST SECONDARY SCHOOL PUPILS**

COUNTRY (% FEMALE) / SECONDARY SCHOOL PUPILS

1 China (48)
100,631,925

2 India (43)
89,461,794

3 Brazil (52)
25,127,503

4 USA (49)
24,431,934

5 Indonesia (49)
15,993,187

6 Russia (49)
12,433,155

7 Mexico (51)
10,564,404

8 Bangladesh (50)
10,354,760

9 Iran (47)
9,942,201

10 Vietnam (49)
9,939,319

Top 10 total (av. 49) 308,880,182
World total (47) 512,553,149

Source: UNESCO, *Global Education Digest 2007*

TOP 10 **COUNTRIES WITH THE HIGHEST PERCENTAGE OF ADULTS IN FURTHER EDUCATION**

	COUNTRY	% SCHOOL LEAVERS OF BOTH SEXES IN FURTHER EDUCATION
1	Finland	92
2	South Korea	91
3	Greece	89
4	USA	83
5	= New Zealand	82
	= Sweden	82
7	Slovenia	81
8	= Denmark	80
	= Norway	80
10	Lithuania	73
	World average	*24*

Source: UNESCO, *Global Education Digest 2007*

TOP 10 **OLDEST UNIVERSITIES AND COLLEGES IN THE USA**

	UNIVERSITY / LOCATION	YEAR CHARTERED
1	Harvard University, Massachusetts	1636
2	College of William and Mary, Virginia	1692
3	Yale University, Connecticut	1701
4	University of Pennsylvania, Pennsylvania	1740
5	Moravian College, Pennsylvania	1742
6	Princeton University, New Jersey	1746
7	Washington and Lee University, Virginia	1749
8	Columbia University, New York	1754
9	Brown University, Rhode Island	1764
10	Rutgers, the State University of New Jersey	1766

Source: National Center for Education Statistics

Books

TOP 10 MOST TRANSLATED AUTHORS

AUTHOR / COUNTRY / DATES	TRANSLATIONS
1 Agatha Christie (UK, 1890–1976)	6,362
2 Jules Verne (France, 1828–1905)	4,021
3 V. I. Lenin (Russia, 1870–1924)	3,497
4 William Shakespeare (England, 1564–1616)	3,435
5 Enid Blyton (UK, 1897–1968)	3,433
6 Barbara Cartland (UK, 1901–2000)	3,315
7 Danielle Steel (USA, b. 1947)	2,767
8 Hans Christian Andersen (Denmark, 1805–75)	2,624
9 Stephen King (USA, b. 1947)	2,591
10 Jakob Grimm (Germany, 1785–1863)	2,382

According to UNESCO's *Index Translationum*, the total number of translations of books in the period 1979–2005 places British crime writer Agatha Christie as the world's most translated novelist by a substantial margin. Just outside the Top 10 are such popular authors as Mark Twain and Arthur Conan Doyle. Although not an "author" as such, by virtue of the total translations of Walt Disney Productions titles, which number 8,677, the company leads the field.

Queen of crime
Agatha Christie (1890–1976) is one of the bestselling authors of all time, and, according to UNESCO, the most translated.

THE 10 FIRST POCKET BOOKS

AUTHOR / TITLE

1 James Hilton, Lost Horizon
2 Dorothea Brande, Wake Up and Live!
3 William Shakespeare, Five Great Tragedies
4 Thorne Smith, Topper
5 Agatha Christie, The Murder of Roger Ackroyd
6 Dorothy Parker, Enough Rope
7 Emily Brontë, Wuthering Heights
8 Samuel Butler, The Way of All Flesh
9 Thornton Wilder, The Bridge of San Luis Rey
10 Felix Saltern, Bambi

All 10 Pocket Books were published in the USA in 1939 (a single title, Pearl S. Buck's Nobel Prize-winning *The Good Earth*, had been test-marketed the previous year, but only in New York). Unlike their British counterparts, Penguin Books, Pocket Books titles all had pictorial covers: the first 10 were created by Isador N. Steinberg and Frank J. Lieberman (who also drew the Pocket Books logo, a kangaroo that he named Gertrude, after his mother-in-law). When a survey of sales was conducted 18 years later, it was discovered that of the first 10, Shakespeare was the bestselling title with over 2,000,000 copies in print, followed by James Hilton's *Lost Horizon* (1,750,000), Thorne Smith's *Topper* (1,500,000), and Emily Brontë's *Wuthering Heights* (more than 1,000,000).

TOP 10 BESTSELLING BOOKS OF ALL TIME

AUTHOR / BOOK / DATE	EST. SALES
1 The Bible, c. 1456–	6,000,000,000
2 Quotations from the Works of Mao Tse-tung, 1966	900,000,000
3 Qur'an (Koran)	800,000,000
4 Miguel de Cervantes, Don Quixote, 1605	500,000,000
5 Xinhua Zidian (Chinese dictionary), 1953–	400,000,000
6 Thomas Cranmer, Book of Common Prayer, 1549	300,000,000
7 John Bunyan, The Pilgrim's Progress, 1678	250,000,000
8 John Foxe, Foxe's Book of Martyrs, 1563	150,000,000
9 J. K. Rowling, Harry Potter and the Philosopher's Stone, 1997	117,000,000
10 Agatha Christie, And Then There Were None, 1939	110,000,000

The publication of multiple editions, translations, and pirated copies—and often exaggerated sales claims—make it notoriously problematic to establish precise sales of recently published books.

THE 10 **LATEST WINNERS OF THE PULITZER PRIZE FOR FICTION**

YEAR	AUTHOR / TITLE
2008	Junot Diaz, The Brief Wondrous Life of Oscar Wao
2007	Cormac McCarthy, The Road
2006	Geraldine Brooks, March
2005	Marilynne Robinson, Gilead
2004	Edward P. Jones, The Known World
2003	Jeffrey Eugenides, Middlesex
2002	Richard Russo, Empire Falls
2001	Michael Chabon, The Amazing Adventures of Kavalier & Clay
2000	Jhumpa Lhiri, Interpreter of Maladies
1999	Michael Cunningham, The Hours

THE 10 **FIRST PENGUIN PAPERBACKS**

AUTHOR / TITLE

1 André Maurois, Ariel
2 Ernest Hemingway, A Farewell to Arms
3 Eric Linklater, Poet's Pub
4 Susan Ertz, Madame Claire
5 Dorothy L. Sayers, The Unpleasantness at the Bellona Club
6 Agatha Christie, The Mysterious Affair at Styles
7 Beverley Nichols, Twenty-five
8 E. H. Young, William
9 Mary Webb, Gone to Earth
10 Compton Mackenzie, Carnival

Paperbacks have a much longer history than most people realize. In 1837 the German publishing company, Tauchnitz, began to issue paperback novels in English. Curiously, for copyright and other reasons, they were available everywhere except Great Britain, but through healthy sales to English-speaking Europeans and British and American travelers, the company was able to add a new title virtually every week for the next 100 years. A rival to Tauchnitz, the Albatross Modern Continental Library, began publishing in 1932—but sales of their English-language paperbacks were similarly restricted to the Continent. Although some books had appeared in paperback in England during this period, they were generally of poor quality. It was the British publisher Allen Lane (1902–70; knighted 1952) who, remarking "I would be the first to admit that there is no fortune in this series for anyone concerned," launched his first Penguin titles in Great Britain on July 30, 1935. Originally Penguins were paperback reprints of books that had been previously published as hardbacks; their quality, range of subjects, and low price established them as the pioneering books in the "paperback revolution."

The importance of being Ernest
Ernest Hemingway's A Farewell to Arms *was one of the first Penguin paperbacks. By the time it was published in 1939, the novel (first issued in 1929) had been made into an Oscar-nominated film.*

Libraries & Loans

TOP 10 MOST BORROWED FICTION TITLES IN THE USA, 2007

1 Khaled Hosseini,
   A Thousand Splendid Suns
2 James Patterson and Howard
   Roughan, You've Been Warned
3 James Patterson and Michael
   Ledwidge, The Quickie
4 Sandra Brown, Play Dirty
5 Khaled Hosseini, The Kite Runner
6 James Patterson and Maxine
   Paetro, The 6th Target
7 Janet Evanovich, Lean Mean Thirteen
8 John Grisham, Playing for Pizza
9 Nora Roberts, High Noon
10 Jeffrey Eugenides, Middlesex

Source: Library Journal

Page-turner Patterson
Author James Patterson has sold over 150
million books worldwide and has established
the PageTurner Awards to encourage reading.

TOP 10 BOOKS FOUND IN MOST LIBRARIES

BOOK / TOTAL LIBRARY HOLDINGS*

1 Bible, 796,882
2 US Census, 460,628
3 Mother Goose, 67,663
4 Dante Alighieri,
   Divine Comedy, 62,414
5 Homer, The Odyssey, 45,551
6 Homer, The Iliad, 44,093
7 Mark Twain, Huckleberry Finn, 42,724
8 J. R. R. Tolkien,
   Lord of the Rings (trilogy), 40,907
9 William Shakespeare,
   Hamlet, 39,521
10 Lewis Carroll, Alice's Adventures
   in Wonderland, 39,277

* Based on WorldCat listings of all editions of
books held in 53,000 libraries in 96 countries

Source: OCLC (Online Computer Library Center)

TOP 10 LARGEST LIBRARIES

	LIBRARY	LOCATION	FOUNDED	BOOKS
1	Library of Congress	Washington DC, USA	1800	32,124,001
2	British Library*	London, UK	1753	29,000,000
3	Deutsche Bibliothek#	Frankfurt, Germany	1990	22,200,000
4	Library of the Russian Academy of Sciences	St Petersburg, Russia	1714	20,500,000
5	National Library of Canada	Ottawa, Canada	1953	19,500,000
6	Russian State Library†	Moscow, Russia	1862	17,000,000
7	Harvard University Library	Cambridge, Massachusetts, USA	1638	15,826,570
8	Boston Public Library	Boston, Massachusetts, USA	1895	15,686,902
9	Vernadsky National Scientific Library of Ukraine	Kiev, Ukraine	1919	15,000,000
10	National Library of Russia	St Petersburg	1795	14,799,267

* Founded as part of the British Museum, 1753; became an independent body in 1973
# Formed in 1990 through the unification of the Deutsche Bibliothek, Frankfurt (founded 1947)
and the Deutsche Bucherei, Leipzig
† Founded 1862 as Rumyantsev Library, formerly State V .I. Lenin Library

Comparisons between libraries based on their holdings vary according to what is included.
The figure for the Library of Congress is for printed books only, but it also has more than
100 million catalogued items, including manuscripts, maps, and photographs.

TOP 10 MOST-VISITED PRESIDENTIAL LIBRARIES IN THE USA

PRESIDENT* / ANNUAL VISITORS

1 Abraham Lincoln, 800,000
2 Thomas Jefferson, 450,112
3 Bill Clinton, 400,000
4 Ronald Reagan, 300,000
5 John Fitzgerald Kennedy, 220,000
6 (John) Adams National
   Historical Park, 185,000
7 Lyndon Johnson, 183,000
8 George Bush, 138,252
9 (George) Washington Birthplace
   National Monument, 131,000
10 = Franklin Delano Roosevelt,
   110,000
   = Harry Truman, 110,000

* Excluding the Richard Nixon Library, which
does not reveal its visitor figures

Source: The Official Museum Directory

TOP 10 **OLDEST NATIONAL LIBRARIES**

LIBRARY / LOCATION	FOUNDED
1 Národní Knihovna Ceské Republiky National Library of the Czech Republic, Prague, Czech Republic	1366
2 Österreichische Nationalbibliothek National Library of Austria, Vienna, Austria	1368
3 Biblioteca Nazionale Marciana, Venice, Italy	1468
4 Bibliothèque Nationale de France National Library of France, Paris, France	1480
5 National Library of Malta, Valletta, Malta	1555
6 Bayerische Staatsbibliothek, Munich, Germany	1558
7 Bibliothèque Royale Albert 1er National Library of Belgium, Brussels, Belgium	1559
8 Nacionalna i Sveucilicna Knjisnica Zagreb National and University Library, Zagreb, Croatia	1606
9 Helsingin Yliopisto Kirjasto National Library of Finland, Helsinki, Finland	1640
10 Det Kongeligie Bibliotek National Library of Denmark, Copenhagen, Denmark	1653

What may claim to be the world's first national library was that in Alexandria, Egypt, founded in about 307 BC by King Ptolemy I Soter. It assembled the world's largest collection of scrolls, which were partly destroyed during Julius Caesar's invasion of 48 BC, and totally by Arab invaders under Amr ibn al'Aas in AD 642, an event that is considered one of the greatest losses to world scholarship.

TOP 10 **MOST BORROWED NONFICTION TITLES IN THE USA, 2007**

1 Elizabeth Gilbert, Eat, Pray, Love

2 Don Piper, 90 Minutes In Heaven: A True Story of Death and Life

3 Jon Krakauer, Into the Wild

4 Kevin Trudeau, Natural Cures "They" Don't Want You to Know About

5 Michael Berg, The Secret: Unlocking the Source of Joy and Fulfillment

6 Dave Pelzer, The Lost Boy

7 Jeannette Walls, The Glass Castle: A Memoir

8 Rhonda Byrne, The Secret

9 Karrine Steffans, Confessions of a Video Vixen

10 Christopher Hitchens, God Is Not Great

Source: *Library Journal*

Austrian National Library
The imperial library founded by Austrian Duke Albrecht III (1349–95) has grown into an institution with a collection of some 7.5 million books.

The Press

TOP 10 **MAGAZINES**

MAGAZINE*	AVERAGE CIRCULATION
1 Reader's Digest	12,078,000
2 Better Homes and Gardens	7,605,000
3 Family Circle	4,634,000
4 Woman's Day	4,205,000
5 Time	4,112,000
6 Ladies' Home Journal	4,101,000
7 Kampioen (Netherlands)	3,756,000
8 People	3,625,000
9 Playboy	3,215,000
10 Newsweek	3,183,000

* All US unless otherwise stated

Source: International Federation of Audit Bureaux of Circulations

TOP 10 **MAGAZINES IN THE USA***

MAGAZINE	AVERAGE CIRCULATION, 2006
1 AARP The Magazine	23,250,882
2 AARP Bulletin	22,621,079
3 Reader's Digest	10,094,284
4 Better Homes and Gardens	7,627,046
5 National Geographic	5,072,478
6 Good Housekeeping	4,675,281
7 Ladies' Home Journal	4,136,462
8 Time	4,082,740
9 Woman's Day	4,014,278
10 Family Circle	4,000,887

* Free and paid-for publications

Source: Audit Bureau of Circulations/Magazine Publishers of America

TOP 10 **DAILY NEWSPAPERS IN THE USA**

NEWSPAPER	AVERAGE US CIRCULATION*
1 USA Today	2,284,219
2 The Wall Street Journal	2,069,463
3 The New York Times	1,476,400
4 Los Angeles Times	1,101,981
5 Chicago Tribune	898,703
6 The Washington Post	890,163
7 New York Daily News	775,543
8 New York Post	702,488
9 Denver Post/Rocky Mountain News	600,026
10 Dallas Morning News	520,215

* Average for six months to March 31, 2008

Source: Audit Bureau of Circulations

Apart from *The Wall Street Journal*, which focuses mainly on financial news, *USA Today* remains the USA's only true national daily newspaper. Historically, America's press has been regionally based, and in consequence the top four listed are the only newspapers with million-plus circulations. This contrasts with, for example, the UK, where, despite its comparatively small population, nationwide newspapers dominate the market, three of them achieving sales in excess of one million.

TOP 10 OLDEST NEWSPAPERS

	NEWSPAPER	COUNTRY	FOUNDED
1	Haarlems Dagblad	Netherlands	1656
2	Gazzetta di Mantova	Italy	1664
3	The London Gazette	UK	1665
4	Wiener Zeitung	Austria	1703
5	Hildesheimer Allgemeine Zeitung	Germany	1705
6	Berrow's Worcester Journal	UK	1709
7	Newcastle Journal	UK	1711
8	Stamford Mercury	UK	1712
9	Northampton Mercury	UK	1720
10	Hanauer Anzeiger	Germany	1725

This list includes only newspapers that have been published continuously since their founding, under the same name—or at least containing the name, as in the case of the *Worcester Journal*, which was founded in 1690 as *Worcester Post Man*, published irregularly until it became the *Worcester Journal* in 1709, and adopted the name of its proprietor, Harvey Berrow, to become *Berrow's Worcester Journal* in 1753. The former No. 1 on this list, the Swedish *Post-och Inrikes Tidningar*, founded in 1645, ceased publication on paper on January 1, 2007, and is now available only online.

TOP 10 OLDEST NEWSPAPERS IN THE USA

	NEWSPAPER / CITY	YEAR ESTABLISHED
1	The Hartford Courant, Hartford, CT	1764
2	= Poughkeepsie Journal, Poughkeepsie, NY	1785
	= The Augusta Chronicle, Augusta, GA	1785
	= The Register Star, Hudson, NY	1785
5	= Pittsburgh Post-Gazette, Pittsburgh, PA	1786
	= Daily Hampshire Gazette, Northampton, MA	1786
7	The Berkshire Eagle, Pittsfield, MA	1789
8	Norwich Bulletin, Norwich, CT	1791
9	The Recorder, Greenfield, MA	1792
10	Intelligencer Journal, Lancaster, PA	1794

Source: *Editor and Publisher Year Book*

Among even older newspapers that are no longer extant is the *Boston News-Letter*, first published in 1704 by New England postmaster John Campbell. It measured just 7.5 x 12 inches and had a circulation of 300 copies.

TOP 10 DAILY NEWSPAPERS

	NEWSPAPER	COUNTRY	AVERAGE DAILY CIRCULATION*, 2006
1	Yomiuri Shimbun	Japan	14,246,000
2	Asahi Shimbun	Japan	12,326,000
3	Mainichi Shimbun	Japan	5,635,000
4	Nihon Keizai Shimbun	Japan	4,737,000
5	Chunichi Shimbun	Japan	4,571,000
6	Bild	Germany	4,220,000
7	The Sun	UK	3,461,000
8	Sankei Shimbun	Japan	2,665,000
9	USA Today	USA	2,603,000
10	Canako Xiaoxi (Beijing)	China	2,530,000

* Averaged over a whole year rather than a period

Source: International Federation of Audit Bureaus of Circulations

Yomiuri Shimbun was founded in Japan 1874. In 1998 it became the country's and the world's bestselling daily newspaper, achieving a record average sale of 14,532,694 copies a day.

Art

TOP 10 BEST-ATTENDED ART EXHIBITIONS, 2007

EXHIBITION	VENUE / CITY / DATES	DAILY AVERAGE	ATTENDANCE* TOTAL#
1 Tutankhamun and the Golden Age of the Pharaohs	Franklin Institute, Philadelphia, USA, Feb 3–Sep 30, 2007	5,375	1,290,000
2 Manet to Picasso	National Gallery, London, UK, Sep 22, 2006–May 23, 2007	4,635	1,110,044
3 Ways of Seeing: John Baldessari Explores	Hirshhorn Museum, Washington DC, USA, Jul 26, 2006–Sep 23, 2007	2,062	874,203
4 The Mind of Leonardo	National Museum, Tokyo, Japan, Mar 20–Jun 17, 2007	10,071	796,004
5 Richard Serra Sculpture: 40 Years	Museum of Modern Art, New York. USA, Jun 3–Sep 10, 2007	8,585	737,074
6 Monet's Art and its Posterity	National Art Center, Tokyo, Japan, Apr 7–Jul 2, 2007	9,273	704,420
7 Masterpieces of French Painting	Neue Nationalgalerie, Berlin, Germany, Jun 1–Oct 7, 2007	6,115	677,000
8 Anselm Kiefer	Museo Guggenheim, Bilbao, Spain, Mar 28–Sep 9, 2007	3,707	576,214
9 Masterpieces of French Painting from the Met	Museum of Fine Arts, Houston, Texas, USA, Feb 4–May 6, 2007	7,268	574,207
10 Heaven or Hell	Royal Ontario Museum, Toronto, Canada, Nov 25, 2006–Oct 8, 2007	1,645	519,747

* With longest part of run in 2007
\# Approximate totals provided by museums

Source: *The Art Newspaper*

Tutankhamun on show
Treasures from the tomb of Tutankhamun formed the centerpiece of a popular exhibition shown in five locations in the USA and in London.

THE 10 MOST-VISITED ART GALLERIES AND MUSEUMS IN THE USA

MUSEUM/GALLERY / LOCATION	ANNUAL VISITORS
1 The Smithsonian Institution*	20,100,000
2 United States Capitol Historical Society*	8,000,000
3 National Museum of American History*	5,900,000
4 National Museum of Natural History*	5,542,000
5 Metropolitan Museum of Art#	5,400,000
6 National Gallery of Art*	4,000,000
7 American Museum of Natural History#	4,000,000
8 Statue of Liberty National Monument and Ellis Island Immigration Museum#	3,408,560
9 Museum of Modern Art#	1,585,000
10 Museum of Science†	1,429,685

* Washington, DC
\# New York, NY
† Boston, MA

Source: The Official Museum Directory

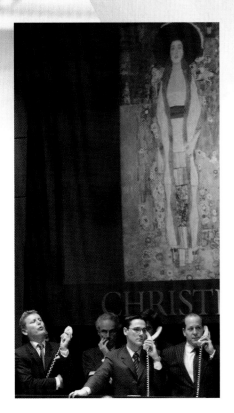

Portraits of a lady

After lengthy litigation to establish their ownership, Gustav Klimt's two portraits of Adele Bloch-Bauer were sold in 2006, the first for an estimated $135 million, setting a world record for a private transaction, while the second fetched almost $88 million at auction.

The Prince of Prints

While paintings are the most expensive works of art sold at auction, in recent years many photographs have sold for increasingly high prices. In 2005 American photographer Richard Prince became the first whose prints sold for more than $1 million when his large *Untitled (Cowboy)* realized $1,248,000 at Christie's New York. Since then, three more prints of the same image have sold for in excess of $1 million.

TOP 10 MOST EXPENSIVE PAINTINGS SOLD AT AUCTION

2008

PAINTING / ARTIST	SALE	PRICE ($)
1 Garçon à la pipe, Pablo Picasso (Spanish; 1881–1973)	Sotheby's New York, May 5, 2004	104,168,000
2 Dora Maar au chat, Pablo Picasso	Sotheby's New York, May 3, 2006	95,216,000
3 Portrait of Adele Bloch-Bauer II, Gustav Klimt (Austrian; 1862–1918)	Christie's New York, Nov 8, 2006	87,936,000
4 Portrait du Dr Gachet, Vincent van Gogh (Dutch; 1853–90)	Christie's New York, May 15, 1990	82,500,000
5 Bal au Moulin de la Galette, Montmartre Pierre-Auguste Renoir (French; 1841–1919)	Sotheby's New York, May 17, 1990	78,100,000
6 The Massacre of the Innocents, Sir Peter Paul Rubens (Flemish; 1577–1640)	Sotheby's London, Jul 10, 2002	75,930,440
7 White Center (Yellow, pink and lavender on rose Mark Rothko (American; 1903–70)	Sotheby's New York, May 15, 2007	72,840,000
8 Green Car Crash – Green Burning Car I, Andy Warhol (American 1928–87)	Christie's New York, May 16, 2007	71,720,000
9 Portrait de l'Artiste Sans Barbe, Vincent van Gogh	Christie's New York, Nov 19, 1998	71,502,496
10 Rideau, Cruchon et Compôtier, Paul Cézanne (French; 1839–1906)	Sotheby's New York, May 10, 1999	60,502,500

1988

PAINTING / ARTIST	SALE	PRICE ($)
1 Irises, Vincent van Gogh, (Dutch; 1853–90)	Sotheby's New York, Nov 11, 1987	53,900,000
2 Sunflowers, Vincent Van Gogh	Christie's London, Mar 30, 1987	39,404,600
3 Acrobate et Jeune Arlequin, Pablo Picasso, (Spanish; 1881–1973)	Christie's London, Nov 28, 1988	38,138,700
4 Dans la Prairie, Claude Monet (French; 1840–1926)	Sotheby's London, Jun 28, 1988	25,417,700
5 Maternité, Pablo Picasso	Christie's New York, Jun 14, 1988	24,750,000
6 Le Pont de Trinquetaille, Vincent van Gogh	Christie's London, Jun 29, 1987	20,622,800
7 False Start, Jasper Johns (American; b.1930)	Sotheby's New York, Nov 10, 1988	17,050,000
8 La Cage d'Oiseaux, Pablo Picasso	Sotheby's New York, Nov 10, 1988	15,400,000
9 Adoration of the Magi, Andrea Mantegna (Italian; 1431–1506)	Christie's London, Apr 18, 1985	10,317,780
10 Paysage au Soleil Levant, Vincent Van Gogh	Sotheby's New York, Apr 24, 1985	9,900,000

Monumental Achievements

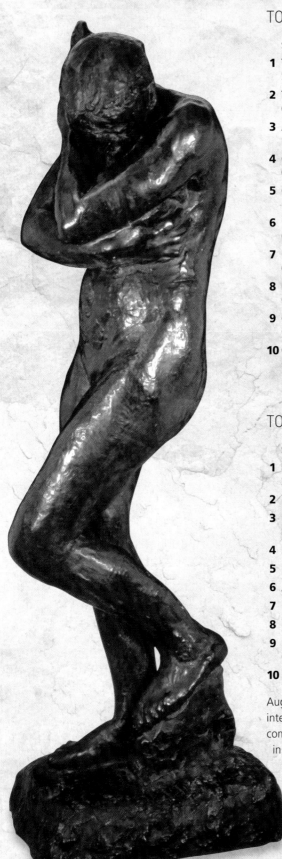

TOP 10 **MOST EXPENSIVE SCULPTURES SOLD AT AUCTION**

SCULPTURE / ARTIST / SALE	PRICE ($)
1 The Guennol Lioness (c. 3000 BC), unknown artist, Sotheby's New York, Dec 5, 2007	57,161,000
2 Tête de femme (Dora Maar) (1941), Pablo Picasso (Spanish; 1881–1973), Sotheby's New York, Nov 7, 2007	29,161,000
3 Artemis and the stag (1st C BC–1st C AD), unknown artist, Sotheby's New York, Jun 10, 2007	28,600,000
4 Oiseau dans l'espace (1922–23), Constantin Brancusi (Romanian; 1876–1957), Christie's New York, May 4, 2005	27,456,000
5 Cubi XXVIII (1965), David Smith (American; 1906–65), Sotheby's New York, Nov 5, 2005	23,816,000
6 Hanging heart (Magenta/Gold) (1994–2006), Jeff Koons (American; b.1955), Sotheby's New York, Nov 14, 2007	23,561,000
7 L'homme qui chavire (1947), Alberto Giacometti (Swiss/Italian; 1901–66), Christie's New York, May 9, 2007	18,520,000
8 Danaïde (1913), Constantin Brancusi (Romanian; 1876–1956), Christie's New York, May 7, 2002	18,159,000
9 Grande Femme Debout I (1960), Alberto Giacometti, Christie's New York, Nov 8, 2000	14,306,000
10 Grande Tete de Diego (1954), Alberto Giacometti, Sotheby's New York, May 8, 2002	13,759,500

TOP 10 **MOST EXPENSIVE SCULPTURES BY AUGUSTE RODIN**

SCULPTURE / SALE	PRICE ($)
1 Iris, messagère des dieux (1890–91), Sotheby's London, Jun 19, 2007	9,114,624
2 Eve (1880–81), Christie's New York, Nov 8, 1999	4,842,500
3 Les Bourgeois de Calais, Grandmodele, Sotheby's New York, May 17, 1990	4,290,000
4 Balzac, Sotheby's New York, May 13, 1998	3,522,500
5 Le penseur (The Thinker) (1880), Sotheby's New York, Nov 7, 2007	3,065,000
6 Andromède (1886), Christie's New York, Nov 8, 2006	3,040,000
7 L'Enfant prodigue (1884), Sotheby's New York, May 3, 2006	2,928,000
8 Le baiser (The Kiss) (1886), Christie's New York, May 8, 2000	2,756,000
9 Eve au rocher, petit modèle – modèle aux pieds détaillés (1883), Christie's New York, May 9, 2007	2,616,000
10 Le baiser (The Kiss) (1886), Sotheby's New York, Nov 7, 2001	2,425,750

Auguste Rodin (1840–1917) was the foremost French sculptor of his day. He achieved international fame through such creations as his *The Thinker* and *The Kiss*, which was commissioned by an American connoisseur, Edward Perry Warren, and kept at his house in Lewes, England, until it was sold to the Tate Gallery, London. Bronze casts of Rodin's works mean that multiple copies exist of a number of them, including *The Burghers of Calais*, one of his most celebrated sculptures, a version of which is in third place in this list, but can also be seen in Calais and in Victoria Tower Gardens in London.

Record Rodin
Rodin's life-sized Eve *set a twentieth-century record for the sculptor when it made $4.8 million at auction. The original sculpture, dating from 1880–81, was cast in bronze in 1897.*

TOP 10 TALLEST FREE-STANDING STATUES

Mighty project
The model of the memorial to Native American warrior Crazy Horse (c.1842–77) is just ¹/₃₄th the size of the actual statue, in progress for 60 years.

STATUE / LOCATION	HEIGHT FT	M
1 **Crazy Horse Memorial**, Thunderhead Mountain, South Dakota, USA	563	172

Started in 1948 by Polish-American sculptor Korczak Ziolkowski and continued after his death in 1982 by his widow and eight of his children, this gigantic equestrian statue, even longer than it is high (641 ft/195 m), is not expected to be completed for several years.

2 **Foshan Jinfo (Vairocana Buddha)**, Lushan, Henan, China	420	128

Completed in 2001, the Buddha sits on a 66-ft (20-m) throne atop a 82 ft (25-m) pedestal.

3 **Ushiku Amida Buddha**, Joodo Teien Garden, Japan	394	120

This Japan-Taiwanese project, unveiled in 1993, took seven years to complete and weighs 1,102 tons.

4 **Nanshan Haishang Guanyin (Avalokitesvara)**, Sanya, Hainan, China	354	108

Depicting the bodhisattva Guan Yin, the statue was completed in 2005 after six years' construction.

5 **Emperors Yan and Huang**, Zhengzhou, Henan, China	348	106

Completed in 2007.

6 **The Indian Rope Trick**, Riddersberg Säteri, Jönköping, Sweden	337	103

Sculptor Calle Örnemark's 159-ton wooden sculpture depicts a long strand of "rope" held by a fakir, while another figure ascends.

7 **Sendai Daikannon (Avalokitesvara)** Sendai, Japan	328	100

Built by a construction company during the late twentieth-century economic boom in Japan.

8 **Peter the Great**, Moscow, Russia	315	96

Georgian sculptor Zurab Tsereteli's statue of the Russian ruler on a galleon was moved from St. Petersburg in 1997.

9 **= Grand Buddha at Ling Shan (Gautama Buddha)**, Wuxi, China	289	88

This gigantic bronze statue was completed in 1996.

= Dai Kannon of Kita no Miyako park (Avalokitesvara) Ashibetsu, Hokkaido, Japan	289	88

Completed in 1989.

MUSIC

Singles

SINGLES THAT STAYED LONGEST IN THE US CHARTS

	TITLE / ARTIST / LONGEST CONSECUTIVE RUN	FIRST CHART ENTRY	WEEKS IN CHART
1	"How Do I Live", LeAnn Rimes (69)	1997	69
2	"Foolish Games"/"You Were Meant For Me", Jewel (41)	1996	65
3	"Before He Cheats", Carrie Underwood (64)	2006	64
4	"Macarena (Bayside Boys Mix)", Los Del Rio (60)	1996	60
5	"Smooth", Santana featuring Rob Thomas (58)	1999	58
6	"Higher", Creed (57)	1999	57
7	="I Don't Want to Wait", Paula Cole (56)	1997	56
	="The Way You Love Me", Faith Hill (56)	2000	56
9	="Amazed", Lonestar (55)	1999	55
	="Barely Breathing", Duncan Sheik (55)	1996	55
	="Missing", Everything But The Girl (55)	1996	55

Source: Music Information Database

Jewel's "You Were Meant For Me" charted for 41 weeks, but then became a double A-side for the remainder of its chart run.

Left: Sweet success
Stefani's Sweet Escape *album generated a world tour and a single of the same name that made the Top 10 of 2007.*

Right: Timbaland
Taken from his album Shock Value, *Timbaland's "The Way I Are" hit No. 1 on the Billboard Top 100 singles chart and was one of 2007's bestsellers.*

TOP 10 **SINGLES OF ALL TIME IN THE USA**

	TITLE / ARTIST	EST. US SALES
1	"Candle in the Wind (1997)"/"Something About the Way You Look Tonight", Elton John	11,000,000
2	"White Christmas", Bing Crosby	8,000,000
3	="Hey Jude", The Beatles	4,000,000
	="We Are the World", USA for Africa	4,000,000
	="I Will Always Love You", Whitney Houston	4,000,000
	="Whoomp! (There it Is)", Tag Team	4,000,000
	="Hound Dog"/"Don't Be Cruel", Elvis Presley	4,000,000
8	="Love Me Tender"/"Any Way You Want Me", Elvis Presley	3,000,000
	="(Every Thing I Do) I Do It For You", Bryan Adams	3,000,000
	="Macarena", Los Del Rio	3,000,000
	="I'll Be Missing You", Puff Daddy and Faith Evans (feat. 112)	3,000,000
	="How Do I Live", LeAnn Rimes	3,000,000

Source: RIAA

TOP 10 **SINGLES IN THE USA IN THE PAST 10 YEARS**

	TITLE	ARTIST	YEAR
1	"Crank That"	Soulja Boy Tell 'Em	2007
2	"Bad Day"	Daniel Powter	2006
3	"Hollaback Girl"	Gwen Stefani	2005
4	"I Believe"	Fantasia	2004
5	"Bridge Over Troubled Water"	Clay Aiken	2003
6	"Before Your Love"/ "A Moment Like This"	Kelly Clarkson	2002
7	"Loverboy"	Mariah Carey	2001
8	"Maria Maria"	Santana feat. the Product G&B	2000
9	"Believe"	Cher	1999
10	"The Boy is Mine"	Brandy & Monica	1998

Source: Music Information Database

The bestselling singles of 2002, 2003, and 2004 were all by the participants of the TV show *American Idol*.

TOP 10 **ARTISTS WITH THE MOST NO. 1 SINGLES IN THE USA**

	ARTIST / TOTAL CHART HITS	NO. 1 SINGLES
1	Elvis Presley (131)	22
2	The Beatles (72)	20
3	Mariah Carey (34)	18
4	Michael Jackson (46)	13
5	= Madonna (52)	12
	= The Supremes (45)	12
7	Whitney Houston (38)	11
8	Janet Jackson (36)	10
9	= The Bee Gees (43)	9
	= Paul McCartney/Wings (46)	9
	= Stevie Wonder (61)	9

Source: Music Information Database

TOP 10 **SINGLES IN THE USA, 2007**

	TITLE / ARTIST	SALES
1	"Crank That", Soulja Boy Tell 'Em	2,909,000
2	"Hey There Delilah", Plain White T's	2,566,000
3	"Big Girls Don't Cry", Fergie	2,525,000
4	"Girlfriend", Avril Lavigne	2,415,000
5	"Apologize", Timbaland featuring OneRepublic	2,371,000
6	"Umbrella", Rihanna	2,359,000
7	"Stronger", Kanye West	2,328,000
8	"Sweet Escape", Gwen Stefani	2,251,000
9	"Glamorous", Fergie feat. Ludacris	2,169,000
10	"The Way I Are", Timbaland feat. D.O.E./Keri Hilson	1,943,000

Source: Nielsen SoundScan

TOP 10 **ARTISTS WITH MOST WEEKS ON THE US SINGLES CHART**

	ARTIST	TOTAL WEEKS*
1	Elvis Presley	1,205
2	Elton John	979
3	Madonna	866
4	Stevie Wonder	770
5	Rod Stewart	692
6	Janet Jackson	690
7	Michael Jackson	689
8	James Brown	681
9	Mariah Carey	676
10	Aretha Franklin	659

* To December 2007

Source: Music Information Database

Albums

TOP 10 ALBUMS IN THE USA, 2007

TITLE / ARTIST / SALES

1 Noel
Josh Groban
3,699,000

2 High School Musical 2
Soundtrack
2,957,000

3 Long Road Out of Eden
Eagles
2,608,000

4 As I Am
Alicia Keys
2,543,000

5 Daughtry
Daughtry
2,497,000

6 Hannah Montana 2 –
Meet Miley, Soundtrack
2,489,000

7 Minutes To Midnight
Linkin Park
2,099,000

8 Dutchess
Fergie
2,064,000

9 Taylor Swift
Taylor Swift
1,951,000

10 Graduation
Kanye West
1,892,000

Source: Nielsen SoundScan

Bob dazzles
Bob Dylan performing at the inaugural Farm Aid concert (1985). His US album career encompasses 52 chart hits.

TOP 10 ARTISTS WITH THE MOST CHART ALBUMS IN THE USA

	ARTIST	CHART ALBUMS
1	Elvis Presley	110
2	Frank Sinatra	82
3	Johnny Mathis	69
4	Willie Nelson	53
5	Bob Dylan	52
6	Ray Conniff	50
7	= James Brown	49
	= The Temptations	49
9	= The Beach Boys	48
	= The Beatles	48

Source: Music Information Database

TOP 10 ALBUMS IN THE USA IN THE PAST 10 YEARS

YEAR	TITLE / ARTIST
2007	Noel, Josh Groban
2006	High School Musical, Soundtrack
2005	The Emancipation of Mimi, Mariah Carey
2004	Confessions, Usher
2003	Get Rich or Die Tryin', 50 Cent
2002	The Eminem Show, Eminem
2001	Hybrid Theory, Linkin Park
2000	No Strings Attached, *NSync
1999	Millennium, Backstreet Boys
1998	Titanic, Soundtrack

Source: Nielsen SoundScan

TOP 10 ALBUMS THAT STAYED LONGEST IN THE US CHARTS

	TITLE / ARTIST / LONGEST CONSECUTIVE RUN	FIRST CHART ENTRY	WEEKS IN CHART
1	The Dark Side of the Moon, Pink Floyd (593)	1973	741
2	Johnny's Greatest Hits, Johnny Mathis (208)	1958	490
3	My Fair Lady, Original Cast (192)	1956	480
4	Highlights from the Phantom of the Opera, Original Cast (331)	1990	331
5	Oklahoma!, Soundtrack (95)	1955	305
6	Tapestry, Carole King (302)	1971	302
7	Heavenly, Johnny Mathis (155)	1959	295
8	MCMXC A.D., Enigma (252)	1991	282
9	Metallica, Metallica (281)	1991	281
10	The King and I, Soundtrack (96)	1956	277

Source: Music Information Database

Long players
Simon & Garfunkel's Bridge Over Troubled Water *is one of the bestselling albums of all time in the USA.*

TOP 10 ALBUMS OF ALL TIME IN THE USA

#	TITLE / ARTIST / YEAR OF ENTRY	EST. SALES
1	Their Greatest Hits, 1971–1975, Eagles, 1976	29,000,000
2	Thriller, Michael Jackson, 1982	27,000,000
3	Led Zeppelin IV, Led Zeppelin, 1971	23,000,000
4	Back in Black, AC/DC, 1980	22,000,000
5	Come on Over, Shania Twain, 1997	20,000,000
6	Rumours, Fleetwood Mac, 1977	19,000,000
7	= No Fences, Garth Brooks, 1990	17,000,000
	= The Bodyguard, Soundtrack, 1992	17,000,000
	= Boston, Boston, 1976	17,000,000
10	= Greatest Hits, Elton John, 1974	16,000,000
	= Physical Graffiti, Led Zeppelin, 1975	16,000,000
	= Hotel California, Eagles, 1976	16,000,000
	= Cracked Rear View, Hootie & the Blowfish, 1994	16,000,000
	= Jagged Little Pill, Alanis Morissette, 1995	16,000,000

Source: RIAA

TOP 10 ALBUMS IN THE USA, 1960–2005

#	TITLE / ARTIST	YEAR
1	The Sound of Music, Original Broadway Cast	1960
2	Mary Poppins, Original Soundtrack	1965
3	Bridge Over Troubled Water, Simon & Garfunkel	1970
4	Captain Fantastic and The Brown Dirt Cowboy, Elton John	1975
5	The Wall, Pink Floyd	1980
6	Like a Virgin, Madonna	1985
7	Please Hammer Don't Hurt 'Em, MC Hammer	1990
8	Cracked Rear View, Hootie & the Blowfish	1995
9	No Strings Attached, *NSync	2000
10	The Emancipation of Mimi, Mariah Carey	2005

Source: Music Information Database

Record Firsts

THE 10 FIRST FEMALE SINGERS TO HAVE A NO. 1 HIT IN THE USA DURING THE ROCK ERA

	ARTIST	TITLE	DATE AT NO. 1
1	Joan Weber	"Let Me Go Lover"	Jan 22, 1955
2	Georgia Gibbs	"Dance With Henry (Wallflower)"	May 21, 1955
3	Kay Starr	"Rock and Roll Waltz"	Feb 18, 1956
4	Gogi Grant	"The Wayward Wind"	Jun 16, 1956
5	Debbie Reynolds	"Tammy"	Aug 31, 1957
6	Connie Francis	"Everybody's Somebody's Fool"	Jul 2, 1960
7	Brenda Lee	"I'm Sorry"	Jul 23, 1960
8	Shelley Fabares	"Johnny Angel"	Apr 7, 1962
9	Little Eva	"The Loco-motion"	Aug 25, 1962
10	Little Peggy March	"I Will Follow Him"	Apr 27, 1963

Source: Music Information Database

By the time Little Peggy March had her first No. 1, Connie Francis had had two more and Brenda Lee one.

THE 10 FIRST US ARTISTS TO TOP THE UK SINGLES CHART

	ARTIST / TITLE	DATE AT NO. 1
1	Al Martino, "Here In My Heart"	Nov 15, 1952
2	Jo Stafford, "You Belong To Me"	Jan 17, 1953
3	Kay Starr, "Comes A-Long A-Love"	Jan 24, 1953
4	Eddie Fisher, "Outside of Heaven"	Jan 31, 1953
5	Perry Como, "Don't Let The Stars Get In Your Eyes"	Feb 7, 1953
6	Guy Mitchell, "She Wears Red Feathers"	Mar 14, 1953
7	Frankie Laine, "I Believe"	Apr 25, 1953
8	Doris Day, "Secret Love"	Apr 17, 1954
9	Johnnie Ray, "Such A Night"	May 1, 1954
10	Kitty Kallen, "Little Things Mean a Lot"	Sep 11, 1954

Source: Music Information Database

To give some perspective of the dominance of US music on the UK market during the 1950s, only two British acts topped the charts during this time period.

THE 10 **FIRST NATIONALITIES TO TOP THE US SINGLES CHART***

NATIONALITY / ARTIST / TITLE	DATE AT NO. 1
1 Cuban, Perez "Prez Prado", "Cherry Pink and Apple Blossom White"	Apr 30, 1955
2 Canadian, Paul Anka, "Diana"	Sep 14, 1957
3 Italian, Domenico Modugno, "Nel Blu Dipinto Di Blue (Volare)"	Aug 23, 1958
4 German, Bert Kaempfert, "Wonderland by Night"	Jan 14, 1961
5 Japanese, Kyu Sakamoto, "Sukiyaki"	Jun 15, 1963
6 Belgian, The Singing Nun, "Dominique"	Dec 7, 1963
7 French, Paul Mauriat, "Love is Blue"	Feb 10, 1968
8 Dutch, Shocking Blue, "Venus"	Feb 7, 1970
9 Irish, Gilbert O'Sullivan, "Alone Again (Naturally)"	Jul 29, 1972
10 Swedish, Blue Swede, "Hooked on a Feeling"	Apr 6, 1974

* Excluding the UK

Source: Music Information Database

Only four nationalities match the corresponding UK list—Cuban, Canadian, Italian, and Irish.

Far left: Jo Stafford
Jo Stafford's "You Belong to Me" was the UK's second No. 1 and the first by a female singer— a position it held for a single week.

Left: Doris Day
Doris Day's Oscar-winning "Secret Love" from the film Calamity Jane (1953) held the UK No. 1 slot for 10 weeks.

Right: Prez Prado
The Cuban bandleader's "Cherry Pink and Apple Blossom White" hit the US No. 1 spot in 1955, the first foreign artist to do so.

THE 10 **FIRST RECORDS TO ENTER THE US CHART AT NO. 1**

ARTIST	TITLE	DATE AT NO. 1
1 Michael Jackson	"You Are Not Alone"	Sep 2, 1995
2 Mariah Carey	"Fantasy"	Sep 30, 1995
3 Whitney Houston	"Exhale (Shoop Shoop)"	Nov 25, 1995
4 Mariah Carey & Boyz II Men	"One Sweet Day"	Dec 2, 1995
5 Mariah Carey	"Honey"	Sep 13, 1997
6 Elton John	"Candle in the Wind 1997"	Oct 11, 1997
7 Celine Dion	"My Heart Will Go On"	Feb 28, 1998
8 Aerosmith	"I Don't Want To Miss A Thing"	Sep 5, 1998
9 Lauryn Hill	"Doo Wop (That Thing)"	Nov 14, 1998
10 R. Kelly & Celine Dion	"I'm Your Angel"	Dec 5, 1998

Source: Music Information Database

The introduction of SoundScan, using new methodology to compile the Hot 100, first made it possible for a single to enter the chart at the summit.

Male Singers

Love Sounds success
Justin Timberlake's album Futuresex/Love Sounds *was the bestselling album of 2006 and just one of several chart-toppers for the artist.*

YOUNGEST MALE SOLO SINGERS TO HAVE A NO. 1 SINGLE IN THE USA

	ARTIST / TITLE	YEAR	YRS	AGE* MTHS	DAYS
1	Stevie Wonder, "Fingertips"	1963	13	2	28
2	Donny Osmond, "Go Away Little Girl"	1971	13	9	2
3	Michael Jackson, "Ben"	1972	14	1	15
4	Laurie London, "He's Got the Whole World in His Hands"	1958	14	3	0
5	Chris Brown, "Run It!"	2005	15	6	21
6	Paul Anka, "Diana"	1957	16	1	16
7	Brian Hyland, "Itsy Bitsy Teenie Weenie Yellow Polkadot Bikini"	1960	16	9	1
8	Soulja Boy, "Crank That Soulja Boy"	2007	17	1	18
9	Mario, "Let Me Love You"	2005	17	4	7
10	Sean Kingston, "Beautiful Girls"	2007	17	6	8

* During first week of debut No. 1 US single

Source: Music Information Database

After no new names on this list in 33 years, four new entrants have been added in a three-year period. If group members were eligible for the list, all three Hanson brothers would be in the Top 10. Isaac was 16 years and 6 months, Taylor 14 years and 2 months, and Zachary 11 years and 7 months when "Mmmbop" topped the charts in 1997.

TOP 10 **MALE SOLO SINGERS WITH THE LONGEST GAPS BETWEEN NO. 1 HIT SINGLES IN THE USA**

	ARTIST	PERIOD	YRS	GAP MTHS	DAYS
1	Paul Anka	Aug 15, 1959–Aug 17, 1974	15	0	2
2	Rod Stewart	Mar 10, 1979–Jan 15, 1994	14	10	5
3	George Harrison	Jul 7, 1973–Jan 9, 1988	14	6	2
4	Neil Sedaka	Aug 25, 1962–Jan 25, 1975	12	5	0
5	Herb Alpert	Jul 20, 1968–13 Oct 1979	11	2	23
6	Stevie Wonder	Aug 31, 1963–Jan 20, 1973	9	4	20
7	Elton John	Sep 4, 1976–Jan 11, 1986	9	4	7
8	Dean Martin	Feb 18, 1956–Aug 8, 1964	8	5	21
9	David Bowie	Oct 3, 1975–May 14, 1983	7	7	11
10	Elvis Presley	May 5, 1962–Oct 25, 1969	7	5	20

Source: Music Information Database

TOP 10 **SINGLES BY MALE SOLO SINGERS IN THE USA**

	TITLE / ARTIST	YEAR
1	"Candle in the Wind (1997)"/"Something About the Way You Look Tonight", Elton John	1997
2	"White Christmas", Bing Crosby	1942
3	"Hound Dog"/"Don't Be Cruel", Elvis Presley	1956
4	"Gangsta's Paradise", Coolio featuring L.V.	1995
5	"(Everything I Do) I Do It For You", Bryan Adams	1991
6	"Love Me Tender"/"Any Way You Want Me", Elvis Presley	1956
7	"All Shook Up", Elvis Presley	1957
8	"Jailhouse Rock", Elvis Presley	1957
9	"Heartbreak Hotel"/"I Was the One", Elvis Presley	1956
10	"Baby Got Back", Sir Mix-A-Lot	1992

Source: Music Information Database

TOP 10 **MALE SOLO ALBUMS IN THE USA IN THE PAST 10 YEARS**

YEAR	TITLE / ARTIST
2007	Noel, Josh Groban
2006	Futuresex/Love Sounds, Justin Timberlake
2005	The Massacre, 50 Cent
2004	Confessions, Usher
2003	Get Rich or Die Tryin', 50 Cent
2002	The Eminem Show, Eminem
2001	Hotshot, Shaggy
2000	The Marshall Mathers LP, Eminem
1999	Ricky Martin, Ricky Martin
1998	Double Live, Garth Brooks

Source: Nielsen SoundScan

Stevie Wonder
Stevie Wonder first topped the US charts at the age of 13—the youngest male solo artist ever.

TOP 10 **BESTSELLING ALBUMS BY A MALE ARTIST IN THE USA**

	TITLE / ARTIST /	YEAR
1	Thriller, Michael Jackson,	1982
2	No Fences, Garth Brooks	1990
3	Greatest Hits, Elton John	1974
4	Born in the USA, Bruce Springsteen	1984
5	=Bat Out of Hell, Meat Loaf	1977
	=Ropin' the Wind, Garth Brooks	1991
7	=Greatest Hits, Kenny Rogers	1980
	=No Jacket Required, Phil Collins	1985
	=Breathless, Kenny G,	1992
10	=James Taylor's Greatest Hits, James Taylor	1976
	=Devil Without a Cause, Kid Rock, 1999	1999

Source: RIAA

TOP 10 **MALE ARTISTS WITH MOST PLATINUM AND MULTI-PLATINUM ALBUMS IN THE USA**

	ARTIST	PLATINUM ALBUMS*
1	Garth Brooks (15)	106
2	Elvis Presley (81)	89
3	Billy Joel (18)	68
4	Elton John (36)	63
5	Michael Jackson (8)	59
6	Bruce Springsteen (20)	54
7	George Strait (36)	53
8	Kenny G (15)	46
9	Kenny Rogers (26)	41
10	Neil Diamond (39)	39

*By number of album awards, rather than number of albums qualifying for awards; gold totals in brackets

Source: RIAA

Female Singers

TOP 10 FEMALE SINGERS WITH THE LONGEST GAPS BETWEEN NO. 1 HIT SINGLES IN THE USA

	ARTIST	PERIOD	YRS	GAP MTHS	DAYS
1	Cher	Mar 23, 1974–Mar 13, 1999	24	11	21
2	Aretha Franklin	Jun 10, 1967–Apr 11, 1987	19	10	1
3	Alicia Keys	Oct 13, 2001–Dec 1, 2007	6	1	18
4	Madonna	Apr 15, 1995–Sep 9, 2000	5	4	25
5	Mariah Carey	Feb 19, 2000–Jun 4, 2005	5	3	16
6	Jennifer Warnes	Nov 27, 1982–Nov 21, 1987	4	11	25
7	Diana Ross	Jul 10, 1976–Aug 30, 1980	4	1	20
8	Janet Jackson	Dec 25, 1993–Jan 24, 1998	4	0	30
9	Olivia Newton-John	Mar 15, 1975–Jun 3, 1978	3	2	19
10	Barbra Streisand	Feb 9, 1974–Feb 26, 1977	3	0	17

Source: Music Information Database

TOP 10 YOUNGEST FEMALE SINGERS TO HAVE A NO. 1 SINGLE IN THE USA

	ARTIST / TITLE / YEAR	YRS	AGE MTHS	DAYS
1	Little Peggy March, "I Will Follow Him", 1963	15	1	20
2	Brenda Lee, "I'm Sorry", 1960	15	7	7
3	Tiffany, "I Think We're Alone", 1987	16	1	5
4	Lesley Gore, "It's My Party", 1963	17	0	30
5	Little Eva, "The Loco-Motion", 1962	17	1	27
6	Britney Spears, "...Baby One More Time", 1999	17	1	29
7	Monica, "The First Night", 1998	17	11	9
8	Shelley Fabares, "Johnny Angel", 1962	18	2	19
9	Rihanna, "SOS", 2006	18	2	24
10	Debbie Gibson, "Foolish Beat", 1988	18	6	4

Source: Music Information Database

Mind the gap
Cher's spaced-out US No. 1s span nearly 25 years, from her third chart-topper in March 1974, "Dark Lady," to the worldwide hit "Believe" in 1999, when she was 52 years old.

TOP 10 BESTSELLING ALBUMS BY A FEMALE ARTIST IN THE USA

	TITLE / ARTIST	YEAR
1	Come On Over, Shania Twain	1997
2	The Bodyguard, Whitney Houston	1992
3	Jagged Little Pill, Alanis Morissette	1995
4	...Baby One More Time, Britney Spears	1999
5	Whitney Houston, Whitney Houston	1986
6	Pieces of You, Jewel	1996
7	The Woman in Me, Shania Twain	1995
8	Up!, Shania Twain	2002
9	Falling into You, Celine Dion	1996
10	The Immaculate Collection, Madonna	1991

Source: RIAA

More than one
Britney Spears' album ...Baby One More Time spawned a single of the same name that hit No. 1 in the USA and every European country.

TOP 10 SINGLES BY FEMALE SOLO SINGERS IN THE USA

	TITLE / ARTIST	YEAR
1	"I Will Always Love You", Whitney Houston	1992
2	"How Do I Live", LeAnn Rimes	1997
3	"Un-break My Heart", Toni Braxton	1996
4	"Fantasy", Mariah Carey	1995
5	"Vogue", Madonna	1990
6	"You're Still the One", Shania Twain	1998
7	"The First Night", Monica	1998
8	"You're Makin' Me High"/ "Let it Flow", Toni Braxton	1996
9	"Because You Loved Me", Celine Dion	1996
10	"You Were Meant For Me", Jewel	1997

Source: Music Information Database

TOP 10 BESTSELLING ALBUMS BY FEMALE SOLO ARTISTS IN THE USA IN THE PAST 10 YEARS

YEAR	TITLE / ARTIST
2007	As I Am, Alicia Keys
2006	Some Hearts, Carrie Underwood
2005	The Emancipation of Mimi, Mariah Carey
2004	Feels Like Home, Norah Jones
2003	Come Away With Me, Norah Jones
2002	Let Go, Avril Lavigne
2001	A Day Without Rain, Enya
2000	Oops! ... I Did it Again, Britney Spears
1999	...Baby One More Time, Britney Spears
1998	Let's Talk About Love, Celine Dion

Source: Music Information Database

TOP 10 FEMALE ARTISTS WITH THE MOST PLATINUM ALBUMS IN THE USA

	ARTIST*	PLATINUM ALBUMS
1	Madonna (17)	62
2	Barbra Streisand (50)	61
3	Mariah Carey (13)	60
4	Whitney Houston (8)	54
5	Celine Dion (12)	48
6	Shania Twain (4)	44
7	Reba McEntire (25)	37
8	Britney Spears (4)	30
9	Linda Ronstadt (17)	28
10	Janet Jackson (8)	26

* Gold totals listed in brackets

Source: RIAA

Groups & Duos

TOP 10 **SINGLES BY GROUPS AND DUOS IN THE USA, 2007**

TITLE / GROUP/DUO

1 "Make Me Wonder", Maroon 5
2 "Hey There Delilah", Plain White T's
3 "Rockstar", Nickelback
4 "Cupid's Chokehold", Gym Class Heroes
5 "This Ain't a Scene, It's an Arms Race", Fall Out Boy
6 "What I've Done", Linkin Park
7 "Paralyzer", Finger Eleven
8 "Thnks Fr Th Mmrs", Fall Out Boy
9 "Party Like a Rock Star", Shop Boyz
10 "How Far We've Come", Matchbox Twenty

Source: Nielsen Soundscan

Satisfaction guaranteed
In a career spanning nearly 40 years, British rock group the Rolling Stones have had eight US No. 1 chart hits.

TOP 10 **GROUPS AND DUOS WITH THE MOST WEEKS AT NO. 1 IN THE USA**

	GROUP/DUO	WEEKS AT NO. 1
1	The Beatles	59
2	Boyz II Men	50
3	Bee Gees	27
4	= (Diana Ross &) The Supremes	22
	= Santana	22
6	The Four Seasons	18
	= TLC	18
8	The Rolling Stones	17
	= Destiny's Child	17
10	The Everly Brothers	15

Source: Music Information Database

TOP 10 **ALBUMS BY GROUPS AND DUOS IN THE USA, 2007**

TITLE / GROUP/DUO

1 Long Road Out of Eden, Eagles
2 Daughtry, Daughtry
3 Minutes to Midnight, Linkin Park
4 All The Right Reasons, Nickelback
5 Still Feels Good, Rascal Flatts
6 It Won't Be Soon Before Long, Maroon 5
7 Infinity on High, Fall Out Boy
8 Enjoy The Ride, Sugarland
9 Lost Highway, Bon Jovi
10 Me and My Gang, Rascal Flatts

Source: Nielsen Soundscan

TOP 10 **GROUPS AND DUOS WITH THE MOST US NO. 1 SINGLES**

	ARTIST	NO. 1 SINGLES
1	The Beatles	20
2	The Supremes	12
3	The Bee Gees	9
4	The Rolling Stones	8
5	Daryl Hall & John Oates	6
	= Paul McCartney & Wings	6
7	= Boyz II Men*	5
	= Eagles	5
	= The Four Seasons	5
	= KC & the Sunshine Band	5

* Including one with Mariah Carey

Source: Music Information Database

TOP 10 **ALBUMS BY GROUPS IN THE USA**

	TITLE / GROUP	YEAR
1	Their Greatest Hits, 1971–1975, Eagles	1976
2	Led Zeppelin IV (untitled), Led Zeppelin	1971
3	Back in Black, AC/DC	1980
4	Rumours, Fleetwood Mac	1977
5	Boston, Boston	1976
6	Hotel California, Eagles	1977
7	Cracked Rear View, Hootie and the Blowfish	1995
8	Supernatural, Santana	1999
9	Appetite For Destruction, Guns N' Roses	1987
10	The Dark Side of the Moon, Pink Floyd	1973

Source: Music Information Database

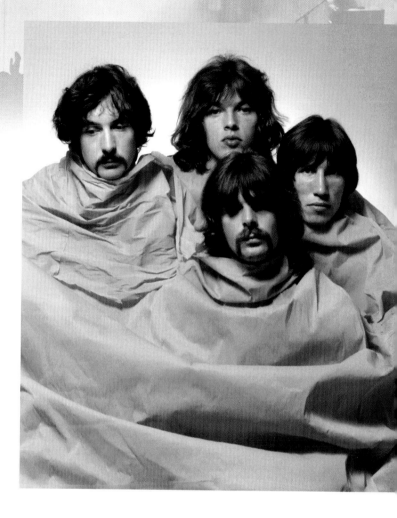

In the pink
Although it held the US No. 1 spot for only one week, Pink Floyd's iconic album The Dark Side of the Moon *has spent a phenomenal 14 years on the Billboard* Top 200 *chart.*

TOP 10 **GROUPS AND DUOS WITH THE LONGEST SINGLES CHART CAREERS IN THE USA**

	GROUP/DUO / CHART SPAN	YEARS	MONTHS	DAYS
1	The Isley Brothers Sep 26, 1959–Aug 16, 2003	43	10	21
2	The Rolling Stones May 2, 1964–Oct 4, 2003	39	5	2
3	Santana Oct 25, 1969–Nov 19, 2005	36	0	24
4	The Beatles Jan 18, 1964–May 4, 1996	32	3	16
5	Bee Gees May 27, 1967–Feb 7, 1998	30	8	11
6	The Righteous Brothers May 11, 1963–Mar 23, 1991	27	10	12
7	The Beach Boys Feb 17, 1962–Sep 9, 1989	27	6	23
8	The Everly Brothers Jun 1, 1957–Nov 17, 1984	27	5	16
9	The Five Satins Oct 13, 1956–Mar 27, 1982	25	5	14
10	Steve Miller Band Nov 23, 1968–Aug 28, 1993	24	9	5

Source: Music Information Database

TOP 10 **SINGLES BY GROUPS AND DUOS IN THE USA, 1960–2005**

	TITLE / GROUP/DUO	YEAR
1	"Cathy's Clown", The Everly Brothers	1960
2	"Help!", The Beatles	1965
3	"Bridge Over Troubled Water", Simon & Garfunkel	1970
4	"Love Will Keep Us Together", The Captain & Tennille	1975
5	"Another One Bites the Dust", Queen	1980
6	"We Are the World", USA For Africa	1985
7	"Pump Up the Jam", Technotronic	1990
8	"One Sweet Day", Mariah Carey & Boyz II Men	1995
9	"Maria Maria", Santana featuring the Product G&B	2000
10	"Beverly Hills", Weezer	2005

Source: Music Information Database

The cumulative total chart occupation of the Top 10 amounts to 315 years 1 month and 144 days.

Music Awards

	ARTIST	AWARDS
1	Madonna	20
2	Peter Gabriel	13
3	R.E.M.	12
4	Aerosmith	10
5	= Fatboy Slim	9
	= Janet Jackson	9
7	= Eminem	8
	= Green Day	8
	= Michael Jackson	8
10	= a-ha	7
	= En Vogue	7
	= 'NSync	7
	= Red Hot Chili Peppers	7
	= The Smashing Pumpkins	7

Source: MTV

THE 10 **ARTISTS WITH MOST GRAMMY AWARDS**

	ARTIST	AWARDS
1	Sir Georg Solti	31
2	Quincy Jones	27
3	Pierre Boulez	26
4	= Vladimir Horowitz	25
	= Stevie Wonder	25
6	U2	22
7	Alison Krauss	21
8	= Henry Mancini	20
	= John Williams	20
10	= Pat Metheny	18
	= Bruce Springsteen	18

Source: NARAS

The Grammy Awards ceremony has been held annually in the United States since its inauguration on May 4, 1959, and the awards are now considered to be the most prestigious in the music industry. The proliferation of classical artists in this Top 10 (not least, conductor Sir George Solti) is largely attributable to the large number of classical award categories at the Grammys, which have been latterly overshadowed by the rise of pop and rock.

THE 10 **LATEST RECIPIENTS OF THE NATIONWIDE MERCURY PRIZE***

	ARTIST / ALBUM	YEAR
1	Klaxons, Myths of the Near Future	2007
2	Arctic Monkeys, Whatever People Say I Am, That's What I'm Not	2006
3	Antony & the Johnsons, I Am a Bird Now	2005
4	Franz Ferdinand, Franz Ferdinand	2004
5	Dizzee Rascal, Boy in Da Corner	2003
6	Ms Dynamite, A Little Deeper	2002
7	PJ Harvey, Stories from the City, Stories from the Sea	2001
8	Badly Drawn Boy, The Hour of Bewilderbeast	2000
9	Talvin Singh, OK	1999
10	Gomez, Bring It On	1998

* Since 2004; originally Mercury Prize, later Mercury Music Prize

Source: Nationwide Mercury Prize

Coldplay and Radiohead have both been nominated three times, but never managed to win.

Madonna
Madonna, who performed at the inaugural MTV Video Music Awards in 1984, has amassed a record tally of 20 MTV awards, ranging from her 1986 Career Achievement Award to Best Video for "Beautiful Stranger" (1999), plus Artist of the Decade special award in 1989.

Yesterday and today
Paul McCartney won two BRIT awards in 1983, but none for the next 25 years, until his Outstanding Contribution to British Music award in 2008.

THE 10 **LATEST RECIPIENTS OF THE BRIT AWARD FOR OUTSTANDING CONTRIBUTION TO BRITISH MUSIC**

	ARTIST	YEAR
1	Paul McCartney	2008
2	Oasis	2007
3	Paul Weller	2006
4	Bob Geldof	2005
5	Duran Duran	2004
6	Tom Jones	2003
7	Sting	2002
8	U2	2001
9	Spice Girls	2000
10	Eurythmics	1999

Source: BRIT Awards

Of the 10 listed artists, only Eurythmics and Fleetwood Mac have never also won a BRIT award.

THE 10 **FIRST ARTISTS TO RECEIVE GRAMMY LIFETIME ACHIEVEMENT AWARDS**

	ARTIST	YEAR
1	Bing Crosby	1962
2	Frank Sinatra	1965
3	Duke Ellington	1966
4	Ella Fitzgerald	1967
5	Irving Berlin	1968
6	Elvis Presley	1971
7	= Louis Armstrong	1972
	= Mahalia Jackson	1972
9	= Chuck Berry	1984
	= Charlie Parker	1984

Source: NARAS

The Grammy Lifetime Achievement Award is presented to "performers who, during their lifetimes, have made creative contributions of outstanding artistic significance to the field of recording."

TOP 10 **LONGEST-SPANNING GRAMMY WINNERS**

	ARTIST	YEARS	SPAN
1	= Tony Bennett	1962–2006	44
	= Ray Charles	1960–2004	44
3	= The Beatles	1964–2007	43
	= Andre Previn	1961–2004	43
5	Al Schmitt	1962–2004	42
6	Phil Ramone	1964–2005	41
7	= Johnny Cash	1967–2007	40
	= Aretha Franklin	1967–2007	40
9	= Burt Bacharach	1967–2005	38
	= Quincy Jones	1963–2001	38
	= Joni Mitchell	1969–2007	38

Source: Music Information Database

Tony Bennett's 44-year span ranges from 1962 Record of the Year "I Left My Heart in San Francisco" to his collaboration with Christina Aguilera, "Steppin' Out With My Baby."

Movie Music

TOP 10 **MOVIE MUSICALS ADAPTED FROM STAGE VERSIONS**

MUSICAL	THEATER OPENING	MOVIE RELEASE
1 Grease	1972	1978
2 Chicago	1975	2002
3 Hairspray	2002	2007
4 The Sound of Music	1959	1965
5 The Phantom of the Opera	1986	2004
6 Evita	1978	1996
7 The Rocky Horror (Picture) Show	1973	1975
8 Dreamgirls	1981	2006
9 Fiddler on the Roof	1964	1971
10 Sweeney Todd: The Demon Barber of Fleet Street	1979	2007

The adapting of stage musicals as movies has a long history, with these the most successful cinematic versions of what, in most instances, were previously long-running theatrical productions.

TOP 10 **MUSICIAN MOVIE BIOGRAPHIES**

MOVIE	SUBJECT	YEAR
1 Walk the Line	Johnny Cash	2005
2 The Sound of Music	von Trapp family	1965
3 Ray	Ray Charles	2004
4 The Pianist	Wladyslaw Szpilman	2002
5 Shine	David Helfgott	1996
6 La Vie en Rose	Edith Piaf	2007
7 Coal Miner's Daughter	Loretta Lynn	1980
8 La Bamba	Ritchie Valens	1987
9 Amadeus	Wolfgang Amadeus Mozart	1984
10 What's Love Got to Do with It	Tina Turner	1993

Biopics on the lives of musicians have been a Hollywood staple for over 60 years, encompassing both classical and popular musicians, including Hank Williams (*Your Cheatin' Heart*, 1964), Peter Tchaikovsky (*The Music Lovers*, 1970), Buddy Holly (*The Buddy Holly Story*, 1978), and Jacqueline du Pré (*Hilary and Jackie*, 1998).

Above: Reverse role
Julie Andrews in Victor/Victoria, *which, in a reverse of the common route, became a musical.*

Left: Role reversal
Hairspray, *the movie (2007) of the musical (2002) of the movie (1988), starred John Travolta, uncharacteristically cast in a female role.*

TOP 10 **BESTSELLING MUSICAL ALBUMS IN THE USA**

	TITLE	YEAR OF RELEASE
1	Grease	1978
2	Evita	1996
3	West Side Story	1961
4	My Fair Lady	1964
5	Beauty and The Beast	1989
6	Oklahoma	1955
7	Chicago	2003
8	The Sound of Music	1965
9	South Pacific	1958
10	The King and I	1956

Source: Music Information Database

TOP 10 **ORIGINAL SOUNDTRACK ALBUMS IN THE USA**

	TITLE	YEAR OF RELEASE
1	The Bodyguard	1992
2	Purple Rain	1984
3	Forrest Gump	1994
4	= Dirty Dancing	1987
	= Titanic	1997
6	The Lion King	1994
7	= Top Gun	1986
	= Footloose	1984
9	= Grease	1978
	= O Brother Where Art Thou?	2000

Source: RIAA

TOP 10 **MGM MUSICALS**

	MUSICAL	YEAR
1	Victor/Victoria	1982
2	That's Entertainment!	1974
3	The Wizard of Oz	1939
4	De-Lovely	2004
5	Gigi	1958
6	Seven Brides For Seven Brothers	1954
7	I'll Cry Tomorrow	1955
8	High Society	1956
9	The Unsinkable Molly Brown	1964
10	Meet Me in St Louis	1944

From the earliest years of talking pictures, MGM established itself as the pre-eminent studio for musicals, making some 200 and winning the first Best Picture Oscar for *The Broadway Melody* (1929) and subsequently for *The Great Ziegfeld* (1936), *An American in Paris* (1951), and *Gigi* (1958). MGM's *That's Entertainment*, like its two sequels (1976 and 1994), was a compilation of clips rather than a single narrative film, while *De-Lovely* is a musical biopic based on the life and songs of Cole Porter.

Classical Music & Opera

The Three Tenors
The Three Tenors' original 1990 concert recording became the world's bestselling classical album and led to a series of immensely popular performances.

THE 10 LATEST CLASSICAL ALBUM GRAMMY WINNERS

	COMPOSER / TITLE	YEAR
1	Joan Tower, Made in America	2007
2	Gustav Mahler, Symphony No. 7	2006
3	William Bolcom, Songs of Innocence and of Experience	2005
4	John Adams, On the Transmigration of Souls	2004
5	Gustav Mahler, Symphony No. 3, Kindertotenlieder	2003
6	Ralph Vaughan Williams, A Sea Symphony (Symphony No. 1)	2002
7	Hector Berlioz, Les Troyens	2001
8	Dmitri Shostakovich, The String Quartets	2000
9	Igor Stravinsky, Firebird, The Rite of Spring, Persephone	1999
10	Samuel Barber, Prayers of Kierkegaard/ Ralph Vaughan Williams, Dona Nobis Pacem/ Bela Bartok, Cantata Profana	1998

Source: NARAS

TOP 10 CLASSICAL ALBUMS IN THE USA

	TITLE	PERFORMER / ORCHESTRA	YEAR
1	The Three Tenors In Concert	José Carreras, Placido Domingo, Luciano Pavarotti	1990
2	Romanza	Andrea Bocelli	1997
3	Sogno	Andrea Bocelli	1999
4	Voice of an Angel	Charlotte Church	1999
5	Chant	Benedictine Monks of Santo Domingo De Silos	1994
6	The Three Tenors – In Concert 1994	José Carreras, Placido Domingo, Luciano Pavarotti	1994
7	Sacred Arias	Andrea Bocelli	1999
8	Tchaikovsky: Piano Concerto No. 1	Van Cliburn	1958
9	Amore	Andrea Bocelli	2006
10	Perhaps Love	Placido Domingo	1982

Source: Music Information Database

Classical recordings held far greater sway in the early years of the US album chart than they have in subsequent decades, and this is partly reflected in the vintage nature of much of the Top 10. The 1990s saw a huge increase in sales of classical and opera music, a change that owes much to the influence of tenors such as Placido Domingo and Luciano Pavarotti, whose rise to international stardom led to opera music becoming a far more accessible genre.

TOP 10 OPERAS MOST FREQUENTLY PERFORMED AT THE ROYAL OPERA HOUSE, COVENT GARDEN, LONDON, 1833–2007

	OPERA / COMPOSER	FIRST PERFORMANCE	TOTAL*
1	La Bohème Giacomo Puccini	Oct 2, 1897	561
2	Carmen Georges Bizet	May 27, 1882	511
3	Aïda Giuseppi Verdi	Jun 22, 1876	481
4	Rigoletto Giuseppi Verdi	May 14, 1853	471
5	Faust Charles Gounod	Jul 18, 1863	448
6	Tosca Giacomo Puccini	Jul 12, 1900	434
7	Don Giovanni Wolfgang Amadeus Mozart	Apr 17, 1834	424
8	La Traviata Giuseppi Verdi	May 25, 1858	408
9	Madama Butterfly Giacomo Puccini	Jul 10, 1905	387
10	Norma Vincenzo Bellini	Jul 12, 1833	355

* To August 31, 2007

TOP 10 OPERAS MOST FREQUENTLY PERFORMED AT THE METROPOLITAN OPERA HOUSE, NEW YORK

	OPERA	COMPOSER	PERFORMANCES*
1	La Bohème	Giacomo Puccini	1,193
2	Aïda	Giuseppi Verdi	1,093
3	Carmen	Georges Bizet	936
4	La Traviata	Giuseppi Verdi	934
5	Tosca	Giacomo Puccini	891
6	Rigoletto	Giuseppi Verdi	815
7	Madama Butterfly	Giacomo Puccini	812
8	Faust	Charles Gounod	733
9	Pagliacci	Ruggero Leoncavallo	705
10	Cavalleria Rusticana	Pietro Mascagni	660

* As at end of the 2007 season

Source: Metropolitan Opera

The Metropolitan Opera House opened on October 22, 1883, with a performance of Charles Gounod's *Faust*.

Carmen
With over 500 performances at the Royal Opera House and more than 900 at the Metropolitan Opera House, Bizet's Carmen, *which premiered in Paris on March 3, 1875, is one of the world's most-performed operas.*

ENTERTAINMENT

In the Long Run

The Bard in brief
Performed by the Reduced Shakespeare Company, the long-running comedy The Complete Works of William Shakespeare (Abridged) *holds the record for its 43-second version of* Hamlet.

TOP 10 **LONGEST-RUNNING NONMUSICALS ON BROADWAY**

SHOW	PERFORMANCES
1 Oh! Calcutta! Sep 24, 1976–Aug 6, 1989	5,959
2 Life with Father Nov 8, 1939–Jul 12, 1947	3,224
3 Tobacco Road Dec 4, 1933–May 31, 1941	3,182
4 Abie's Irish Rose May 23, 1922–Oct 1, 1927	2,327
5 Gemini May 21, 1977–Sep 6, 1981	1,819
6 Deathtrap Feb 26, 1978–Jun 13, 1982	1,793
7 Harvey Nov 1, 1944–Jan 15, 1949	1,775
8 Born Yesterday Feb 4, 1946–Dec 31, 1949	1,642
9 Mary, Mary Mar 6, 1961–Mar 8, 1964	1,572
10 The Voice of the Turtle Dec 8, 1943–Jan 3, 1948	1,557

Off Broadway, *The Golden Horseshoe Revue* performed at Disneyland from July 16, 1955 to October 12, 1986, a record-breaking total of 47,250 performances.

TOP 10 **LONGEST-RUNNING COMEDIES ON BROADWAY**

COMEDY	PERFORMANCES
1 Life with Father Nov 8, 1939–Jul 12, 1947	3,224
2 Abie's Irish Rose May 23, 1922–Oct 1, 1927	2,327
3 Gemini May 21, 1977–Sep 6, 1981	1,819
4 Harvey Nov 1, 1944–Jan 15, 1949	1,775
5 Born Yesterday Feb 4, 1946–Dec 31, 1949	1,642
6 Mary, Mary Mar 8, 1961–Dec 12, 1964	1,572
7 The Voice of the Turtle Dec 8, 1943–Jan 3, 1948	1,557
8 Barefoot in the Park Oct 23, 1963–Jun 25, 1967	1,530
9 Same Time, Next Year Mar 14, 1975–Sep 3, 1978	1,453
10 Brighton Beach Memoirs Mar 27, 1983–May 11, 1986	1,299

Howard Lindsay and Russel Crouse's *Life with Father* owed its success in part to the show's nostalgic view of bygone America that appeared under threat as it opened on the eve of World War II.

TOP 10 **LONGEST-RUNNING MYSTERIES AND THRILLERS ON BROADWAY**

SHOW	RUN	PERFORMANCES
1 Deathtrap	Feb 26, 1978–Jul 13, 1982	1,793
2 Arsenic and Old Lace	Jan 10, 1941–Jun 17, 1944	1,444
3 Angel Street	Dec 5, 1941–Dec 30, 1944	1,295
4 Sleuth	Nov 12, 1970–13 Oct, 1973	1,222
5 The Bat	Aug 23, 1920–Sep 1922	867
6 Dracula	Oct 20, 1977–Jan 6, 1980	925
7 Witness for the Prosecution	Dec 16, 1954–Jun 30, 1956	645
8 Dial 'M' for Murder	Oct 29, 1952–Feb 27, 1954	552
9 Sherlock Holmes	Nov 12, 1974–Jan 4, 1976	471
10 An Inspector Calls	Apr 27, 1994–May 28, 1995	454

Deathtrap by Ira Levin opened at the Music Box Theatre. Though nominated for four Tony Awards, it failed to win any, but went on to achieve a record four-year run, transferring for the last six months to the Biltmore Theatre.

THE 10 **LONGEST-RUNNING SHOWS OF ALL TIME**

SHOW / LOCATION / RUN	PERFORMANCES
1 The Golden Horseshoe Revue (Disneyland, California, 1955–86)	47,250
2 The Mousetrap (London, 1952–)	23,026*
3 The Fantasticks (New York, 1960–2002)	17,162
4 La Cantatrice Chauve (The Bald Soprano) (Paris, 1957–)	16,743*
5 Shear Madness (Boston, 1980–)	11,783*
6 Les Misérables (London, 1985–)	9,934*
7 The Mousetrap (Toronto, 1977–2004)	over 9,600
8 The Drunkard (Los Angeles, 1933–59)	9,477
9 Cats (London, 1981–2002)	8,949
10 Shear Madness (Washington D.C., 1987–)	8,930*

* Still running, total as at March 1, 2008

Chorus of approval
In 2006 Les Misérables, *the musical based on Victor Hugo's 1862 novel, became the longest-running on the London stage. On Broadway it takes a lowlier third place.*

TOP 10 LONGEST-RUNNING MUSICALS ON BROADWAY

	SHOW	RUN	PERFORMANCES
1	The Phantom of the Opera	Jan 26, 1988–	8,355*
2	Cats	Sep 23, 1982–Sep 10, 2000	7,485
3	Les Misérables	Mar 12, 1987–May 18, 2003	6,680
4	A Chorus Line	Jul 25, 1975–Apr 28, 1990	6,137
5	Beauty and the Beast	Mar 9, 1994–Jul 28, 2007	5,461
6	Rent	Apr 29, 1996–	4,908*
7	Chicago	Nov 14, 1996–	4,685*
8	The Lion King	Nov 13, 1997–	4,270*
9	Miss Saigon	Apr 11, 1991–Jan 28, 2001	4,092
10	42nd Street	Aug 18, 1980–Jan 8, 1989	3,486

* Still running, total as at March 1, 2008

All the longest-running musicals date from the past 40 years. Prior to these record-breakers, the longest runner of the 1940s was *Oklahoma!*, which debuted in 1943 and ran for 2,212 performances up to 1948, and from the 1950s *My Fair Lady*, which opened in 1956 and closed in 1962 after 2,717 performances.

TOP 10 LONGEST-RUNNING RODGERS & HAMMERSTEIN PRODUCTIONS ON BROADWAY

	SHOW	PERFORMANCES
1	Oklahoma! (1943–48)	2,212
2	South Pacific (1949–54)	1,925
3	The Sound of Music (1959–63)	1,443
4	The King and I (1951–54)	1,246
5	Carousel (1945–47)	890
6	The King and I (1996–98)	780
7	The King and I (1977–78)	695
8	The Flower Drum Song (1958–60)	600
9	The Sound of Music (1998–99)	533
10	Oklahoma! (2002–03)	388

Movie Industry

TOP 10 **FILM-PRODUCING COUNTRIES**

COUNTRY	FEATURE FILMS PRODUCED (2006)
1 India	1,091
2 USA	490
3 Japan	417
4 China	330
5 France	203
6 Russia	200
7 Spain	150
8 Brazil	142
9 UK	134
10 Germany	122

Source: *Screen Digest*

TOP 10 **COUNTRIES BY BOX-OFFICE REVENUE**

COUNTRY	EST. TOTAL BOX-OFFICE GROSS 2006 ($)
1 USA	9,420,000,000
2 Japan	1,839,600,000
3 UK	1,397,000,000
4 France	1,387,600,000
5 Germany	1,018,300,000
6 Spain	788,300,000
7 Canada	685,900,000
8 Italy	680,200,000
9 Australia	661,000,000
10 Mexico	557,900,000

Source: *Screen Digest*

Lording the lists
The Lord of the Rings *trilogy makes up three of the 14 highest-earning movies of all time worldwide.*

TOP 10 **MOVIES IN THE USA**

MOVIE	YEAR	US GROSS ($)
1 Titanic*	1997	600,788,188
2 Star Wars: Episode IV— A New Hope#	1977	460,998,007
3 Shrek 2†	2004	441,226,247
4 E.T. the Extra-Terrestrial	1982	435,110,554
5 Star Wars: Episode I— The Phantom Menace	1999	431,088,297
6 Pirates of the Caribbean: Dead Man's Chest	2006	421,284,468
7 Spider-Man	2002	403,706,375
8 Star Wars: Episode III— Revenge of the Sith	2005	380,270,577
9 The Lord of the Rings: The Return of the King	2003	377,027,325
10 Spider-Man 2	2004	373,585,825

* Won Best Picture Oscar
\# Originally titled *Star Wars*
† Animated

TOP 10 **BIGGEST MOVIE BUDGETS**

Up to 2007

	MOVIE	YEAR	BUDGET ($)
1	Pirates of the Caribbean: At World's End	2007	300,000,000
2	Superman Returns	2006	270,000,000
3	Spider-Man 3	2007	258,000,000
4	Pirates of the Caribbean: Dead Man's Chest	2006	225,000,000
5	X-Men: The Last Stand	2006	210,000,000
6	King Kong	2005	207,000,000
7	= Titanic	1997	200,000,000
	= Terminator 3: Rise of the Machines	2003	200,000,000
	= Spider-Man 2	2004	200,000,000
10	The Chronicles of Narnia: The Lion, the Witch and the Wardrobe	2005	180,000,000

Above: World's End *world's biggest*
Pirates of the Caribbean: At World's End *had the biggest budget ever, but earned almost $1 billion globally.*

Up to 1987

	MOVIE	YEAR	BUDGET ($)
1	War and Peace (Russia)	1967	100,000,000
2	= Superman	1978	55,000,000
	= Ishtar	1987	55,000,000
4	Superman II	1980	54,000,000
5	= Annie	1982	50,000,000
	= Santa Claus	1985	50,000,000
	= Zimnyaya Vishnya (Russia)	1985	50,000,000
8	The Cotton Club	1984	47,000,000
9	Inchon	1981	46,000,000
10	Dune	1984	45,000,000

The state-sponsored eight-hour Russian epic *War and Peace* took seven years to film. Allowing for inflation since 1967, it would cost over $630 million to make today. It was not until 1991 that a commercially produced movie, *Terminator 2: Judgment Day*, commanded a budget of over $100 million. Its director, James Cameron, went on to make $200-million budget *Titanic*.

Opening Weekends

TOP 10 **OPENING WEEKENDS WORLDWIDE**

MOVIE	YEAR	OPENING WEEKEND WORLD TOTAL ($ MILLION)
1 Spider-Man 3	2007	381.7
2 Pirates of the Caribbean: At World's End	2007	344.0
3 Harry Potter and the Order of the Phoenix	2007	332.7
4 Star Wars: Episode III— Revenge of the Sith	2005	303.9
5 The Lord of the Rings: The Return of the King	2003	250.0
6 The Da Vinci Code	2006	232.1
7 Harry Potter and the Prisoner of Azkaban	2004	207.2
8 War of the Worlds	2005	203.1
9 The Matrix Revolutions	2003	201.4
10 Transformers	2007	191.7

Above: Magic numbers
Potter stars Rupert Grint, Daniel Radcliffe, and Emma Watson at the Hollywood opening of Harry Potter and the Order of the Phoenix. *This film and* Harry Potter and the Prisoner of Azkaban *are among the biggest-opening movies ever.*

Top right: Third time lucky
Spider-Man 3 *broke all records with its opening weekend, setting a new benchmark for worldwide daily and opening weekend earnings.*

Right: Monster hit
The opening weekend earnings of the original Shrek *was far exceeded by its two eagerly awaited sequels.*

TOP 10 **ANIMATED OPENING WEEKENDS IN THE USA**

	MOVIE	YEAR	OPENING WEEKEND GROSS ($)
1	Shrek the Third	2007	121,629,270
2	Shrek 2	2004	108,037,878
3	The Simpsons Movie	2007	74,036,787
4	The Incredibles	2004	70,467,623
5	Finding Nemo	2003	70,251,710
6	Ice Age: The Meltdown	2006	68,033,544
7	Monsters, Inc.	2001	62,577,067
8	Cars	2006	60,119,509
9	Toy Story 2*	1999	57,388,839
10	Shark Tale	2004	47,604,606

* Second weekend; opening weekend release in limited number of cinemas only

TOP 10 **OPENING WEEKENDS IN THE USA**

	MOVIE	YEAR	OPENING WEEKEND GROSS ($)
1	Spider-Man 3	2007	151,116,516
2	Harry Potter and the Order of the Phoenix	2007	139,715,157
3	Pirates of the Caribbean: Dead Man's Chest	2006	135,634,554
4	Shrek the Third*	2007	121,629,270
5	Spider-Man	2002	114,844,116
6	Pirates of the Caribbean: At World's End	2007	114,732,820
7	Star Wars: Episode III— Revenge of the Sith	2005	108,435,841
8	Shrek 2*	2004	108,037,878
9	X-Men: The Last Stand	2006	102,750,665
10	Harry Potter and the Goblet of Fire	2005	102,335,066

* Animated

Movie Genres

TOP 10 **WEDDING MOVIES**

	MOVIE	YEAR
1	My Big Fat Greek Wedding	2002
2	Runaway Bride	1999
3	My Best Friend's Wedding	1997
4	Wedding Crashers	2005
5	Four Weddings and a Funeral	1994
6	American Wedding	2003
7	Sweet Home Alabama	2002
8	In & Out	1997
9	The Wedding Singer	1998
10	Father of the Bride Part II	1995

These are all movies in which a wedding or weddings are central, rather than incidental, to the plot. All those in the Top 10 have earned upwards of $100 million worldwide.

TOP 10 **HORROR SPOOF MOVIES**

	MOVIE	YEAR
1	Scary Movie	2000
2	Scary Movie 3	2003
3	Scary Movie 4	2006
4	Scream	1996
5	Scream 2	1997
6	Scream 3	2000
7	Scary Movie 2	2001
8	The Rocky Horror Picture Show	1975
9	Young Frankenstein	1974
10	Lake Placid	1999

While many films combine comedy and horror elements, those in this Top 10 represent the most successful of a species of parodies of classic horror films that began 60 years ago with such examples as *Abbott and Costello Meets Frankenstein* (1948).

TOP 10 **GHOST MOVIES**

	MOVIE	YEAR
1	The Sixth Sense	1999
2	Ghost	1990
3	Ghostbusters	1984
4	What Lies Beneath	2000
5	Casper	1995
6	The Ring	2002
7	Scary Movie 3	2003
8	Ghostbusters II	1989
9	The Others	2001
10	Sleepy Hollow	1999

Wedding Crashers
The spectacle and social interaction offered by weddings has made them a popular and often successful staple of both Hollywood and—with films such as Monsoon Wedding *(2001)— international cinema.*

TOP 10 **SUPERHERO MOVIES**

	MOVIE	YEAR
1	Spider-Man 3	2007
2	Spider-Man	2002
3	Spider-Man 2	2004
4	The Incredibles*	2004
5	X-Men: The Last Stand	2006
6	Batman	1989
7	X2: X-Men United	2003
8	Superman Returns	2006
9	Batman Begins	2005
10	The Mask	1994

* Animated

Marching on
The highest-earning natural-history film of all time, French-made March of the Penguins *has made in excess of $127 million worldwide.*

TOP 10 **MAGIC, WITCHES, AND WIZARDS MOVIES**

	MOVIE	YEAR
1	The Lord of the Rings: The Return of the King	2003
2	Harry Potter and the Sorcerer's Stone	2001
3	Harry Potter and the Order of the Phoenix	2007
4	The Lord of the Rings: The Two Towers	2002
5	Shrek 2*	2004
6	Harry Potter and the Goblet of Fire	2005
7	Harry Potter and the Chamber of Secrets	2002
8	The Lord of the Rings: The Fellowship of the Ring	2001
9	Harry Potter and the Prisoner of Azkaban	2004
10	Shrek the Third*	2007

* Animated

TOP **DOCUMENTARY MOVIES**

	MOVIE	SUBJECT	YEAR
1	Fahrenheit 9/11	War on terrorism	2004
2	The Dream is Alive	Space Shuttle	1985
3	Everest	Mountaineering	1998
4	March of the Penguins	Emperor penguins	2005
5	To Fly	History of flying	1976
6	Grand Canyon: The Hidden Secrets	Exploration	1984
7	Mysteries of Egypt	Historical	1998
8	Space Station 3-D	International Space Station	2002
9	Jackass: Number Two	Comedy stunts	2006
10	Jackass: The Movie	Comedy stunts	2002

Comedy Stars

TOP 10 **MIKE MYERS MOVIES**

	MOVIE	YEAR
1	Austin Powers: The Spy Who Shagged Me	1999
2	Austin Powers in Goldmember	2002
3	Wayne's World	1992
4	The Cat in the Hat	2003
5	Austin Powers: International Man of Mystery	1997
6	Wayne's World 2	1993
7	54	1998
8	View from the Top	2003
9	So I Married an Axe Murderer	1993
10	Mystery, Alaska	1999

The power of Austin
Mike Myers as Austin Powers, eponymous star of three of his highest-earning movies.

TOP 10 **BILL MURRAY MOVIES**

	MOVIE	YEAR
1	Ghostbusters	1984
2	Charlie's Angels	2000
3	Ghostbusters II	1989
4	Tootsie	1982
5	Lost in Translation	2003
6	Groundhog Day	1993
7	Stripes	1981
8	The Royal Tenenbaums	2001
9	Wild Things	1998
10	Scrooged	1988

Bill Murray appeared, uncredited, as himself in *Space Jam* (1996)—if included in his personal Top 10, based on global box-office income, it would appear in third place. He also provided the voice of Garfield in the animated *Garfield: The Movie* (2004) and *Garfield: A Tail of Two Kitties* (2006).

TOP 10 **OWEN WILSON MOVIES**

	MOVIE	YEAR
1	Night at the Museum	2006
2	Armageddon	1998
3	Meet the Fockers	2004
4	Meet the Parents	2000
5	Wedding Crashers	2005
6	The Haunting	1999
7	Starsky and Hutch	2004
8	Anaconda	1997
9	You, Me and Dupree	2006
10	The Cable Guy	1996

Assuming his cameo role in *Meet the Fockers* is included, every one of Owen Wilson's films has earned more than $100 million—the first three more than $500 million—at the global box office. He also provided the voice of Lightning McQueen in the animated *Cars* (2006).

TOP 10 **JIM CARREY MOVIES**

	MOVIE	YEAR
1	Bruce Almighty	2003
2	Dr Seuss's How the Grinch Stole Christmas	2000
3	The Mask	1994
4	Batman Forever	1995
5	Liar Liar	1997
6	The Truman Show	1998
7	Dumb & Dumber	1994
8	Ace Ventura: When Nature Calls	1995
9	Lemony Snicket's A Series of Unfortunate Events	2004
10	Fun with Dick and Jane	2005

One click
Adam Sandler's fantasy comedy Click *has earned more than 10 times its $25 million budget.*

TOP 10 **STEVE MARTIN MOVIES**

	MOVIE	YEAR
1	Cheaper by the Dozen	2003
2	Bringing Down the House	2003
3	The Pink Panther	2006
4	Cheaper by the Dozen 2	2005
5	Parenthood	1989
6	Father of the Bride Part II	1995
7	Bowfinger	1999
8	HouseSitter	1992
9	Father of the Bride	1991
10	The Jerk	1979

TOP 10 **ADAM SANDLER MOVIES**

	MOVIE	YEAR
1	Click	2006
2	Big Daddy	1999
3	50 First Dates	2004
4	Anger Management	2003
5	The Longest Yard	2005
6	The Waterboy	1998
7	I Now Pronounce You Chuck and Larry	2007
8	Mr Deeds	2002
9	The Wedding Singer	1998
10	Little Nicky	2000

TOP 10 **BEN STILLER MOVIES**

	MOVIE	YEAR
1	Night at the Museum	2006
2	Meet the Fockers	2004
3	There's Something About Mary	1998
4	Meet the Parents	2000
5	Along Came Polly	2004
6	Starsky and Hutch	2004
7	DodgeBall: A True Underdog Story	2004
8	The Cable Guy	1996
9	The Heartbreak Kid	2007
10	The Royal Tenenbaums	2001

Oscar-winning Movies

TOP 10 **MOVIES TO WIN THE MOST OSCARS***

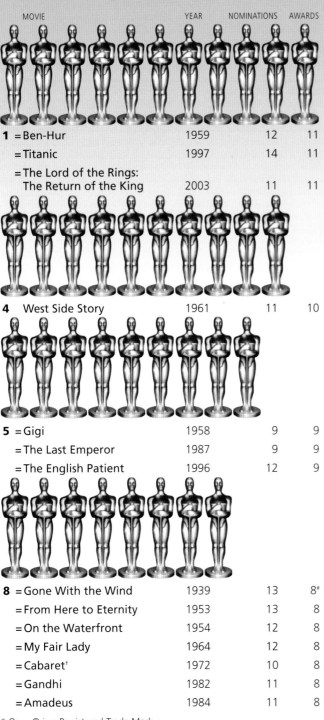

MOVIE	YEAR	NOMINATIONS	AWARDS
1 = Ben-Hur	1959	12	11
= Titanic	1997	14	11
= The Lord of the Rings: The Return of the King	2003	11	11
4 West Side Story	1961	11	10
5 = Gigi	1958	9	9
= The Last Emperor	1987	9	9
= The English Patient	1996	12	9
8 = Gone With the Wind	1939	13	8#
= From Here to Eternity	1953	13	8
= On the Waterfront	1954	12	8
= My Fair Lady	1964	12	8
= Cabaret†	1972	10	8
= Gandhi	1982	11	8
= Amadeus	1984	11	8

* Oscar® is a Registered Trade Mark
\# Plus two special awards
† Did not win Best Picture Oscar

Titanic matched the previous record of 14 nominations of *All About Eve* (1950), but outshone it by winning 11, compared with the latter's six. *Shakespeare in Love* (1998) and *Schindler's List* (1993) are the most recent of 10 movies that have won seven Oscars each.

Titanic success
Kate Winslet was nominated as Best Actress for her role in Titanic. *In addition to Oscars for Best Picture and Best Director, the movie won nine others.*

TOP 10 **MOVIES NOMINATED FOR THE MOST OSCARS**

MOVIE	YEAR	AWARDS	NOMINATIONS
1 = All About Eve	1950	6	14
= Titanic	1997	11	14
3 = Gone With the Wind	1939	8*	13
= From Here to Eternity	1953	8	13
= Mary Poppins#	1964	5	13
= Who's Afraid of Virginia Woolf?#	1966	5	13
= Forrest Gump	1994	6	13
= Shakespeare in Love	1998	7	13
= The Lord of the Rings: The Fellowship of the Ring#	2001	4	13
= Chicago	2002	6	13

* Plus two special awards
\# Did not win Best Picture Oscar

Thirteen is not an unlucky number where Oscar nominations are concerned, no fewer than eight movies having received that total. They and the two with 14 are those that received the greatest share of votes from Academy members (currently over 5,500, who include previous nominees and winners), using a system that creates a shortlist of five nominees in each of 24 categories.

"There are no clean getaways"
Josh Brolin as Llewelyn Moss in No Country for Old Men, *the Oscar-winning movie based on Cormac McCarthy's novel.*

TOP 10 **HIGHEST-EARNING BEST PICTURE OSCAR WINNERS**

MOVIE	YEAR*	WORLD BOX OFFICE ($)
1 Titanic	1997	1,845,034,188
2 The Lord of the Rings: The Return of the King	2003	1,129,219,252
3 Forrest Gump	1994	677,386,686
4 Gladiator	2000	457,640,427
5 Dances With Wolves	1990	424,208,842
6 Rain Man	1988	416,011,462
7 Gone With the Wind	1939	400,176,459
8 American Beauty	1999	356,296,601
9 Schindler's List	1993	321,267,179
10 A Beautiful Mind	2001	313,542,341

* Of release; Academy Awards are made the following year

THE 10 **LATEST BEST PICTURE OSCAR WINNERS**

YEAR	MOVIE	DIRECTOR
2007	No Country for Old Men	Ethan Coen and Joel Coen
2006	The Departed	Martin Scorsese
2005	Crash	Paul Haggis*
2004	Million Dollar Baby	Clint Eastwood
2003	The Lord of the Rings: The Return of the King	Peter Jackson
2002	Chicago	Rob Marshall*
2001	A Beautiful Mind	Ron Howard
2000	Gladiator	Ridley Scott*
1999	American Beauty	Sam Mendes
1998	Shakespeare in Love	John Madden*

* Did not also win Best Director Oscar

Oscar-winning Stars

Hepburn's hat-trick
Katharine Hepburn is the only actress to win three Best Actress Oscars, with almost 50 years between her first and last.

THE 10 FIRST STARS TO WIN TWO BEST ACTOR/ACTRESS OSCARS

	STAR	FIRST WIN / YEAR	SECOND WIN / YEAR
1	Luise Rainer	The Great Ziegfeld* 1936	The Good Earth 1937
2 =	Bette Davis	Dangerous 1935	Jezebel 1938
=	Spencer Tracy	Captains Courageous 1937	Boys Town 1938
4	Fredric March	Dr Jekyll and Mr Hyde 1931/32	The Best Years of Our Lives* 1946
5	Olivia de Havilland	To Each His Own 1946	The Heiress 1949
6	Vivien Leigh	Gone With the Wind* 1939	A Streetcar Named Desire 1951
7	Gary Cooper	Sergeant York 1941	High Noon 1952
8	Ingrid Bergman	Gaslight 1944	Anastasia 1956
9	Elizabeth Taylor	Butterfield 8 1960	Who's Afraid of Virginia Woolf? 1966
10	Katharine Hepburn	Morning Glory 1932/33	Guess Who's Coming to Dinner? 1967

* Won Best Picture Oscar

Uniquely, Katharine Hepburn went on to win a third Best Actress Oscar with *The Lion in Winter* (1968) and a fourth for *On Golden Pond* (1981).

THE 10 LATEST STARS TO WIN TWO BEST ACTOR/ACTRESS OSCARS

	ACTRESS	FIRST WIN / YEAR	SECOND WIN / YEAR
1	Hilary Swank	Boys Don't Cry 1999	Million Dollar Baby* 2004
2	Jack Nicholson	One Flew Over the Cuckoo's Nest 1975	As Good as it Gets 1997
3	Tom Hanks	Phildelphia 1993	Forrest Gump* 1994
4	Jodie Foster	The Accused 1988	The Silence of the Lambs* 1991
5	Dustin Hoffman	Kramer vs. Kramer* 1979	Rain Man* 1988
6	Sally Field	Norma Rae 1979	Places in the Heart 1984
7	Jane Fonda	Klute 1971	Coming Home 1978
8	Glenda Jackson	Women in Love 1970	A Touch of Class 1973
9	Katharine Hepburn	The Lion in Winter 1968	On Golden Pond 1981
10	Marlon Brando	On the Waterfront* 1954	The Godfather* 1972

* Won Best Picture Oscar

TOP 10 ACTORS AND ACTRESSES WITH THE MOST NOMINATIONS*

	ACTOR /	WINS: SUPPORTING/BEST /	NOMINATIONS
1	Meryl Streep	1 1	14
2 =	Katharine Hepburn	0 4	12
=	Jack Nicholson	1 2	12
4 =	Bette Davis	0 2	10
=	Laurence Olivier	0 1	10
6 =	Paul Newman	0 1	9
=	Spencer Tracy	0 2	9
8 =	Marlon Brando	0 2	8
=	Jack Lemmon	1 1	8
=	Peter O'Toole	0 0	8
=	Al Pacino	0 1	8
=	Geraldine Page	0 1	8

* In all acting categories

THE 10 **LATEST BEST ACTOR OSCAR WINNERS**

YEAR	ACTOR	MOVIE
2007	Daniel Day-Lewis	There Will Be Blood
2006	Forest Whitaker	The Last King of Scotland
2005	Philip Seymour Hoffman	Capote
2004	Jamie Foxx	Ray
2003	Sean Penn	Mystic River
2002	Adrien Brody	The Pianist
2001	Denzel Washington	Training Day
2000	Russell Crowe	Gladiator*
1999	Kevin Spacey	American Beauty*
1998	Roberto Benigni	Life is Beautiful

* Won Best Picture Oscar

THE 10 **LATEST BEST ACTRESS OSCAR WINNERS**

YEAR	ACTRESS	MOVIE
2007	Marion Cotillard	La Vie en Rose
2006	Helen Mirren	The Queen
2005	Reese Witherspoon	Walk the Line
2004	Hilary Swank	Million Dollar Baby*
2003	Charlize Theron	Monster
2002	Nicole Kidman	The Hours
2001	Halle Berry	Monster's Ball
2000	Julia Roberts	Erin Brockovich
1999	Hilary Swank	Boys Don't Cry
1998	Gwyneth Paltrow	Shakespeare in Love*

* Won Best Picture Oscar

Blood and roses
Above: Daniel Day-Lewis (center) won his second Best Actor Oscar for his role as oilman Daniel Plainview in There Will be Blood.
Below: French actress Marion Cotillard gained her Best Actress Oscar for her performance as Edith Piaf in La Vie en Rose.

Actors

TOP 10 **GEORGE CLOONEY MOVIES**

	MOVIE	YEAR
1	Ocean's Eleven	2001
2	Ocean's Twelve	2004
3	The Perfect Storm	2000
4	Ocean's Thirteen	2007
5	Batman & Robin	1997
6	Spy Kids	2001
7	Intolerable Cruelty	2003
8	The Peacemaker	1997
9	Three Kings	1999
10	One Fine Day	1996

Already well-known as Dr. Doug Ross in the TV series *ER*—as well as some best-forgotten early film parts, such as *Return of the Killer Tomatoes!* (1988)—George Clooney has appeared in a run of successful movies during the past decade. His cameo role in *Spy Kids 3D: Game Over* (2003) has been discounted here. He also provided voices for the animated *South Park: Bigger, Longer, & Uncut* (1999) and the title role in the forthcoming *The Fantastic Mr Fox* (2009).

TOP 10 **LEONARDO DICAPRIO MOVIES**

	MOVIE	YEAR
1	Titanic*	1997
2	Catch Me If You Can	2002
3	The Departed	2006
4	The Aviator	2004
5	Gangs of New York	2002
6	The Man in the Iron Mask	1998
7	Blood Diamond	2006
8	Romeo + Juliet	1996
9	The Beach	2000
10	The Quick and the Dead	1995

* Won Best Picture Oscar

Leonardo DiCaprio is in the enviable position of having starred in *Titanic*, the highest-earning movie of all time, in addition to eight further films that have generated more than $100 million at the global box office.

Ocean swell
George Clooney as crime caper hero Danny Ocean. The three Ocean's movies have earned a total of over $1.1 billion at the world box office.

TOP 10 **JOHN TRAVOLTA MOVIES**

	MOVIE	YEAR
1	Grease	1978
2	Look Who's Talking	1989
3	Saturday Night Fever	1977
4	Wild Hogs	2007
5	Face/Off	1997
6	Pulp Fiction	1994
7	Hairspray	2007
8	Phenomenon	1996
9	Broken Arrow	1996
10	The General's Daughter	1999

TOP 10 **NICOLAS CAGE MOVIES**

	MOVIE	YEAR
1	National Treasure: Book of Secrets	2007
2	National Treasure	2004
3	The Rock	1996
4	Face/Off	1997
5	Gone in 60 Seconds	2000
6	Ghost Rider	2007
7	Con Air	1997
8	City of Angels	1998
9	World Trade Center	2006
10	The Family Man	2000

TOP 10 **BRAD PITT MOVIES**

	MOVIE	YEAR
1	Troy	2004
2	Mr & Mrs Smith	2005
3	Ocean's Eleven	2001
4	Ocean's Twelve	2004
5	Se7en	1995
6	Ocean's Thirteen	2007
7	Interview with the Vampire: The Vampire Chronicles	1994
8	Twelve Monkeys	1995
9	Sleepers	1996
10	Legends of the Fall	1994

Bourne again
The Bourne Ultimatum, *the third outing for Matt Damon in the role of Jason Bourne, earned twice as much globally as the original movie,* The Bourne Identity.

TOP 10 **MATT DAMON MOVIES**

	MOVIE	YEAR
1	Saving Private Ryan	1998
2	Ocean's Eleven	2001
3	The Bourne Ultimatum	2007
4	Ocean's Twelve	2004
5	Ocean's Thirteen	2006
6	The Departed	2006
7	The Bourne Supremacy	2004
8	Good Will Hunting	1997
9	The Bourne Identity	2002
10	The Talented Mr Ripley	1999

TOP 10 **JOHNNY DEPP MOVIES**

	MOVIE	YEAR
1	Pirates of the Caribbean: Dead Man's Chest	2006
2	Pirates of the Caribbean: At World's End	2007
3	Pirates of the Caribbean: The Curse of the Black Pearl	2003
4	Charlie and the Chocolate Factory	2004
5	Sleepy Hollow	1999
6	Platoon	1986
7	Chocolat	2000
8	Sweeney Todd: The Demon Barber of Fleet Street	2007
9	Donnie Brasco	1997
10	Finding Neverland	2004

TOP 10 **DANIEL CRAIG MOVIES**

	MOVIE	YEAR
1	Casino Royale	2006
2	The Golden Compass	2004
3	Lara Croft: Tomb Raider	2001
4	Road to Perdition	2002
5	Munich	2005
6	Elizabeth	1998
7	The Invasion	2007
8	The Jacket	2005
9	I Dreamed of Africa	2000
10	A Kid in King Arthur's Court	1995

Actresses

TOP 10 CATE BLANCHETT MOVIES

MOVIE	YEAR
1 The Lord of the Rings: The Return of the King	2003
2 The Lord of the Rings: The Two Towers	2002
3 The Lord of the Rings: The Fellowship of the Ring	2001
4 The Aviator	2004
5 Babel	2006
6 The Talented Mr Ripley	1999
7 Elizabeth: The Golden Age	2007
8 Bandits	2001
9 Elizabeth	1998
10 Notes on a Scandal	2006

Cate Blanchett has been nominated for five Oscars, winning the 2004 Best Supporting Actress award for playing the part of a previous Oscar-winner, Katharine Hepburn, in *The Aviator*.

Screen queen
Cate Blanchett's Top 10 is dominated by the commercially successful Lord of the Rings *trilogy.*

TOP 10 KEIRA KNIGHTLEY MOVIES

MOVIE	YEAR
1 Pirates of the Caribbean: Dead Man's Chest	2006
2 Pirates of the Caribbean: At World's End	2007
3 Star Wars: Episode I – The Phantom Menace	1999
4 Pirates of the Caribbean: The Curse of the Black Pearl	2003
5 Love Actually	2003
6 King Arthur	2004
7 Atonement	2007
8 Pride and Prejudice	2005
9 Bend it Like Beckham	2003
10 Domino	2005

The Top 10 movies in which Keira Knightley has starred have earned a total of $4.4 billion worldwide. All were made before she was 21, her Academy Award Best Actress nomination at 20 (for *Pride and Prejudice*) being the third youngest ever.

TOP 10 DREW BARRYMORE MOVIES

MOVIE	YEAR
1 E.T.: The Extra-Terrestrial	1982
2 Batman Forever	1995
3 Charlie's Angels	2000
4 Charlie's Angels: Full Throttle	2003
5 50 First Dates	2004
6 Scream	1996
7 Music and Lyrics	2007
8 The Wedding Singer	1998
9 Ever After: A Cinderella Story	1998
10 Never Been Kissed	1999

Granddaughter of Hollywood legend John Barrymore, Drew Barrymore's first film role was in *Altered States* (1980), when she was five; by the time of her part in *E.T.: The Extra-Terrestrial* she was aged seven. Her bankability has increased in recent years to enable her to command a reputed $15 million for her role in *Music and Lyrics* (2007).

TOP 10 JUDI DENCH MOVIES

MOVIE	YEAR
1 Casino Royale	2006
2 Die Another Day	2002
3 The World is Not Enough	1999
4 GoldenEye	1995
5 Tomorrow Never Dies	1997
6 Shakespeare in Love	1998
7 Chocolat	2000
8 Pride and Prejudice	2005
9 The Chronicles of Riddick	2004
10 Notes on a Scandal	2006

While her highest-earning films are her five Bond appearances as "M," all but one in Dame Judi Dench's personal Top 10 earned in excess of $100 million worldwide. She won a Best Supporting Actress Oscar for an appearance in *Shakespeare in Love* that lasts barely six minutes. She also provided the voice of Mrs Calloway in the animated *Home on the Range*.

TOP 10 CAMERON DIAZ MOVIES

MOVIE	YEAR
1 There's Something About Mary	1998
2 The Mask	1994
3 My Best Friend's Wedding	1997
4 Charlie's Angels	2000
5 Charlie's Angels: Full Throttle	2003
6 The Holiday	2006
7 Vanilla Sky	2001
8 Gangs of New York	2002
9 Any Given Sunday	1999
10 In Her Shoes	2005

Cameron Diaz's Top 10 movies include some of the highest-earning of recent years, the Top 10 cumulatively making $2.3 billion worldwide. She also provided the voice of Princess Fiona in all three *Shrek* films (2001–07), which have outearned those listed.

TOP 10 **RACHEL WEISZ MOVIES**

	MOVIE	YEAR
1	The Mummy Returns	2001
2	The Mummy	1999
3	Constantine	2005
4	About a Boy	2002
5	Fred Claus	2007
6	Enemy at the Gates	2001
7	The Constant Gardener	2005
8	Runaway Jury	2003
9	Chain Reaction	1996
10	Confidence	2003

While the two *Mummy* films top Rachel Weisz's list based on earnings, it was her role in *The Constant Gardener* that earned her the Best Actress Oscar.

Dual role
Based on the comic Hellblazer *horror film,* Constantine *starred Rachel Weisz in two parts, as a detective and her deceased twin sister.*

TOP 10 **UMA THURMAN MOVIES**

	MOVIE	YEAR
1	Batman & Robin	1997
2	Pulp Fiction	1994
3	Kill Bill: Vol. 1	2003
4	Kill Bill: Vol. 2	2004
5	Paycheck	2003
6	Be Cool	2005
7	Prime	2005
8	My Super Ex-Girlfriend	2006
9	The Truth About Cats & Dogs	1996
10	The Avengers	1998

Although in the Top 10 by virtue of its global-box office income, *The Avengers* did not earn back its substantial production budget, estimated at $60 million. Conversely, *Pulp Fiction* had a budget of some $8 million, but went on to make more than $200 million worldwide. Uma Thurman's Top 10 films have earned more than $1.2 billion.

Directors

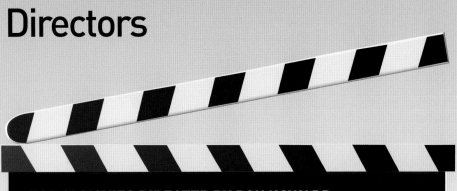

TOP 10 MOVIES DIRECTED BY RON HOWARD

MOVIE	YEAR
1 The Da Vinci Code	2006
2 Dr. Seuss's How the Grinch Stole Christmas	2000
3 Apollo 13	1995
4 A Beautiful Mind*	2001
5 Ransom	1996
6 Backdraft	1991
7 Far and Away	1992
8 Parenthood	1989
9 Cinderella Man	2005
10 Cocoon	1985

* Won Best Director Oscar; film won Best Picture Oscar

Above: Ron Howard's The Da Vinci Code *Starring Tom Hanks, the movie has earned over $750 million internationally.*

TOP 10 MOVIES DIRECTED BY RIDLEY SCOTT

MOVIE	YEAR
1 Gladiator	2000
2 Hannibal	2001
3 American Gangster	2007
4 Kingdom of Heaven	2005
5 Black Hawk Down	2001
6 Black Rain	1989
7 Alien	1979
8 G.I. Jane	1997
9 Matchstick Men	2003
10 Thelma and Louise	1991

TOP 10 MOVIES DIRECTED OR PRODUCED BY GEORGE LUCAS

MOVIE	YEAR
1 Star Wars: Episode I— The Phantom Menace*#	1999
2 Star Wars: Episode III— Revenge of the Sith*#	2005
3 Star Wars: Episode IV— A New Hope*#	1977
4 Star Wars: Episode II— Attack of the Clones*#	2002
5 Star Wars: Episode VI— Return of the Jedi#	1983
6 Star Wars: Episide V— The Empire Strikes Back#	1980
7 Indiana Jones and the Last Crusade#	1989
8 Raiders of the Lost Ark#	1981
9 Indiana Jones and the Temple of Doom#	
10 American Graffiti*	1973

* Directed
\# Produced

George Lucas made the move from directing to producing after the phenomenal success of the first of the *Star Wars* films, but he has a Midas touch in both fields, the first six on this list ranking among the 50 highest-earning movies ever, and his Top 10 cumulatively earning more than $5.6 billion worldwide.

TOP 10 MOVIES DIRECTED BY CHRISTOPHER COLUMBUS

MOVIE	YEAR
1 Harry Potter and the Sorcerer's Stone	2001
2 Harry Potter and the Chamber of Secrets	2002
3 Home Alone	1990
4 Mrs Doubtfire	1993
5 Home Alone 2: Lost in New York	1992
6 Stepmom	1998
7 Nine Months	1995
8 Bicentennial Man	1999
9 Adventures in Babysitting	1987
10 Rent	2005

Burton directs
Tim Burton on the set of Batman Returns *(1992), with Michael Keaton as Batman and Michelle Pfeiffer as Catwoman. It had a budget of $80 million and earned over $283 million.*

TOP 10 **MOVIES DIRECTED BY TIM BURTON**

	MOVIE	YEAR
1	Charlie and the Chocolate Factory	2005
2	Batman	1989
3	Batman Returns	1992
4	Planet of the Apes	2001
5	Sleepy Hollow	1999
6	Big Fish	2003
7	Sweeney Todd: The Demon Barber of Fleet Street	2007
8	Tim Burton's Corpse Bride	2005
9	Mars Attacks!	1996
10	Edward Scissorhands	1990

Director-producer-writer Tim Burton is one of a handful of successful Hollywood directors whose name features as part of the titles of movies he has directed. The first two films in his list have each earned in excess of $400 million globally, and all but No. 10 in this list over $100 million. The recent success of *Sweeney Todd: The Demon Barber of Fleet Street* displaced cult film *Beetlejuice* from his Top 10.

TOP 10 **MOVIES DIRECTED BY STEVEN SPIELBERG**

	MOVIE	YEAR
1	Jurassic Park	1993
2	E.T.: The Extra-Terrestrial	1982
3	The Lost World: Jurassic Park	1997
4	War of the Worlds	2005
5	Indiana Jones and the Last Crusade	1989
6	Saving Private Ryan	1998
7	Jaws	1975
8	Raiders of the Lost Ark	1981
9	Minority Report	2002
10	Catch Me If You Can	2002

If Spielberg's credits as producer were also included, further blockbusters such as *Transformers* (2007), *Shrek* (2001; uncredited) and *Men in Black* (1997) would rank highly. Spielberg has been nominated for Oscars on 12 occasions, winning Best Director and Best Picture for *Schindler's List* and Best Director for *Saving Private Ryan*. He has also received the Academy's Irving G. Thalberg Memorial Award.

TOP 10 **MOVIES DIRECTED BY CLINT EASTWOOD**

	MOVIE	YEAR
1	Million Dollar Baby*	2004
2	The Bridges of Madison County	1995
3	Unforgiven*	1992
4	Mystic River	2003
5	A Perfect World	1993
6	Space Cowboys	2000
7	Absolute Power	1997
8	The Rookie	1990
9	Letters from Iwo Jima	2006
10	Sudden Impact	1983

* Won Best Director Oscar; film won Best Picture Oscar

Animation

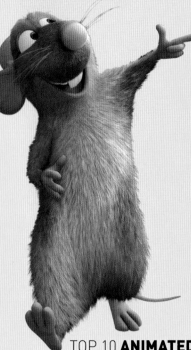

Rat rates
Set in Paris, Best Animated Feature Oscar-winning Ratatouille established a new French record for the highest-earning opening weekend for an animated movie.

TOP 10 **ANIMATED MOVIES**

MOVIE	YEAR	WORLDWIDE TOTAL GROSS ($)
1 Shrek 2*	2004	920,665,658
2 Finding Nemo#	2003	864,625,978
3 Shrek the Third*	2007	797,750,521
4 The Lion King#	1994	783,841,776
5 Ice Age: The Meltdown†	2006	651,564,512
6 The Incredibles#	2004	631,442,092
7 Ratatouille#	2007	620,720,969
8 Madagascar*	2005	532,680,671
9 Monsters, Inc.#	2001	529,061,238
10 The Simpson's Movie†	1992	526,622,545

* DreamWorks
\# Disney
† 20th Century Fox Animation

TOP 10 **ANIMATED MOVIES IN THE USA**

MOVIE	YEAR	US TOTAL GROSS ($)
1 Shrek 2*	2004	441,226,247
2 Finding Nemo#	2003	339,714,978
3 The Lion King#	1994	328,541,776
4 Shrek the Third*	2007	322,719,944
5 Shrek*	2001	267,665,011
6 The Incredibles#	2004	261,441,092
7 Monsters, Inc.#	2001	255,873,250
8 Toy Story 2#	1999	245,852,179
9 Cars#	2006	244,082,982
10 Aladdin*	1992	217,350,219

* DreamWorks
\# Disney
† 20th Century Fox Animation

THE 10 **LATEST WINNERS OF ANNIE AWARDS FOR BEST ANIMATED FEATURE**

YEAR* / MOVIE

2007	Ratatouille
2006	Cars
2005	Wallace & Gromit in The Curse of the Were-Rabbit
2004	The Incredibles
2003	Finding Nemo
2002	Spirited Away
2001	Shrek
2000	Toy Story 2
1999	The Iron Giant
1998	Mulan

* Of movie—awards are made the following year

The Annie Awards have been presented by the International Animated Film Society (ASIFA-Hollywood) since 1972. In addition to the individual and specialist category awards presented from then, it has been honoring Best Animated Feature (originally Outstanding Achievement in an Animated Theatrical Feature) since 1992, when it was won by *Beauty and the Beast*. The equivalent Academy Award (Oscar) for Best Animated Feature was first presented in 2001.

Worth the wait
It took 10 years from its original conception to release, but The Simpsons Movie *has earned a place in the Top 10 highest-earning animated movies of all time.*

TOP 10 **ANIMATED MOVIE BUDGETS**

	MOVIE	YEAR	BUDGET ($)
1	The Polar Express	2004	170,000,000
2	Shrek the Third	2007	160,000,000
3	= Bee Movie	2007	150,000,000
	= Beowulf	2007	150,000,000
	= Ratatouille	2007	150,000,000
	= Shrek 2	2007	150,000,000
7	Flushed Away	2006	149,000,000
8	Tarzan	1999	145,000,000
9	Treasure Planet	2002	140,000,000
10	Final Fantasy: The Spirits Within	2001	137,000,000

Snow White and the Seven Dwarfs (1937) established a record animated film budget of $1.49 million. The $2.6 million budget for *Pinocchio* (1940) and $2.28 million for *Fantasia* (1940) were the two biggest of the 1940s, while *Sleeping Beauty* (1959) at $6 million was the highest of the 1950s. Since the 1990s budgets of $50 million or more have become commonplace: *The Lion King* (1994) cost $79.3 million, *Tarzan* becoming the first to break through $100 million.

TOP 10 **ANIMATED MOVIES BASED ON TV SHOWS**

	MOVIE	TV SHOW*	FILM YEAR
1	The Simpsons Movie	1987	2007
2	Pokemon: The First Movie	1997	1999
3	The Rugrats Movie	1991	1998
4	The SpongeBob SquarePants Movie	1999	2004
5	Pokemon: The Movie 2000	1997	2000
6	Rugrats in Paris: The Movie – Rugrats II	1991	2000
7	TMNT	1987	2007
8	South Park: Bigger, Longer & Uncut	1997	1999
9	Beavis and Butt-head Do America	1993	1996
10	Pokémon 3: The Movie	1997	2001

* Launched on TV in USA

Prior to these releases, popular animated TV shows including *Flintstones, Jetsons,* and *Transformers* made the transition to the big screen. Such is their long-established fan following that such movies often attract huge audiences: the first six films in this list each earned in excess of $100 million.

Radio

THE 10 **LATEST NAB MARCONI LEGENDARY STATIONS OF THE YEAR**

YEAR   STATION / LOCATION

2007 WWL-AM New Orleans, Louisiana
2006 WBEB-FM Philadelphia, Pennsylvania
2005 WIBC-AM Indianapolis, Indiana
2004 WOR, New York, New York
2003 WABC, New York, New York
2002 WSB-AM, Atlanta, Georgia
2001 KNIX, Phoenix, Arizona
2000 WEBN, Cincinnati, Ohio
1999 KOA, Denver, Colorado
1998 WCBS-FM, New York, New York

Unlike the National Association of Broadcasters' other awards, the "Legendary Station" award can only be presented once to a station. It recognizes overall excellence in radio, and considers the station's history and heritage. Established in 1989, it is named after Nobel Prize winner and "Father of Wireless Telegraphy" Guglielmo Marconi (1874–1937). A task force of broadcasters chooses five finalists, with the eventual winner being voted on by their peers.

THE 10 **LATEST GEORGE FOSTER PEABODY AWARDS FOR BROADCASTING WON BY NATIONAL PUBLIC RADIO***

YEAR   BROADCAST

2004 = On the Media
          = The War in Iraq
2002   The Yiddish Radio Project
2001 = Coverage of September 11, 2001
          = Jazz Profiles
2000   The NPR 100
1999 = Lost & Found Sound
          = Morning Edition with Bob Edwards
1998 = Coverage of Africa
          = I Must Keep Fightin': The Art of Paul Robeson
          = Performance Today

* Includes only programs made or co-produced by NPR

Source: Peabody Awards

In 1938, the National Association of Broadcasters formed a committee to establish a "Pulitzer Prize" for radio. These awards were inaugurated the following year and named in honor of George Foster Peabody, a native Georgian and noted philanthropist. The Awards are now regarded as the most prestigious in American broadcasting.

TOP 10 **RADIO FORMATS IN THE USA**

FORMAT / SHARE (%)*

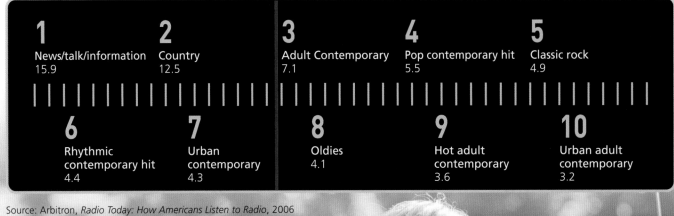

1 News/talk/information 15.9
2 Country 12.5
3 Adult Contemporary 7.1
4 Pop contemporary hit 5.5
5 Classic rock 4.9
6 Rhythmic contemporary hit 4.4
7 Urban contemporary 4.3
8 Oldies 4.1
9 Hot adult contemporary 3.6
10 Urban adult contemporary 3.2

Source: Arbitron, *Radio Today: How Americans Listen to Radio*, 2006

THE 10 **LATEST NAB HALL OF FAME INDUCTEES**

YEAR	INDUCTEE
2007	Rick Dees
2006	Dick Purtan
2005	Jack Buck
2004	Mormon Tabernacle Choir
2003	Scott Shannon
2002	Dick Orkin
2001	Bruce Morrow
2000	Tom Joyner
1999	Wolfman Jack
1998	Rush Limbaugh

Since 1977, the National Association of Broadcasters' Hall of Fame has been honoring radio personalities and programs that have earned a place in US broadcasting history. Among its earlier inductees were Orson Welles and Bing Crosby, while two US Presidents have also been included: Herbert Hoover in 1977, and former radio sportscaster Ronald Reagan in 1981.

TOP 10 **LONGEST-RUNNING PROGRAMS ON NATIONAL PUBLIC RADIO**

	PROGRAM	FIRST BROADCAST
1	All Things Considered	1971
2	Weekend All Things Considered	1977
3	Fresh Air with Terry Gross	1977
4	Marian McPartland's Piano Jazz	1978
5	Morning Edition	1979
6	Weekend Edition/ Saturday with Scott Simon	1985
7	Performance Today	1987
8	Weekend Edition/ Sunday with Liane Hansen	1987
9	Car Talk	1987
10	Talk of the Nation	1991

Source: National Public Radio

All Things Considered, the longest-running NPR program, was first broadcast on May 3, 1971.

Sound waves
Telecommunication towers for radio and TV broadcasts, as well as cell-phone masts, are now a notable feature of the world's skylines.

TV

THE 10 LATEST WINNERS OF THE PRIMETIME EMMY "OUTSTANDING LEAD ACTRESS IN A DRAMA SERIES" AWARD

SEASON ENDING	ACTRESS / SERIES
2007	Sally Fields, Brothers & Sisters
2006	Mariska Hargitay, Law & Order: Special Victims Unit
2005	Patricia Arquette, Medium
2004	Allison Janney, The West Wing
2003	Edie Falco, The Sopranos
2002	Allison Janney, The West Wing
2001	Edie Falco, The Sopranos
2000	Sela Ward, Once and Again
1999	Edie Falco, The Sopranos
1998	Christine Lahti, Chicago Hope

THE 10 LATEST WINNERS OF THE PRIMETIME EMMY OUTSTANDING LEAD ACTOR IN A DRAMA SERIES AWARD

SEASON ENDING	ACTOR / PROGRAM
2007	James Spader, Boston Legal
2006	Kiefer Sutherland, 24
2005	James Spader, Boston Legal
2004	James Spader, The Practice
2003	James Gandolfini, The Sopranos
2002	Michael Chiklis, The Shield
2001	James Gandolfini, The Sopranos
2000	James Gandolfini, The Sopranos
1999	Dennis Franz, NYPD Blue
1998	Andre Braugher, Homicide: Life on the Street

THE 10 LATEST EMMY COMEDY AWARD WINNNG SERIES*

YEAR	SHOW / NETWORK
2007	30 Rock, NBC
2006	The Office, NBC
2005	Everybody Loves Raymond, CBS
2004	Arrested Development, Fox
2003	Everybody Loves Raymond, CBS
2002	Friends, NBC
2001	Sex and the City, HBO
2000	Will & Grace, NBC
1999	Ally McBeal, FOX
1998	Frasier, NBC

* Primetime Emmy Award for Outstanding Comedy Series

TOP 10 SATELLITE TV COUNTRIES

	COUNTRY / SATELLITE TV HOUSEHOLDS*
1	USA 43,574,750
2	Japan 23,777,360
3	Germany 16,533,870
4	Egypt 10,587,910
5	India 9,925,410
6	UK 9,913,460
7	Italy 7,144,960
8	France 7,132,170
9	Turkey 6,397,580
10	Algeria 5,328,320

Top 10 total 140,315,790
World total 205,503,210

* Households with satellite TV, 2009 forecast

Source: Euromonitor International, Global Market Information Database

THE 10 **LATEST WINNERS OF THE PRIMETIME EMMY "OUTSTANDING DRAMA" AWARD**

SEASON ENDING	PROGRAM
2007	The Sopranos
2006	24
2005	Lost
2004	The Sopranos
2003	The West Wing
2002	The West Wing
2001	The West Wing
2000	The West Wing
1999	The Practice
1998	The Practice

The first Emmy awards were presented on January 25, 1949. Emmy awards are awarded by the National Academy of Television Arts and Sciences and are considered the ultimate accolade for those in American television.

TOP 10 **CABLE TV COUNTRIES**

COUNTRY / CABLE TV HOUSEHOLDS*

1	China	191,998,950
2	USA	85,017,870
3	India	76,216,660
4	Japan	31,684,190
5	Germany	22,367,950
6	Russia	20,551,350
7	South Korea	16,608,320
8	Canada	8,237,540
9	Philippines	6,886,740
10	Netherlands	6,418,690

Top 10 total 465,988,260
World total 556,067,040

* Households with cable TV, 2009 forecast

Source: Euromonitor International, Global Market Information Database

TOP 10 **TV AUDIENCES IN THE USA**

	PROGRAM	DATE	TOTAL	VIEWERS %
1	M*A*S*H Special	Feb 28, 1983	50,150,000	60.2
2	Dallas	Nov 21, 1980	41,470,000	53.3
3	Roots Part 8	Jan 30, 1977	36,380,000	51.1
4	Super Bowl XVI	Jan 24, 1982	40,020,000	49.1
5	Super Bowl XVII	Jan 30, 1983	40,480,000	48.6
6	XVII Winter Olympics	Feb 23, 1994	45,690,000	48.5
7	Super Bowl XX	Jan 26, 1986	41,490,000	48.3
8	Gone With the Wind Pt. 1	Nov 7, 1976	33,960,000	47.7
9	Gone With the Wind Pt. 2	Nov 8, 1976	33,750,000	47.4
10	Super Bowl XII	Jan 15, 1978	34,410,000	47.2

Source: Nielsen Media Research

DVD & Video

Gold disk
After earning almost $300 million worldwide from its cinema release and winning four Oscars, The
Departed, *starring Jack Nicholson and Matt Damon, went on to become the year's most-rented DVD.*

TOP 10 **DVD RENTALS IN THE USA, 2007**

1 The Departed
2 The Pursuit of Happyness
3 Blood Diamond
4 Shooter
5 Wild Hogs
6 Night at the Museum
7 Déjà Vu
8 The Guardian
9 Premonition
10 The Illusionist

Source: *Video Business*

TOP 10 **BESTSELLING DVDS IN THE USA, 2007**

DVD	SALES (UNITS)
1 Transformers	13,740,000
2 Happy Feet	13,480,000
3 Pirates of the Caribbean: At World's End	13,200,000
4 300	12,910,000
5 Ratatouille	12,060,000
6 Shrek the Third	11,840,000
7 Harry Potter and the Order of the Phoenix	10,140,000
8 The Departed	8,940,000
9 Night at the Museum	8,660,000
10 The Bourne Ultimatum	7,360,000

Source: Redhill Group/Home Media

In 2007, total sales and rentals of DVDs were $23.4 billion, some
3 percent lower than in 2006—the first time sale declined since
1997. Total sales were $16 billion and rentals $7.5 billion.

TOP 10 **VIDEO CITIES IN THE USA**

CITY / PERCENTAGE*

1 Salt Lake City, Utah 73

2 Colorado Springs/
  Pueblo, Colorado 65

3 = Columbus, Ohio 64

  = Las Vegas, Nevada 64

  = Norfolk/Portsmouth/
    Newport News, Virginia 64

6 Denver, Colorado 63

7 = Oklahoma City, Oklahoma 62

  = Phoenix, Arizona 62

  = Spokane, Washington 62

  = Tulsa, Oklahoma 62

* Of adults in households that purchased a pre-recorded DVD during the previous year (2007)

Source: Nielsen/Scarborough Research

TOP 10 **DVD RELEASES BY GENRE**

GENRE	REGION 1 TITLES RELEASED*
1 Special interest	2,214
2 Music, opera, stage performances	1,033
3 Foreign language feature films	910
4 Theatrical catalog (pre-1997)	906
5 Direct to video feature films	926
6 New theatrical (1997–)	445
7 TV series (multi-disk sets)	428
8 Children's (non-feature)	396
9 Anime	375
10 Adult-themed (non-feature)	236
Total (all genres)	*8,478*

* During the first three-quarters of 2007

Source: *DVD Release Report/Screen Digest*

The total number of Region 1 (USA, US territories, Canada, and Bermuda) DVDs released in 2007 fell 15.9 percent below the 10,079 total for the same period in 2006. By 2008, it has been estimated that, excluding discontinued and adult genre disks, some 85,536 DVDs were currently available for purchase.

Big fish
Finding Nemo *(2003) still tops the list of bestselling DVDs, although Shrek 2 is not far behind.*

TOP 10 **BESTSELLING DVDS IN THE USA**

MOVIE	YEAR*	REVENUE ($)#
1 Finding Nemo	2003	320,400,000
2 Shrek 2	2004	316,000,000
3 Transformers	2007	302,706,311
4 Pirates of the Caribbean: Dead Man's Chest	2006	293,800,000
5 The Incredibles	2005	285,000,000
6 The Chronicles of Narnia: The Lion, the Witch, and the Wardrobe	2006	282,300,000
7 The Lord of the Rings: The Two Towers	2003	280,500,000
8 Pirates of the Caribbean: At World's End	2007	279,046,391
9 Cars	2006	269,000,000
10 The Lord of the Rings: The Fellowship of the Ring	2002	257,300,000

* Of DVD release
# In release year

Source: *Video Business*

THE COMMERCIAL WORLD

Workers of the World

A million workers
Created in 1988, the China National Petroleum Corporation is one of the world's biggest employers.

TOP 10 **COMPANIES WITH THE MOST EMPLOYEES**

	COMPANY / COUNTRY	INDUSTRY	EMPLOYEES
1	Wal-Mart Stores, USA	Retail	1,900,000
2	State Grid, China	Electric power	1,504,000
3	China National Petroleum, China	Oil and gas	1,086,966
4	US Postal Service, USA	Mail	796,199
5	Sinopec, China	Oil and gas	681,900
6	Siemens, Germany	Electronics	475,000
7	McDonald's, USA	Fast-food restaurants	465,000
8	Deutsche Post, Germany	Post and courier	463,350
9	Carrefour, France	Hypermarkets	456,295
10	Agricultural Bank of China, China	Banking	452,464

Source: *Fortune Global 500 2007*

TOP 10 **OCCUPATIONS IN THE USA**

	OCCUPATION	EMPLOYEES (2007)
1	Retail salespersons	3,492,000
2	Drivers/sales workers and truck drivers	3,460,000
3	Retail supervisors and managers	3,445,000
4	Secretaries and administrative assistants	3,401,000
5	Managers (unspecified)	3,398,000
6	Cashiers	3,022,000
7	Elementary and middle-school teachers	2,943,000
8	Registered nurses	2,629,000
9	Janitors and building cleaners	2,080,000
10	Waiters and waitresses	1,978,000
	Total (all occupations)	*146,047,000*

Source: Bureau of Labor Statistics

TOP 10 **COUNTRIES WORKING THE LONGEST HOURS**

	COUNTRY	AVERAGE ANNUAL HOURS PER PERSON*
1	South Korea	2,354
2	Greece	2,053
3	Czech Republic	2,002
4 =	Hungary	1,994
=	Poland	1,994
6	Mexico	1,909
7	New Zealand	1,809
8	USA	1,804
9	Italy	1,801
10	Iceland	1,794

* In employment, 2005—total (employed and self-employed) or employed only, depending on source; OECD countries only

Source: OECD

Among OECD member countries, Norway works the fewest hours per annum—an average of 1,360. Historical assessments of hours worked show that in the mid-nineteenth century, the average US employee worked up to 3,650 hours a year, equivalent to 10 hours a day, seven day a week, or more than double the contemporary figure.

TOP 10 **COUNTRIES WITH THE MOST WORKERS**

	COUNTRY	WORKERS*
1	China	803,300,000
2	India	516,400,000
3	USA	153,100,000
4	Indonesia	108,000,000
5	Brazil	99,470,000
6	Russia	75,100,000
7	Bangladesh	69,400,000
8	Japan	66,070,000
9	Nigeria	50,130,000
10	Pakistan	49,180,000
	World total	*3,001,000,000*

* 2007 or latest year available; based on people aged 15–64 who are currently employed; excluding unpaid groups

Source: CIA, *The World Factbook 2008*/ International Labour Organization

As defined by the ILO, the "labor force" includes people aged 15 to 64 currently employed and those who are unemployed, but excludes unpaid groups such as students, housewives, and retired people.

Call center
Although a fraction of its huge labor force, over one million Indians are employed in call centers, such as this one in Bangalore.

TOP 10 **COUNTRIES WITH THE HIGHEST PROPORTION OF WORKERS**

	COUNTRY	WORKERS PER 1,000 OF POPULATION
1	Monaco	1,347
2	San Marino	691
3	United Arab Emirates	668
4	Azerbaijan	639
5	China	604
6	Myanmar	601
7	Papua New Guinea	600
8	Andorra	591
9	Trinidad and Tobago	585
10	The Bahamas	577
	USA	*503*

Source: CIA, *The World Factbook 2008*

Wealth—Countries

TOP 10 AREAS OF FEDERAL GOVERNMENT EXPENDITURE

AREA OF EXPENDITURE	ESTIMATED FEDERAL EXPENDITURE 2009 ($)
1 Social security	649,332,000,000
2 National defense	675,084,000,000
3 Medicare	413,324,000,000
4 Income security	401,711,000,000
5 Health	299,393,000,000
6 Interest payments	260,231,000,000
7 Veterans/benefits and services	91,875,000,000
8 Education, training, employment, and social services	88,313,000,000
9 Transportation	83,901,000,000
10 Administration of justice	51,143,000,000
Total Federal expenditure:	3,107,355,000,000

TOP 10 SOURCES OF US GOVERNMENT INCOME

SOURCE	ESTIMATED FEDERAL INCOME 2009 ($)
1 Individual income tax	1,259,041,000,000
2 Old-age and survivors' insurance	594,598,000,000
3 Corporation income tax	339,224,000,000
4 Hospital insurance	199,716,000,000
5 Disability insurance	100,966,000,000
6 Unemployment insurance	44,953,000,000
7 Highway trust funds	39,928,000,000
8 Airport and airway trust funds	12,570,000,000
9 Alcohol excise taxes	8,915,000,000
10 Tobacco excise taxes	7,526,000,000
Total Federal income	2,699,947,000,000

TOP 10 COINS AND BILLS IN CIRCULATION IN THE USA

DENOMINATION	UNITS IN CIRCULATION 2006 (£)
1 Penny	106,000,000,000
2 Dime	18,400,000,000
3 Quarter	16,300,000,000
4 Nickel	12,100,000,000
5 $1 bill	9,302,326,502
6 $20 bill	6,089,160,181
7 $100 bill	5,692,539,414
8 $5 bill	2,153,459,388
9 $10 bill	1,615,589,394
10 $50 bill	1,259,580,007
Total currency (value)	$792,159,288,292

* As at December 31, 2007

THE 10 COUNTRIES WITH THE HIGHEST INFLATION

COUNTRY	ANNUAL INFLATION RATE (%, 2007)
1 Zimbabwe	16,170
2 Myanmar	36.9
3 Guinea	23.4
4 Eritrea	22.7
5 Iran	19.0
6 Venezuela	18.0
7 Ethiopia	17.8
8 Dem. Rep. of Congo	17.5
9 Sri Lanka	17.0
10 = Azerbaijan	16.6
= São Tomé and Príncipe	16.6
USA	2.7

Source: International Monetary Fund

These figures indicate the rise in consumer prices over the previous year. An inflation rate of 100 percent would mean that consumer prices had doubled since the previous year. High though they are, and immensely painful to consumers and governments alike, these levels seem almost insignificant when compared with the multimillion percent hyperinflation experienced by Germany in 1923, or Hungary in 1946.

TOP 10 **RICHEST COUNTRIES**

	COUNTRY	GROSS DOMESTIC PRODUCT PER CAPITA 2008 ($)
1	Luxembourg	110,032
2	Norway	83,702
3	Qatar	80,211
4	Iceland	63,875
5	Ireland	62,482
6	Denmark	59,728
7	Switzerland	58,412
8	Sweden	49,091
9	Netherlands	48,169
10	UK	48,072
	USA	*46,820*

Source: International Monetary Fund, World Economic Outlook Database

Sky high
Qatar has a population of fewer than one million, but its oil wealth results in a substantial GDP, reflected in its high-rise and exotic architecture, such as the coffee-pot monument— a symbol of welcome—in Doha, the capital city.

African tragedy
Despite its considerable natural resources, warfare and other problems have so damaged the economy of the Democratic Republic of Congo that, while it has a population similar to that of the UK, its GDP is just 1/276th.

THE 10 **POOREST COUNTRIES**

	COUNTRY	GROSS DOMESTIC PRODUCT PER CAPITA, 2008 ($)
1	Burundi	140
2	Dem. Rep. of Congo	174
3	Liberia	206
4	Guinea-Bissau	211
5	Ethiopia	225
6	Myanmar	230
7	The Gambia	259
8	Malawi	269
9	Sierra Leone	287
10	Niger	331

Source: International Monetary Fund, World Economic Outlook Database

Richest of the Rich

TOP 10 **COUNTRIES WITH THE MOST DOLLAR BILLIONAIRES**

COUNTRY* / $ BILLIONAIRES

1 USA
435

2 Russia
82

3 China (including Hong Kong)
78

4 India
50

5 = Germany 49
= UK 49

7 Turkey
35

8 Switzerland
27

9 Japan
25

10 Canada
23

World total 946

* Of residence, irrespective of citizenship

Source: *Forbes* magazine, *The World's Billionaires*, 2008

TOP 10 **RICHEST MEN***

	NAME / COUNTRY (CITIZEN/RESIDENCE, IF DIFFERENT)	SOURCE	NET WORTH ($)
1	Warren Edward Buffett, USA	Berkshire Hathaway (investments)	62,000,000,000
2	Carlos Slim Helu, Mexico	Communications	60,000,000,000
3	William H. Gates III, USA	Microsoft (software)	58,000,000,000
4	Lakshmi Mittal, India/UK	Mittal Steel	45,000,000,000
5	Mukesh Ambani, India	Reliance Industries (petrochemicals)	43,000,000,000
6	Anil Ambani, India	Reliance Communications (petrochemicals)	42,000,000,000
7	Ingvar Kamprad, Sweden/Switzerland	Ikea (home furnishings)	31,000,000,000
8	K. P. Singh, India	DLF (property)	30,000,000,000
9	Oleg Deripaska, Russia	UC Russal (aluminium)	28,000,000,000
10	Karl Albrecht, Germany	Aldi (supermarkets)	27,000,000,000

* Excluding rulers and family fortunes

Source: *Forbes* magazine, *The World's Billionaires*, 2008

TOP 10 **HIGHEST-EARNING CELEBRITIES**

CELEBRITY*	PROFESSION	EARNINGS# ($)
1 Oprah Winfrey	Talkshow host/producer	260,000,000
2 Jerry Bruckheimer	Movie and TV producer	120,000,000
3 Steven Spielberg	Movie producer/director	110,000,000
4 Tiger Woods	Golfer	100,000,000
5 Johnny Depp	Movie actor	92,000,000
6 Jay-Z	Rap artist	83,000,000
7 Tom Hanks	Movie actor	74,000,000
8 Madonna	Singer	72,000,000
9 Howard Stern	Radio shock jock	70,000,000
10 Bon Jovi	Singer	67,000,000

* Individuals, excluding groups; all US
\# 2006–07

Source: *Forbes* magazine, *The Celebrity 100*, 2007

Earning élite
Oprah and Elvis, respectively the world's highest-earning living and deceased celebrities. Elvis is one of a select group of individuals who, through ongoing royalty and other earnings, are worth more dead than alive.

TOP 10 **HIGHEST-EARNING SPORTSMEN**

SPORTSMAN / COUNTRY*	SPORT	ESTIMATED EARNINGS, 2006–07
1 Tiger Woods	Golf	100,000,000
2 Oscar de la Hoya	Boxing	43,000,000
3 Phil Mickelson	Golf	42,200,000
4 Kimi Räikkönen, Finland	Motor racing	40,000,000
5 Michael Schumacher, Germany	Motor racing	36,000,000
6 David Beckham, UK	Soccer	33,000,000
7 Kobe Bryant	Basketball	32,900,000
8 Shaquille O'Neal	Basketball	31,900,000
9 = Michael Jordan	Basketball	31,000,000
= Ronaldinho, Brazil	Soccer	31,000,000

* All from the USA unless otherwise stated

Source: *Forbes* magazine

TOP 10 **HIGHEST-EARNING DEAD CELEBRITIES**

CELEBRITY / PROFESSION	DEATH	EARNINGS 2006–07 ($)
1 Elvis Presley Rock star	16 Aug 1977	49,000,000
2 John Lennon Rock star	8 Dec 1980	44,000,000
3 Charles Schultz "Peanuts" cartoonist	12 Feb 2000	35,000,000
4 George Harrison Rock star	29 Nov 2001	22,000,000
5 Albert Einstein Scientist	18 Apr 1955	18,000,000
6 Andy Warhol Artist	22 Feb 1987	15,000,000
7 Theodor "Dr Seuss" Geisel Author	24 Sep 1991	13,000,000
8 Tupac Shakur Musician	13 Sep 1996	9,000,000
9 Marilyn Monroe Actress	5 Aug 1962	7,000,000
10 Steve McQueen Actor	30 Nov 1980	6,000,000

Source: *Forbes* magazine, *Top-Earning Dead Celebrities*, 2007

Natural Resources

TOP 10 **ALUMINIUM PRODUCERS**

COUNTRY / PRODUCTION 2006 (TONS)

1 China 9,590,108

2 Russia 4,100,598

3 Canada 3,306,934

4 USA 2,535,316

5 Australia 2,094,391

6 Brazil 1,763,698

7 Norway 1,499,143

8 India 1,102,311

9 South Africa 981,057

10 Bahrain 914,918

World 36,486,504

Source: US Geological Survey, *Minerals Yearbook*

TOP 10 **SALT PRODUCERS**

COUNTRY / PRODUCTION* 2006 (TONS)

1 China 52,910,942

2 USA 50,706,320

3 Germany 20,502,990

4 India 17,636,981

5 Canada 16,534,670

6 Australia 13,668,660

7 Mexico 9,369,646

8 Brazil 8,046,872

9 France 7,716,179

10 UK 7,047,523

World 264,554,712

* Includes salt in brine

Source: US Geological Survey, *Minerals Yearbook*

TOP 10 **CEMENT PRODUCERS**

COUNTRY / PRODUCTION 2006 (TONS)

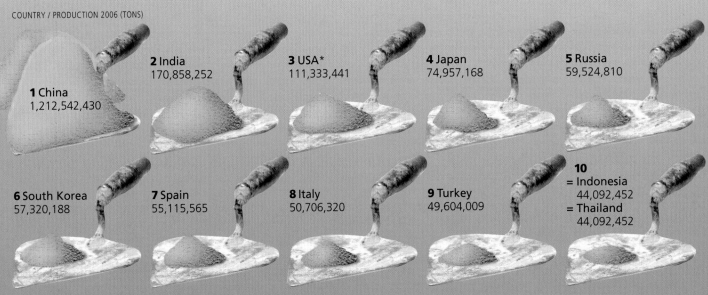

1 China 1,212,542,430

2 India 170,858,252

3 USA* 111,333,441

4 Japan 74,957,168

5 Russia 59,524,810

6 South Korea 57,320,188

7 Spain 55,115,565

8 Italy 50,706,320

9 Turkey 49,604,009

10
= Indonesia 44,092,452
= Thailand 44,092,452

* Including Puerto Rico   Source: US Geological Survey, *Minerals Yearbook*

World 2,500,000,000

TOP 10 **STEEL PRODUCERS**

COUNTRY / PRODUCTION (TONS 2006)

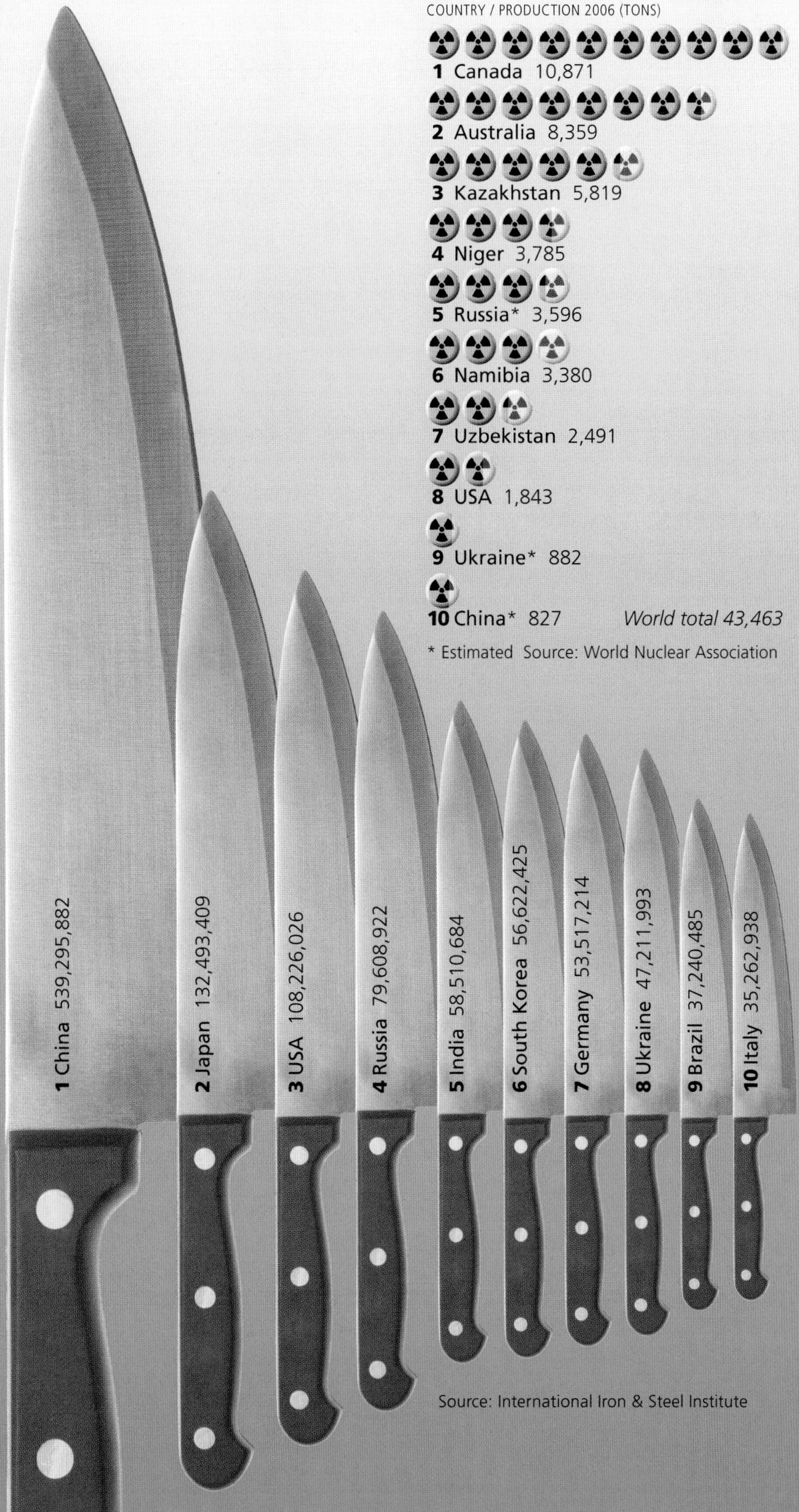

1 China 539,295,882
2 Japan 132,493,409
3 USA 108,226,026
4 Russia 79,608,922
5 India 58,510,684
6 South Korea 56,622,425
7 Germany 53,517,214
8 Ukraine 47,211,993
9 Brazil 37,240,485
10 Italy 35,262,938

Source: International Iron & Steel Institute

TOP 10 **URANIUM-PRODUCING COUNTRIES**

COUNTRY / PRODUCTION 2006 (TONS)

1 Canada 10,871
2 Australia 8,359
3 Kazakhstan 5,819
4 Niger 3,785
5 Russia* 3,596
6 Namibia 3,380
7 Uzbekistan 2,491
8 USA 1,843
9 Ukraine* 882
10 China* 827   *World total 43,463*

* Estimated Source: World Nuclear Association

TOP 10 **LEAD PRODUCERS**

COUNTRY / PRODUCTION 2006 (TONS)

1 China 1,157,427
2 Australia 859,803
3 USA 473,994
4 Peru 352,740
5 Mexico 154,324
6 Canada 87,083
7 Ireland 71,650
8 Sweden 67,241
9 = India 66,139
  = Poland 66,139

Precious Things

TOP 10 **LARGEST UNCUT DIAMONDS**

DIAMOND / DATE / LOCATION OF DISCOVERY / DETAILS — CARATS

1 Cullinan, 1905, Premier Mine, South Africa — 3,106.75
Measuring approximately 4 x 2.5 x 2 in (100 x 65 x 50 mm) and weighing
1 lb 6 oz (621 g) it was bought by the Transvaal government for £150,000
and presented to King Edward VII, who had it cut. The most important of
the separate gems are now among the British Crown Jewels.

2 Excelsior, Jun 30, 1893, Jagersfontein Mine, South Africa — 971.75
Cut by the celebrated Amsterdam firm of I. J. Asscher in 1903, the Excelsior
produced 21 superb stones, which were sold mainly through Tiffany's of
New York.

3 Star of Sierra Leone, Feb 14, 1972, Sierra Leone — 968.90
The uncut diamond weighed 8 oz (225 g) and measured 2.5 x 1.5 in
(63.5 x 38.1 mm).

4 Incomparable, c. 1980, Mbuji-Mayi ("Goat Water") village,
Dem. Rep. of Congo (then Zaïre) — 890.00
The four-year cutting process yielded a stone of 407.48 carats and 14 "satellite"
gems. In 2002 it was offered for sale on eBay with a reserve of $15 million.
It did not reach its reserve and was unsold.

5 Great Mogul, 1650, Kollur Diggings, India — 787.50
Upon its discovery, this diamond was presented to Shah Jahan, the builder
of the Taj Mahal.

6 De Beers Millennium Star, 1990, near Mbuji-Mayi,
Dem. Rep. of Congo (then Zaïre) — 777.00
The dimensions of the rough diamond from which the Millennium Star was
cut are shrouded in secrecy. The polished stone, which was featured in the
celebrations at the Millennium Dome, London, on December 31, 1999
(and later figured in an averted attempt by an armed gang to steal it), is
203.04 carats and measures 2 x 1.5 x 0.75 in (50.06 x 36.56 x 18.5 mm).

7 Woyie River, 1945, Woyie River, Sierra Leone — 770.00
Cut into 30 stones, the largest of which, known as Victory and weighing
31.35 carats, was auctioned at Christie's, New York, in 1984 for $880,000.

8 Golden Jubilee, c. 1985–86, Premier Mine, South Africa — 755.50
Found in 1986 in the Premier Mine (the home of the Cullinan), the polished
diamond cut from it is, at 545.67 carats, the largest in the world.

9 Presidente Vargas, 1938, San Antonio River, Brazil — 726.60
Named after the then president, Getúlio Dornelles Vargas.

10 Jonker, Jan 17, 1934, Elandsfontein, South Africa — 726.00
This massive diamond was found on a claim owned by Johannes Jacobus
Jonker, after it had been exposed by a heavy storm. Acquired by Harry Winston,
it was exhibited in the American Museum of Natural History and attracted
enormous crowds.

Source: De Beers

The weight of diamonds is measured in carats (the word derives from the carob bean,
which was once used as a measure). There are approximately 142 carats to the ounce.
Fewer than 1,000 rough diamonds weighing more than 100 carats have ever been
recorded. In 2007, an 8,000-carat diamond was alleged to have been discovered in an
unnamed mine in South Africa. As the world's press speculated on what could have been
a stone more than twice the size of the record-holding Cullinan, it was exposed as a fake.

TOP 10 **DIAMOND PRODUCERS**

	COUNTRY	VOLUME 2006 (CARATS)
1	Russia	38,400,000
2	Botswana	32,000,000
3	Australia	29,220,000
4	Dem. Rep. of Congo	28,000,000
5	South Africa	15,370,000
6	Canada	12,350,000
7	Angola	7,800,000
8	Namibia	2,200,000
9	China	1,065,000
10	Ghana	970,000
	World total	*171,200,000*

Source: The Diamond Registry

TOP 10 **SILVER PRODUCERS**

	COUNTRY	% OF WORLD TOTAL	PRODUCTION 2006 (TONS)
1	Peru	17.2	3,826
2	Mexico	14.9	3,305
3	China	11.5	2,554
4	Australia	8.6	1,906
5	Chile	8.0	1,766
6	Poland	6.3	1,386
7	Russia	6.1	1,358
8	USA	5.7	1,258
9	Canada	4.8	1,069
10	Kazakhstan	4.0	895
	World total	*100.0*	*22,152*

Source: The Silver Institute/GFMS, *World Silver Survey 2007*

Good as gold
The manufacture of gold jewelry in India has a long tradition. Although some gold is recycled, the country's total demand is equivalent to more than one-fifth of all the gold mined in a year worldwide.

TOP 10 **GOLD JEWELRY MANUFACTURING COUNTRIES**

	COUNTRY	GOLD CONSUMPTION 2006* (TONS)
1	India	574.9
2	USA	340.3
3	China	269.7
4	Turkey	182.2
5	Saudi Arabia	115.0
6	United Arab Emirates	97.2
7	Russia	76.6
8	Italy	70.4
9	Indonesia	63.6
10	Pakistan	60.3

* Including scrap

Source: Gold Fields Mineral Services Ltd, Gold Survey 2007

TOP 10 **COUNTRIES WITH THE MOST GOLD**

COUNTRY / GOLD RESERVES* (TONS)

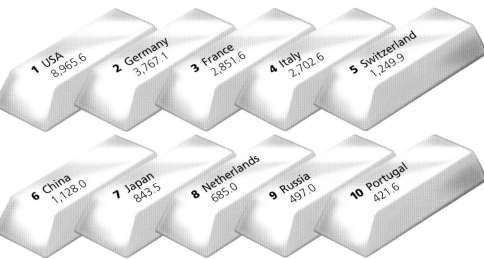

1 USA 8,965.6
2 Germany 3,767.1
3 France 2,851.6
4 Italy 2,702.6
5 Switzerland 1,249.9
6 China 1,128.0
7 Japan 843.5
8 Netherlands 685.0
9 Russia 497.0
10 Portugal 421.6

World total 32,929

* As at March 2008

Source: World Gold Council

Gold reserves are the government holdings of gold in each country – which are often far greater than the gold owned by private individuals. Although less important today, in the days of the 'Gold Standard', this provided a way of measuring a country's wealth, guaranteeing the convertibility of its currency, and determined such factors as exchange rates.

Shopping Lists

TOP 10 GLOBAL RETAILERS

COMPANY / BASE / RETAIL SALES 2006* ($)

* Financial year

Source: *Stores* magazine,
2008 Global Powers of Retailing

2 Carrefour, France
97,861,000,000

3 Home Depot, Inc., USA
90,837,000,000

4 Tesco plc, UK
79,976,000,000

5 METRO AG,
Germany
74,857,000,000

6 Kroger Co., USA
66,111,000,000

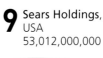

7 Target Corp., USA
59,490,000,000

8 Costco Wholesale
Corp., USA
58,963,000,000

9 Sears Holdings,
USA
53,012,000,000

10 Schwarz Unternehmens
Treuhand KG, Germany
52,422,000,000

1 Wal-Mart Stores, Inc., USA
344,992,000,000

TOP 10 ITEMS OF CONSUMER EXPENDITURE IN THE USA

ITEM	AVERAGE ANNUAL PER CAPITA EXPENDITURE, 2005 ($)
1 Housing	15,167
2 Transportation	8,344
3 Food	5,931
4 Personal insurance and pensions	5,204
5 Utilities, fuels, and public services	3,183
6 Healthcare	2,664
7 Entertainment	2,388
8 Apparel and services	1,886
9 Household furnishings and equipment	1,767
10 Education	940
Total (including items not in Top 10)	*46,409*

Source: U.S. Bureau of Labor Statistics

TOP 10 CONSUMER COMPLAINTS IN THE USA

1 Home improvement/repairs
2 Automobile sales
3 Automobile repairs
4 Credit
5 Telecommunications/cable/satellite
6 Debt collections/billing practices
7 ID theft/deceptive practices
8 Internet/ISP/e-commerce
9 Major purchases/household goods
10 Telemarketing/sales practices

Source: Consumer Federation of America, *Thirteenth Annual NACAA/CFA Consumer Complaint Survey Report*, 2005

Great Mall of China
Until recently the world's largest shopping complex, the Jin Yuan shopping Mall, Beijing, with more than 1,000 stores, caters for the Chinese capital's emerging middle class.

TOP 10 **LARGEST SHOPPING MALLS IN THE WORLD**

	MALL / LOCATION	OPENED	GLA* SQ FT
1	**South China Mall**, Dongguan, China	2005	7,104,174
2	**Jin Yuan**, Beijing, China	2004	6,027,784
3	**Mall of Asia**, Pasay City, Philippines	2006	4,154,865
4	**West Edmonton Mall**, Edmonton, Alberta, Canada	1981	3,767,365
5	**Cevahir Istanbul**, Istanbul, Turkey	2005	3,745,837
6 =	**City North Edsa**, Quezon City, Philippines	1985	3,573,615
=	**Megamall**, Mandaluyong City, Philippines	1991	3,573,615
8 =	**Beijing Mall**, Beijing, China	2005	3,444,448
=	**Berjaya Times Square**, Kuala Lumpur, Malaysia	2003	3,444,448
10	**Zhengjia Plaza**, Guangzhou, China	2005	3,013,892

* Gross Leasable Area

Source: Emil Pocock, Eastern Connecticut State University

TOP 10 **US RETAILERS**

	COMPANY	RETAIL SALES, 2005* ($)
1	Wal-Mart Stores, Inc.	312,427,000,000
2	Home Depot, Inc.	81,511,000,000
3	Kroger Co.	60,553,000,000
4	Target Corp.	52,620,000,000
5	Costco Wholesale Corp.	51,862,000,000
6	Sears Holdings	49,124,000,000
7	Lowe's	43,243,000,000
8	Walgreen	42,202,000,000
9	Albertsons	40,358,000,000
10	Safeway	38,416,000,000

* Financial year

Source: Stores *magazine*, 2007 Global Powers of Retailing

Advertising & Brands

TOP 10 COUNTRIES SPENDING THE MOST ON ADVERTISING

	COUNTRY	TOTAL AD SPEND FORECAST (2009)
1	USA	210,955,280,000
2	Japan	41,755,480,000
3	UK	26,620,310,000
4	Germany	23,311,560,000
5	China	22,702,710,000
6	France	16,014,470,000
7	Russia	13,931,960,000
8	Italy	13,340,400,000
9	Brazil	11,659,150,000
10	Spain	11,337,030,000
	Top 10 total	*391,628,350,000*
	World total	*549,627,610,000*

Source: Euromonitor International, Global Market Information Database

TOP 10 ADVERTISERS BY CATEGORY IN THE USA

	CATEGORY	ADVERTISING SPENDING 2006 ($)
1	Automotive	19,799,000,000
2	Retail	19,114,000,000
3	Telecommunications	10,950,200,000
4	Medicines and remedies	9,192,900,000
5	General services	8,702,000,000
6	Financial services	8,689,000,000
7	Food, beverages, and candy	7,225,000,000
8	Personal care	5,732,000,000
9	Airlines, hotels, car rental, travel	5,415,600,000
10	Movies, video, music	5,379,900,000

Source: *Advertising Age*

TOP 10 COUNTRIES SPENDING THE MOST ON ONLINE ADVERTISING

	COUNTRY	ONLINE AD SPEND FORECAST (2009)
1	USA	21,937,370,000
2	UK	5,721,140,000
3	Japan	5,712,250,000
4	Canada	1,427,310,000
5	Australia	1,158,430,000
6	South Korea	1,143,150,000
7	Germany	1,027,510,000
8	Norway	926,120,000
9	France	790,990,000
10	Italy	788,730,000
	Top 10 total	*40,633,000,000*
	World total	*45,470,600,000*

Source: Euromonitor International, Global Market Information Database

TOP 10 ADVERTISERS IN THE USA

	ADVERTISER	TOTAL US AD SPENDING 2006 ($)			
1	Procter & Gamble	4,898,000,000	6	Ford Motor Company	2,576,800,000
2	AT&T	3,344,700,000	7	GlaxoSmithKline	2,444,200,000
3	General Motors	3,296,100,000	8	Walt Disney	2,320,000,000
4	Time-Warner	3,088,800,000	9	Johnson & Johnson	2,290,500,000
5	Verizon Communications	2,821,800,000	10	Unilever	2,098,300,000

Source: *Advertising Age*

Signs of the times
While the USA dominates world advertising expenditure by a considerable margin, Japan is solidly in second place.

Russian bear brand
Once regarded a symbol of the decadent West, Coca-Cola, the world's most valuable brand, is now widely available throughout Russia, as this, one of 18 such advertisements in Irkutsk, Siberia, testifies.

TOP 10 **GLOBAL MARKETERS**

COMPANY / COUNTRY	WORLD ADVERTISING* SPENDING 2006 ($)
1 Procter & Gamble Company, USA	8,522,000,000
2 Unilever, UK/Netherlands	4,537,000,000
3 General Motors Corporation, USA	3,353,000,000
4 L'Oréal, France	3,119,000,000
5 Toyota Motor Corporation, Japan	3,098,000,000
6 Ford Motor Company, USA	2,869,000,000
7 Time Warner, USA	2,136,000,000
8 Nestlé, Switzerland	2,114,000,000
9 Johnson & Johnson, USA	2,025,000,000
10 DaimlerChrysler, Germany/USA	2,003,000,000

* Includes newspapers, magazines, billboards, television, radio, Internet and Yellow Pages

Source: *Advertising Age*, "Global Marketers," 2007

TOP 10 **MOST VALUABLE GLOBAL BRANDS**

BRAND NAME*	INDUSTRY	BRAND VALUE 2007 ($)
1 Coca-Cola	Beverages	65,324,000,000
2 Microsoft	Technology	58,709,000,000
3 IBM	Technology	57,091,000,000
4 General Electric	Diversified	51,569,000,000
5 Nokia (Finland)	Technology	33,696,000,000
6 Toyota (Japan)	Automotive	32,070,000,000
7 Intel	Technology	30,594,000,000
8 McDonald's	Food retail	29,398,000,000
9 Disney	Leisure	29,210,000,000
10 Mercedes-Benz (Germany)	Automotive	23,568,000,000

* All US-owned unless otherwise stated

Source: Interbrand/*BusinessWeek*

Brand consultants Interbrand use a method of estimating value that takes account of the profitability of individual brands within a business (rather than the companies that own them), as well as such factors as their potential for growth.

Food

TOP 10 ICE-CREAM CONSUMERS

	COUNTRY	CONSUMPTION PER CAPITA (2007) PINTS	LITERS
1	USA	24.55	13.95
2	Australia	23.84	13.55
3	Finland	21.10	11.99
4	Norway	18.44	10.48
5	Sweden	17.79	10.11
6	Canada	17.49	9.94
7	Italy	15.12	8.59
8	New Zealand	15.01	8.53
9	Chile	12.48	7.09
10	UK	12.46	7.08

Source: Euromonitor International, Global Market Information Database

TOP 10 BEAN* CONSUMERS

	COUNTRY	EST. CONSUMPTION PER CAPITA (2007) LB	OZ	KG
1	UK	12	12	5.78
2	Ireland	9	3	4.18
3	Portugal	6	14	3.13
4	Australia	4	15	2.25
5	Spain	4	10	2.10
6	Canada	4	10	2.09
7	USA	3	15	1.79
8	New Zealand	3	11	1.68
9	Saudi Arabia	3	11	1.66
10	France	3	5	1.49
	World average	0	10	0.29

* Including baked beans, flageolet beans, kidney beans, chick peas, lentils, broad beans, white beans, black beans, etc.; excludes beans canned with sausages, which are categorized as "canned ready meals"

Source: Euromonitor International, Global Market Information Database

The world eats 1,890,610 tons of beans a year, of which the UK consumes 386,703 tons, including 1.2 million cans of Heinz baked beans per day.

TOP 10 CHOCOLATE CONSUMERS

	COUNTRY	EST. CONSUMPTION PER CAPITA (2007) LB	OZ	KG
1	UK	22	14	10.37
2	Ireland	22	5	10.11
3	Switzerland	21	4	9.65
4	Germany	17	13	8.09
5	Norway	14	10	6.64
6	Austria	13	9	6.15
7	USA	12	10	5.72
8	Belgium	12	8	5.67
9	Denmark	12	0	5.44
10	Sweden	11	2	5.05
	World average	2	5	1.04

Source: Euromonitor International, Global Market Information Database

The estimated world total consumption of chocolate in 2007 was 7,575,943 tons.

TOP 10 BREAD CONSUMERS

COUNTRY / RETAIL VOLUME PER CAPITA (2007) LB OZ/KG

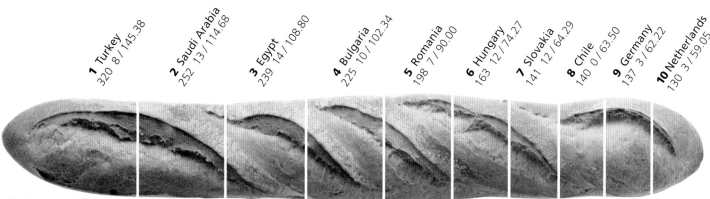

1 Turkey 320 8 / 145.38
2 Saudi Arabia 252 13 / 114.68
3 Egypt 239 14 / 108.80
4 Bulgaria 225 10 / 102.34
5 Romania 198 7 / 90.00
6 Hungary 163 12 / 74.27
7 Slovakia 141 12 / 64.29
8 Chile 140 0 / 63.50
9 Germany 137 3 / 62.22
10 Netherlands 130 3 / 59.05

USA 39 10 / 17.98

Source: Euromonitor International, Global Market Information Database

Breadwinner
Making bread by traditional methods in Egypt,
one of the world's foremost consumers: some
of the earliest archeological evidence of
breadmaking comes from the region.

TOP 10 **FOOD, DRINK, AND RESTAURANT BRANDS**

BRAND*	BRAND VALUE, 2007 ($)
1 Coca-Cola	65,324,000,000
2 McDonald's	29,398,000,000
3 Nescafé, Swizerland	12,950,000,000
4 Pepsi	12,888,000,000
5 Budweiser	11,652,000,000
6 Kellogg's	9,341,000,000
7 Heinz	6,544,000,000
8 Wrigley's	5,777,000,000
9 KFC	5,682,000,000
10 Nestlé, Switzerland	5,314,000,000

* US unless otherwise stated

Source: Interbrand, *Best Global Brands 2007*

TOP 10 **MEAT* CONSUMERS**

		AVERAGE CONSUMPTION PER CAPITA (2007)	
COUNTRY	LB	OZ	KG
1 Spain	251	0	113.85
2 Argentina	249	3	113.02
3 Australia	233	14	106.07
4 New Zealand	227	8	103.18
5 Austria	226	1	102.55
6 Portugal	225	9	102.32
7 Greece	224	2	101.66
8 USA	206	2	93.51
9 Ireland	184	12	83.80
10 France	184	7	83.67
World average	*81*	*0*	*36.74*

* Includes beef, veal, lamb, mutton, goat, pork, poultry, and other meat

Source: Euromonitor International, Global Market Information Database

The world devours a total of 265,329,471 tons of meat a year.

TOP 10 **FOODS CONSUMED IN THE USA***

		ANNUAL PER CAPITA CONSUMPTION (2005)	
ITEM	LB	OZ	KG
1 Dairy products (milk, cream, cheese)	600	8	272.4
2 Fresh fruit	273	1	123.9
3 Processed vegetables	216	5	98.3
4 Fresh vegetables	198	4	90.1
5 Flour and cereal products	192	2	87.2
6 Meat (red meat 110 lb 0 oz/49.9 kg)	183	4	83.3
7 Processed fruit	147	1	66.8
8 Sweeteners (sugar 62 lb 5 oz/ 28.5 kg)	141	4	64.2
9 Fats and oils	85	8	38.8
10 Fish and shellfish	16	1	7.3

* By weight

Source: US Department of Agriculture, Economic Research Service

Drink

TOP 10 **SPIRIT DRINKERS**

COUNTRY / CONSUMPTION PER CAPITA (2007) PINTS/LITERS

1 South Korea
24.46 / 13.90

2 Russia
23.04 / 13.09

3 Ukraine
15.64 / 8.89

4 Thailand
14.25 / 8.10

5 Poland
11.54 / 6.56

6 Japan
11.16 / 6.34

7 Finland
10.33 / 5.87

8 Czech Republic
9.36 / 5.32

9 Bulgaria
8.55 / 4.86

10 France
8.17 / 4.64

USA 6.79 / 3.86 World average 3.55 / 2.02

Source: Euromonitor International, Global Market Information Database

TOP 10 **WINE DRINKERS**

COUNTRY	CONSUMPTION PER CAPITA (2005)	
	PINTS	LITERS
1 Vatican	35.24	62.02
2 Andorra	34.17	60.13
3 France	31.74	55.85
4 Luxembourg	29.95	52.70
5 Italy	27.37	48.16
6 Portugal	26.52	46.67
7 Slovenia	24.87	43.77
8 Croatia	24.02	42.27
9 Switzerland	22.66	39.87
10 Spain	19.70	34.66
USA	*4.94*	*8.69*

Source: Wine Institute

TOP 10 **BEER DRINKERS (PER CAPITA)**

COUNTRY / CONSUMPTION PER CAPITA (2004) PINTS/LITERS

Ireland
230.7 / 131.1

Germany
203.8 / 115.8

Czech Republic
276.1 / 156.9

Australia
193.4 / 109.9

Source: Kirin

Tea break
Tea-drinking is part in of the culture of Morocco and other Islamic countries where alcohol is prohibited.

TOP 10 **TEA DRINKERS**

	COUNTRY	LB	OZ	KG	CUPS*
		CONSUMPTION PER CAPITA (2007)			
1	Ireland	5	8	2.48	1,091
2	UK	4	4	1.92	849
3	Turkey	3	6	1.52	669
4	Poland	2	13	1.27	559
5	Russia	2	9	1.15	506
6	Morocco	2	4	1.02	449
7	Egypt	2	4	1.01	444
8	Japan	1	10	0.75	330
9	New Zealand	1	8	0.69	304
10	Australia	1	8	0.67	295
	USA	*–*	*57*	*0.13*	*57*
	World average	*0*	*10*	*0.27*	*119*

* Based on 440 cups per kg/2 lb 3 oz

Source: Euromonitor International, Global Market Information Database

TOP 10 **COFFEE DRINKERS**

	COUNTRY	LB	OZ	KG	CUPS*
		CONSUMPTION PER CAPITA (2007)			
1	Finland	18	10	8.46	1,269
2	Norway	14	11	6.66	999
3	Sweden	13	11	6.20	930
4	Denmark	10	13	4.91	737
5	Netherlands	10	11	4.85	728
6	Switzerland	10	4	4.64	696
7	Austria	10	2	4.58	687
8	Germany	9	4	4.20	630
9	Belgium	9	3	4.16	624
10	Brazil	7	14	3.57	536
	USA	*5*	*10*	*2.54*	*381*
	World average	*1*	*6*	*0.62*	*93*

* Based on 150 cups per 2 lb 3 oz (1 kg)

Source: Euromonitor International, Global Market Information Database

TOP 10 **CARBONATED SOFT DRINK CONSUMERS**

	COUNTRY	PINTS	LITERS
		ANNUAL CONSUMPTION PER CAPITA (2007)	
1	USA	303.38	137.61
2	Mexico	257.96	117.01
3	Norway	249.92	113.36
4	Argentina	248.50	112.72
5	Chile	227.94	103.39
6	New Zealand	184.90	83.87
7	Belgium	184.81	83.83
8	Canada	184.35	83.62
9	Australia	179.83	81.57
10	Saudi Arabia	154.85	70.24
	World average	*50.84*	*23.06*

Source: Euromonitor International, Global Market Information Database

Austria
190.6 / 108.3

UK
174.2 / 99.0

Belgium
163.7 / 93.0

Denmark
158.2 / 89.9

Finland
149.6 / 85

Luxembourg
148.5 / 84.4

Communications

TOP 10 **COUNTRIES WITH THE MOST TELEPHONES**

COUNTRY / TELEPHONE LINES PER 100 / TOTAL 2006

1 China 27.79
367,786,000

2 USA 28.31
172,031,900

3 Japan 43.02
55,165,000

4 Germany 65.94
54,550,000

5 India 3.64
40,770,000

6 Russia 27.94
40,100,000

7 Brazil 20.54
38,799,200

8 France 55.82
33,897,000

9 UK 56.15
33,602,500

***** Top 10 —
861,750,600

10 Italy 43.12
25,049,000

World 19.34
1,267,252,000

Source: International Telecommunications Union

2007 NOW & THEN 1988

TOP 10 **CELL-PHONE COUNTRIES**

2007		1988	
COUNTRY	SUBSCRIBERS	COUNTRY	SUBSCRIBERS
1 China	500,000,000	**1** USA	1,230,000
2 USA	233,000,000	**2** UK	290,000
3 India	166,000,000	**3** Sweden	160,000
4 Russia	150,000,000	**4** Japan	150,773
5 Japan	100,000,000	**5** Norway	120,029
6 Brazil	99,919,000	**6** Canada	120,000
7 Germany	84,300,000	**7** Denmark	77,432
8 Italy	71,500,000	**8** Finland	71,598
9 UK	69,675,000	**9** West Germany	48,747
10 Indonesia	63,803,000	**10** France	39,234
World total	3,300,000,000		

Source: Siemens, International Telecom Statistics

The first cell-phone network was established in Japan in 1979. Within a decade, most industrialized countries had established national systems, but increasingly, in many developing countries, cell phones have replaced often defunct, inefficient, or nonexistent fixed lines, enabling their telephone systems rapidly to adopt twenty-first-century technology.

Phone line
Like-minded commuters in Japan, where the ownership of cell phones has grown by a factor of 663 in the past 20 years.

U.S. Mail
Despite the growth of e-mail, texting and other forms of communication, the number of domestic mail items in the USA has increased in recent years.

TOP 10 COUNTRIES SENDING AND RECEIVING THE MOST LETTERS (DOMESTIC)

1 ENVELOPE REPRESENTS APPROX 5,000,000,000 ITEMS

COUNTRY	ITEMS OF MAIL HANDLED (2006)
1 USA	201,001,000,000
2 Japan	22,284,166,000
3 Germany	20,887,000,000
4 UK	20,323,000,000
5 France	17,165,000,000
6 Brazil	8,095,400,000
7 China	7,090,414,021
8 Italy	6,779,772,929
9 India	5,923,300,000
10 Spain	5,446,600,000
Top 10 total	*314,995,652,950*
World total	*429,769,752,361*

Source: Universal Postal Union

THE 10 OLDEST POST OFFICES IN THE USA

	CITY	POST-OFFICE ADDRESS	OPENED
1	Galena, IL	110 Green Street	Nov 1, 1858
2	Memphis, TN	1 N. Front Street	Jun 1, 1887
3	Brooklyn, NY	271 Cadman Plaza East	Feb 1, 1892
4	Hoboken, NJ	89 River Street	Jan 1, 1893
5	Port Townsend, WA	1322 Washington Street	Jun 1, 1893
6	Atchison, KS	621 Kansas Avenue	Jun 1, 1894
7	Mankato, MN	401 S. Second Street	Jun 1, 1895
8	Pueblo, CO	421 N. Main Street	Jan 1, 1898
9	Omaha, NE	4730 S. 24th Street	Jun 1, 1898
10	Carrollton, KY	520 Highland Avenue	Jun 1, 1901

Source: United States Postal Service

Galena Post Office and Customs House, which was founded by Galena Congressman Elihu B. Washburne, was the first to be named by the Smithsonian Institution as a "Great American Post Office." It is an unspoiled example of a mid-nineteenth-century post office, replete with elegant mahogany counters and marble flooring. While it is identified by the U.S. Postal Service as its oldest continuously operating, offices in Castine, Maine, and Windsor, Vermont, claim even earlier foundation dates.

THE 10 FIRST CITIES AND COUNTRIES TO ISSUE POSTAGE STAMPS

	CITY/COUNTRY	STAMPS ISSUED
1	Great Britain	May 1, 1840
2	New York City, USA	Feb 1, 1842
3	Zurich, Switzerland	Mar 1, 1843
4	Brazil	Aug 1, 1843
5	Geneva, Switzerland	Sep 30, 1843
6	Basle, Switzerland	Jul 1, 1845
7	USA	Jul 1, 1847
8	Mauritius	Sep 21, 1847
9	Bermuda	unknown date 1848
10	France	Jan 1, 1849

The first adhesive postage stamps issued in the UK were the Penny Blacks that went on sale on May 1, 1840. The first issued in the USA were designed for local delivery (as authorized by an 1836 Act of Congress) and produced by the City Despatch Post, New York City, inaugurated on February 1, 1842, and later that year incorporated into the US Post Office Department. The rest of the United States followed suit in 1847 when the Post Office Department issued its first national stamps.

Tourism

TOP 10 **TOURIST DESTINATIONS**

	COUNTRY	INTERNATIONAL VISITORS (2006)
1	France	79,100,000
2	Spain	58,500,000
3	USA	51,100,000
4	China	49,600,000
5	Italy	41,100,000
6	UK	30,700,000
7	Germany	23,600,000
8	Mexico	21,400,000
9	Austria	20,300,000
10	Russia	20,200,000
	World total	*846,000,000*

Source: World Tourism Organization

French leave
Tourists on the Seine, Paris. France has long been the world's most-visited country for international travelers.

TOP 10 **TOURISM SPENDING COUNTRIES**

	COUNTRY	INTERNATIONAL TOURISM EXPENDITURE, 2006 ($)
1	Germany	74,800,000,000
2	USA	72,000,000,000
3	UK	63,100,000,000
4	France	32,200,000,000
5	Japan	26,900,000,000
6	China	24,300,000,000
7	Italy	23,100,000,000
8	Canada	20,500,000,000
9	Russia	18,800,000,000
10	South Korea	16,200,000,000
	World total	*733,000,000,000*

Source: World Tourism Organization

TOP 10 **TOURIST EARNING COUNTRIES**

	COUNTRY	INTERNATIONAL TOURISM RECEIPTS, 2006 ($)
1	USA	85,694,000,000
2	Spain	51,115,000,000
3	France	42,910,000,000
4	Italy	38,129,000,000
5	China	33,949,000,000
6	UK	33,695,000,000
7	Germany	32,760,000,000
8	Australia	17,840,000,000
9	Turkey	16,853,000,000
10	Austria	16,658,000,000
	World total	*733,000,000,000*

Source: World Tourism Organization

TOP 10 COUNTRIES WITH THE BIGGEST INCREASE IN TOURISM

	COUNTRY	VISITORS INCREASE, 2005–06 (%)
1	Zimbabwe	46.7
2	Sudan	33.4
3	Syria	31.3
4	Cape Verde	22.3
5	Panama	20.1
6	Thailand	20.0
7	Cambodia	19.6
8	Lesotho	17.6
9	El Salvador	17.4
10	Bahrain	15.5

TOP 10 COUNTRIES OF ORIGIN OF OVERSEAS VISITORS TO THE USA

	COUNTRY	OVERSEAS VISITORS (2007)
1	Canada	17,735,000
2	Mexico	15,089,000
3	UK	4,497,858
4	Japan	3,531,489
5	Germany	1,524,151
6	France	997,506
7	South Korea	806,175
8	Australia	669,536
9	Brazil	639,431
10	Italy	634,152
	Top 10 total	*46,124,298*
	Total (all countries)	*56,716,277*

On the beach
Thailand's bustling resorts and unspoilt beaches have made the country an increasingly popular long-haul tourist destination.

TOP 10 MOST-VISITED ART GALLERIES AND MUSEUMS IN THE USA

	MUSEUM/GALLERY / LOCATION	APPROX. ANNUAL VISITORS
1	The Smithsonian Institution, Washington, D.C.	20,100,000
2	US Capitol Historical Society, Washington, D.C.	8,000,000
3 =	National Museum of American History, Washington, D.C.	5,500,000
=	National Museum of Natural History, Washington, D.C.	5,500,000
5	Metropolitan Museum of Art, New York, NY	5,400,000
6	National Air & Space Museum, Washington, D.C.	5,000,000
7 =	Grand Canyon National Park Museum Collection, Grand Canyon, AZ	5,000,000
=	The Print Center, Philadelphia, PA	5,000,000
9 =	American Museum of Natural History, New York, NY	4,000,000
=	National Gallery of Art, Washington, D.C.	4,000,000

Source: *The Official Museum Directory*

World Wide Web

TOP 10 **FASTEST SUPERCOMPUTERS**

COMPUTER / LOCATION	SPEED*
1 IBM eServer Blue Gene Solution BlueGene/L Department of Energy National Nuclear Security Administration, Lawrence Livermore National Laboratory, Livermore, California, USA	478.2
2 IBM Blue Gene/P Solution JUGENE Jülich Research Center, Jülich, Germany	167.3
3 SGI Altix ICE 8200 New Mexico Computing Applications Center, Rio Rancho, New Mexico, USA	126.9
4 Hewlett-Packard Cluster Platform 3000 EKA Computational Research Laboratories, Tata Sons, Ltd, Pune, India	117.9
5 Hewlett-Packard Cluster Platform 3000 Swedish National Defence Radio Establishment, Lovön, Sweden	102.8
6 Cray XT3 Red Storm Sandia National Laboratories, Albuquerque, New Mexico, USA	102.2
7 Cray XT4/XT3 Jaguar Oak Ridge National Laboratory, Tennessee, USA	101.7
8 IBM – eServer Blue Gene Solution BGW Thomas J. Watson Research Center, Yorktown Heights, New York, USA	91.29
9 Cray XT4 Franklin National Energy Rsearch Scientific Computing Center, Oakland, California, USA	85.37
10 eServer Blue Gene Solution New York Blue Brookhaven National Laboratory, Stony Brook, New York, USA	82.16

* Teraflops (trillions of calculations per second)

Source: TOP500® Supercomputer Sites, TOP500.org

TOP 10 **MOST-VISITED WEBSITES***

WEBSITE

1 Yahoo—yahoo.com
2 YouTube—youtube.com
3 Windows Live—live.com
4 Google—google.com
5 Myspace—myspace.com
6 Facebook—facebook.com
7 Microsoft Network—msn.com
8 Hi5—hi5.com
9 Wikipedia—wikipedia.org
10 Orkut—orkut.com

* Based on Alexa traffic rankings

Founded in 1996, California-based Internet information company Alexa was acquired by Amazon.com in 1999. Its traffic rankings are widely regarded as providing the most accurate snapshot of the world's most-visited websites and indicate the variations from country to country.

Search engine
Established in 1998, Google has become a major corporation with almost 17,000 employees and annual revenue of $16.6 billion.

Brazilian surfer
The Internet has been avidly adopted as valuable educational tool in countries such as Brazil,
which now ranks with many industrialized nations for its computer usage.

TOP 10 **INTERNET** COUNTRIES

COUNTRY	% OF WORLD TOTAL	INTERNET USERS (2007)
1 USA	18.0	210,575,287
2 China	13.8	162,000,000
3 Japan	7.4	86,300,000
4 Germany	4.3	50,426,117
5 India	3.6	42,000,000
6 Brazil	3.3	39,140,000
7 UK	3.2	37,600,000
8 South Korea	2.9	34,120,000
9 France	2.8	32,925,953
10 Italy	2.7	31,481,928
Top 10 total	62.0	726,569,285
World total	100.0	1,173,109,925

Source: Internet World Stats

TOP 10 **BROADBAND** COUNTRIES

COUNTRY	BROADBAND SUBSCRIBERS*
1 USA	72,914,000
2 China	66,464,000
3 Japan	28,426,000
4 Germany	19,965,000
5 UK	15,679,000
6 France	15,551,000
7 South Korea	14,710,000
8 Italy	10,861,000
9 Canada	8,659,000
10 Spain	8,035,000
World total	349,966,000

* As at January 1, 2008

Source: OECD/Point Topic, *World Broadband Statistics*

TOP 10 **COMPUTER** COUNTRIES

COUNTRY	% OF WORLD TOTAL	COMPUTERS (2006)
1 USA	25.15	240,500,000
2 Japan	7.83	77,950,000
3 China	7.44	74,110,000
4 Germany	5.47	54,480,000
5 UK	4.17	41,530,000
6 France	3.61	35,990,000
7 South Korea	3.07	30,620,000
8 Italy	2.94	29,310,000
9 Russia	2.71	26,970,000
10 Brazil	2.61	25,990,000
Top 10 total	65.00	637,450,000
World total	100.00	996,100,000

Source: Computer Industry Almanac Inc.

Energy

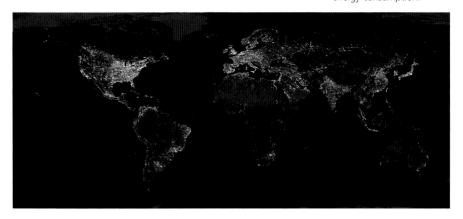

Below: City lights
The world's major cities at night graphically portray the extent of the planet's energy consumption.

TOP 10 **ENERGY-CONSUMING COUNTRIES**

COUNTRY	ENERGY CONSUMPTION (2006)*					
	OIL	GAS	COAL	NUCLEAR	HEP#	TOTAL
1 USA	938.8	566.9	567.3	187.5	65.9	2,326.4
2 China†	363.0	52.2	1,198.8	12.3	94.3	1,720.6
3 Russia	128.5	388.9	112.5	35.4	39.6	704.9
4 Japan	235.0	76.1	119.1	68.6	21.5	520.3
5 India	120.3	35.8	237.7	4.0	25.4	423.2
6 Germany	123.5	78.5	82.4	37.9	6.3	328.5
7 Canada	98.8	87.0	25.0	22.3	79.3	322.3
8 France	92.8	40.6	13.1	102.1	13.9	262.6
9 UK	82.2	81.7	43.8	17.0	1.9	226.6
10 South Korea	105.3	30.8	54.8	33.7	1.2	225.8
World total	*3,889.8*	*2,574.9*	*3,090.1*	*635.5*	*688.1*	*10,878.5*

* Millions of tons of oil equivalent # Hydroelectric power † Including Hong Kong

Source: *BP Statistical Review of World Energy 2007*

TOP 10 **WIND-POWER COUNTRIES**

COUNTRY	% OF TOTAL	CAPACITY (MEGAWATTS)
1 Germany	27.8	20,622
2 Spain	15.6	11,615
3 USA	15.6	11,603
4 India	8.4	6,270
5 Denmark	4.2	3,136
6 China	3.5	2,604
7 Italy	2.9	2,123
8 UK	2.6	1,963
9 Portugal	2.3	1,716
10 France	2.1	1,567
World total		*74,223*

Source: Global Wind 2006 Report

TOP 10 **COUNTRIES MOST RELIANT ON NUCLEAR POWER**

COUNTRY	NUCLEAR ELECTRICITY AS % OF TOTAL (2005)
1 France	78.1
2 Lithuania	69.6
3 Slovakia	56.1
4 Belgium	55.6
5 Ukraine	48.5
6 Sweden	44.9
7 South Korea	44.7
8 Bulgaria	44.1
9 Armenia	42.7
10 Slovenia	42.4
USA	*19.3*

Source: International Atomic Energy Agency

TOP 10 **RENEWABLE POWER-CONSUMING COUNTRIES***

COUNTRY	CONSUMPTION KW/HR (2004)
1 USA	97,090,000,000
2 Germany	39,410,000,000
3 Spain	21,170,000,000
4 Brazil	17,200,000,000
5 Japan	15,010,000,000
6 Italy	12,800,000,000
7 Finland	10,230,000,000
8 Canada	10,020,000,000
9 Philippines	9,770,000,000
10 Denmark	9,720,000,000
UK	*8,100,000,000*
World total	*334,270,000,000*

* Includes geothermal, solar, wind, wood and waste electric power

Source: Energy Information Administration

2006   1986

TOP 10 **OIL-CONSUMING COUNTRIES**

	COUNTRY	CONSUMPTION (TONS) 2006	1986
1	USA	1,034,849,848	825,961,857
2	China*	400,139,002	110,231,130
3	Japan	259,043,156	229,831,906
4	Russia	141,647,002	272,932,277
5	Germany	136,135,446	146,938,096
6	India	132,608,049	50,155,164
7	South Korea	105,300,000	30,203,330
8	Canada	116,073,379	78,264,102
9	France	102,294,489	94,798,772
10	Saudi Arabia	102,074,026	51,037,013
	World total	*4,287,770,495*	*3,188,435,435*

* Including Hong Kong

Source: *BP Statistical Review of World Energy 2007*

In the past 20 years, such factors as population expansion, economic growth, increased industrial production, and especially transport—the number of vehicles on the world's roads almost doubled in this period—have resulted in a 34 percent increase in global oil consumption. This has been most marked in China and South Korea, which contrast sharply with a decline in Russia as its once-mighty industrial base has shrunk. It has been forecast that the inexorable rise in vehicle use in China and India will see these countries' demand for oil for transport alone increase by 75 percent by 2025. It is predicted that worldwide demand for oil will increase from 86 million barrels a day to 118 million by 2030.

TOP 10 **NATURAL GAS- PRODUCING COUNTRIES**

	COUNTRY	PRODUCTION 2006 (TONNES OF OIL EQUIVALENT)
1	Russia	550,900,000
2	USA	479,300,000
3	Canada	168,300,000
4	Iran	94,500,000
5	Norway	78,900,000
6	Algeria	76,000,000
7	UK	72,000,000
8	Indonesia	66,600,000
9	Saudi Arabia	66,300,000
10	Turkmenistan	56,000,000
	World total	*2,586,400,000*

Source: *BP Statistical Review of World Energy 2007*

Above: Water power
Still under construction, the Three Gorges Dam on the Yangtze River, China, controls flooding and generates 22,500 megawatts of electricity, making it the world's greatest hydroelectric plant.

Below: Wind of change
Globally, the number of wind turbines has increased fourfold since the beginning of the twenty-first century, but still accounts for only one percent of all electricity.

Environment

TOP 10 CARBON DIOXIDE-EMITTING COUNTRIES

	COUNTRY	CO₂ EMISSIONS (2004) (TONS OF CO₂)
1	USA	1,818,835,691
2	China	1,506,367,916
3	Russia	458,507,488
4	India	403,777,734
5	Japan	378,221,746
6	Germany	243,165,464
7	Canada	192,244,193
8	UK	176,567,122
9	South Korea	140,001,251
10	Italy	135,282,257
	Top 10 total	5,452,970,859
	World total	8,264,305,599

Carbon emissions

CO₂ and other contaminants from steel production in Benxi, China, make it one of the country's most polluted cities. Such problems were highlighted in 2008 as Olympic athletes considered the health hazards posed.

THE 10 MOST COMMON TYPES OF WASTE IN THE USA

	MATERIAL	TONS (2006)
1	Paper and paperboard	85,300,000
2	Yard trimmings	32,400,000
3	Food wastes	31,300,000
4	Plastics	29,500,000
5	Metals	29,500,000
6	Wood	13,900,000
7	Glass	13,200,000
8	Textiles	11,800,000
9	Rubber and leather	6,540,000
10	Other materials	4,550,000
	Total (including materials not in Top 10)	251,300,000

Source: Environmental Protection Agency, *Municipal Solid Waste Generation, Recycling, and Disposal in the United States: Facts and Figures for 2006*

TOP 10 GARBAGE PRODUCERS

COUNTRY* / DOMESTIC WASTE PER CAPITA 2003# LB/KG

Ireland
1,676 / 760

USA
1,631 / 740

Iceland
1,609 / 730

Norway
1,543 / 700

Australia
1,521 / 690

Denmark
1,477 / 670

Switzerland
1,455 / 660

Luxembourg
1,433 / 650

Spain
1,433 / 650

Germany
1,411 / 640

* OECD countries only
# Or latest year for which data available

Source: Organization for Economic Co-operation and Development

Urban slum
Along with certain other African countries, Angola scores poorly on the EPI. Extensive slum areas known locally as musseques, *with high levels of pollution, blight its capital, Luanda.*

TOP 10 **PAPER-RECYCLING COUNTRIES**

COUNTRY	PRODUCTION 2006 (TONS)
1 USA	49,231,926
2 Japan	24,598,526
3 China	18,622,447
4 Germany	15,887,613
5 UK	8,551,731
6 South Korea	7,810,978
7 France	6,562,059
8 Italy	6,049,731
9 Spain	4,765,292
10 Brazil	3,854,783
Top 10 total	*146,562,823*
World total	*181,141,748*

Source: Food and Agrigulture Organization of the United Nations

TOP 10 **ENVIRONMENTAL PERFORMANCE INDEX COUNTRIES**

	COUNTRY	EPI SCORE*
1	Switzerland	95.5
2	= Norway	93.1
	= Sweden	93.1
4	Finland	91.4
5	Costa Rica	90.5
6	Austria	89.4
7	New Zealand	88.9
8	Latvia	88.8
9	Colombia	88.3
10	France	87.8
	USA	*81.0*

* Environmental Performance Index score out of 100

Source: Environmental Performance Index 2008

THE 10 **WORST ENVIRONMENTAL PERFORMANCE INDEX COUNTRIES**

	COUNTRY	EPI SCORE*
1	Niger	39.1
2	Angola	39.5
3	Sierra Leone	40.0
4	Mauritania	44.2
5	= Burkina Faso	44.3
	= Mali	44.3
7	Chad	45.9
8	Dem. Rep. of Congo	47.3
9	= Guinea-Bissau	49.7
	= Yemen	49.7

* Environmental Performance Index score out of 100

Source: Environmental Performance Index

The Environmental Performance Index is a measure of environmental health and ecosystem vitality based on an assessment of 16 indicators in each country. These include air quality, water resources, biodiversity and habitat, productive natural resources, and sustainable energy.

Hazards

THE 10 **LEADING CAUSES OF INJURY IN THE USA**

PRODUCT/ACTIVITY	ESTIMATED ANNUAL INJURIES
1 Beds, mattresses, pillows	531,280
2 Basketball	512,213
3 Bicycles and accessories	494,712
4 Chairs, sofas, sofa beds	453,424
5 Football	418,260
6 Tables	298,949
7 Bathroom structures and fixtures	293,432
8 Baseball, softball	262,529
9 ATVs, mopeds, minibikes, etc.	250,553
10 Exercise, exercise equipment	243,751

Source: Consumer Product Safety Council, National Electronic Injury Surveillance System

Extending this list beyond the Top 10, other sports and recreational equipment responsible for more than 100,000 annual injuries includes playground equipment (218,506 injuries), soccer (174,686), swimming, and pool equipment (150,553), skateboards (112,544), and trampolines (108,029). Ironically, boxing—where inflicting injury is integral to the sport—results in a comparatively lowly 12,238 incidents.

THE 10 **COUNTRIES WITH THE MOST WORK FATALITIES**

COUNTRY	RATE (FATALITIES PER 100,000)	TOTAL FATALITIES
1 China	10.5	73,615
2 India	11.5	48,176
3 Indonesia	20.9	18,220
4 Bangladesh	26.4	14,403
5 Brazil	16.6	11,304
6 Vietnam	27.0	9,988
7 Nigeria	20.1	9,631
8 Thailand	23.3	7,490
9 Russia	11.0	6,974
10 USA	5.2	6,821
Top 10 total		*206,622*
World total		*345,719*

Source: International Labour Organization, *Global Estimates of Occupational Accidents*, 2005

THE 10 **HOME APPLIANCE INJURIES IN THE USA**

HOME APPLIANCE*	ESTIMATED ANNUAL INJURIES
1 Workshop manual tools	121,676
2 Power saws	92,547
3 Lawn mowers	84,316
4 Lawn and garden equipment	73,611
5 Hand garden tools	48,822
6 Cooking ranges, ovens, etc.	43,602
7 Refrigerators, freezers	37,439
8 Small kitchen appliances	30,878
9 Chain saws	26,939
10 Power tools except saws	23,091

* Incuding tools, yard, and garden equipment

Source: Consumer Product Safety Council, National Electronic Injury Surveillance System

The Great Molasses Flood
One of the strangest industrial accidents was that in Boston, USA, on January 15, 1919, when a gigantic tank containing some 2.3 million gallons (8.7 million liters) of molasses burst and a 40-ft (12-m) wave surged through the streets killing 21 and injuring 150, while horses were drowned, a train derailed, and buildings destroyed.

Guadalajara gas blast
The catastrophic 1992 explosion resulted in an official death toll of 206,
but was believed to be as high as 230, with almost 500 injured.

THE 10 **WORST EXPLOSIONS***

LOCATION / DATE / INCIDENT	ESTIMATED NO. KILLED
1 Rhodes, Greece, Apr 3, 1856 Lightning strike of gunpowder store	4,000
2 Breschia, Italy, Aug 18, 1769 Church of San Nazaire caught fire after being struck by lightning, gunpowder store exploded	>3,000
3 Salang Tunnel, Afghanistan, Nov 3, 1982 Petrol tanker collision	>2,000
4 Lanchow, China, Oct 26, 1935 Arsenal	2,000
5 Halifax, Nova Scotia, Dec 6, 1917 Ammunition ship *Mont Blanc*	1,963
6 Hamont Station, Belgium, Aug 3, 1918 Ammunition trains	1,750
7 Memphis, USA, Apr 27, 1865 *Sultana* paddlesteamer boiler explosion	1,547
8 = Archangel, Russia, Feb 20, 1917 Munitions ship	1,500
= Smederovo, Yugoslavia, Jun 9, 1941 Ammunition dump	1,500
10 Bombay, India, Apr 14, 1944 Ammunition ship *Fort Stikine*	1,376

* Excluding mining disasters, terrorist and military bombs, and natural
explosions, such as volcanoes

THE 10 **WORST INDUSTRIAL DISASTERS***

LOCATION / DATE / INCIDENT	NO. KILLED
1 Bhopal, India, Dec 3, 1984 Methylisocyante gas escape at Union Carbide plant	3,849
2 Jesse, Nigeria, Oct 17, 1998 Oil pipeline explosion	>700
3 Oppau, Germany, Sep 21, 1921 Bradishe Aniline chemical plant explosion	561
4 San Juanico, Mexico, Nov 19, 1984 Explosion at a PEMEX liquefied petroleum gas plant	540
5 Cubatão, Brazil, Feb 25, 1984 Oil pipeline explosion	508
6 Durunkah, Egypt, Nov 2, 1994 Fuel storage depot fire	>500
7 Mexico City, Mexico, Nov 19, 1984 Butane storage explosion	>400
8 Adeje, Nigeria, Jul 10, 2000 Oil pipeline explosion	>250
9 Guadalajara, Mexico, Apr 22, 1992 Explosions caused by a gas leak into sewers	230
10 Oakdale, Pennsylvania, May 18, 1918 TNT explosion at Aetna Chemical Company	210

* Including industrial sites, factories, fuel depots, and pipelines; excluding
military, munitions, bombs, mining, marine and other transport disasters,
dam failures, and mass poisonings

ON THE MOVE

The Need for Speed

THE 10 **LATEST HOLDERS OF THE WATER-SPEED RECORD**

DRIVER* / BOAT / LOCATION / DATE	SPEED MPH	KM/H
1 Dave Villwock, Miss Budweiser, Lake Oroville, California, USA Mar 13, 2004	220.493	354.849
2 Russ Wicks, Miss Freei, Lake Washington, Washington, USA Jun 15, 2000	205.494	330.711
3 Roy Duby, Miss US1, Lake Guntersville, Alabama, USA Apr 17, 1962	200.419	322.543
4 Bill Muncey, Miss Thriftaway, Lake Washington, Feb 16, 1960	192.001	308.996
5 Jack Regas, Hawaii Kai III, Lake Washington, Nov 30, 1957	187.627	301.956
6 Art Asbury (Canada), Miss Supertest II, Lake Ontario, Canada, Nov 1, 1957	184.540	296.988
7 Stanley Sayres, Slo-Mo-Shun IV, Lake Washington, Jul 7, 1952	178.497	287.263
8 Stanley Sayres, Slo-Mo-Shun IV, Lake Washington, Jun 26, 1950	160.323	258.015
9 Malcolm Campbell (UK), Bluebird K4, Coniston Water, UK, Aug 19, 1939	141.740	228.108
10 Malcolm Campbell, Bluebird K3, Hallwiler See, Switzerland, Aug 17, 1938	130.910	210.679

* USA unless otherwise stated

THE 10 **LATEST HOLDERS OF THE LAND-SPEED RECORD**

DRIVER (COUNTRY) / CAR	DATE	SPEED MPH	KM/H
1 Andy Green (UK), ThrustSSC*	Oct 15, 1997	763.04	1,227.99
2 Richard Noble (UK), Thrust2*	Oct 4, 1983	633.47	1,013.47
3 Gary Gabelich (USA), The Blue Flame	Oct 23, 1970	622.41	995.85
4 Craig Breedlove (USA), Spirit of America – Sonic 1	Nov 15, 1965	600.60	960.96
5 Art Arfons (USA), Green Monster	Nov 7, 1965	576.55	922.48
6 Craig Breedlove (USA), Spirit of America – Sonic 1	Nov 2, 1965	555.48	888.76
7 Art Arfons (USA), Green Monster	Oct 27, 1964	536.71	858.73
8 Craig Breedlove (USA), Spirit of America	Oct 15, 1964	526.28	842.04
9 Craig Breedlove (USA), Spirit of America	Oct 13, 1964	468.72	749.95
10 Art Arfons (USA), Green Monster	Oct 5, 1964	434.02	694.43

* Location Black Rock Desert, Nevada, USA; all other speeds were achieved at Bonneville Salt Flats, Utah, USA

Land-Speed Pioneers

The first official Land Speed Record of 39.24 mph (62.78 km/h) was set on December 18, 1898 by Comte Gaston de Chasseloup-Laubat in an electric car. In 1902 a steam-driven car, driven by Leon Serpollet, broke the record. In the same year William Vanderbilt became the first to take the record in a gasoline-powered vehicle.

Fastest man on wheels
British jet pilot Wing Commander Andy Green was the first to break the sound barrier on land, setting the latest Land-Speed Record.

Higher and faster
The SR-71 Blackbird was both the fastest and highest-flying aircraft ever, reaching over 16 miles (25.9 km).

THE 10 **LATEST AIR-SPEED RECORDS HELD BY JETS** *

	PILOT	COUNTRY	LOCATION	AIRCRAFT	SPEED		DATE
					MPH	KM/H	
1	Eldon W. Joersz/ George T. Morgan Jr	USA	Beale AFB, California, USA	Lockheed SR-71A	2,193.167	3,529.560	Jul 28, 1976
2	Adolphus Bledsoe/ John T. Fuller	USA	Beale AFB, USA	Lockheed SR-71A	2,092.294	3,367.221	Jul 27, 1976
3	Robert L. Stephens/ Daniel Andre	USA	Edwards AFB, California, USA	Lockheed YF-12A	2,070.102	3,331.507	May 1, 1965
4	Georgi Mossolov	USSR USSR	Podmoskownoe, Mikoyan E-166		1,665.896	2,681.000	Jul 7, 1962
5	Robert B. Robinson	USA	Edwards AFB, USA	McDonnell F4H-1F Phantom II	1,606.509	2,585.425	Nov 22, 1961
6	Joseph W. Rogers	USA	Edwards AFB, USA	Convair F-106A Delta Dart	1,525.924	2,455.736	Dec 15, 1959
7	Georgi Mossolov	USSR	Jukowski-Petrowskol, USSR	Mikoyan E-66	1,483.834	2,388.000	Oct 31, 1959
8	Walter W. Irwin	USA	Edwards AFB, USA	Lockheed YF-104A Starfighter	1,404.012	2,259.538	May 16, 1958
9	Adrian E. Drew	USA	Edwards AFB, USA	McDonnell F-101A Voodoo	1,207.635	1,943.500	Dec 12, 1957
10	Peter Twiss	UK	Chichester, UK	Fairey Delta Two	1,132.138	1,822.000	Mar 10, 1956

* Ground-launched only, hence excluding X-15 records

On the Road

TOP 10 **CAR-PRODUCING COUNTRIES**

COUNTRY	CAR PRODUCTION (2007)
1 Japan	9,944,637
2 China	6,381,116
3 Germany	5,709,139
4 USA	3,924,268
5 South Korea	3,723,482
6 France	2,554,000
7 Brazil	2,388,402
8 Spain	2,195,780
9 India	1,707,839
10 UK	1,534,567

Source: OICA Statistics Committee

1 steering wheel = approx. 1,000,000

Driving force
The Volkswagen group, which also owns brands from Bentley to Skoda, is a major component of the internationally important German car industry.

TOP 10 **MOTOR VEHICLE-OWNING COUNTRIES**

COUNTRY	CARS	COMMERCIAL VEHICLES	TOTAL (2005)
1 USA	132,908,828	104,788,269	237,697,097
2 Japan	57,090,789	16,733,871	73,824,660
3 Germany	46,090,303	3,133,197	49,223,500
4 Italy	34,667,485	4,422,269	39,089,754
5 France	29,990,000	6,139,000	36,039,000
6 UK	30,651,700	3,942,700	34,594,400
7 Russia	25,285,000	5,705,000	30,990,000
8 China	8,900,000	21,750,000	30,650,000
9 Spain	20,250,377	4,907,867	25,158,244
10 Brazil	18,370,000	4,653,000	23,023,000
World total	*617,020,169*	*245,108,745*	*862,128,914*

Source: *Ward's Motor Vehicle Facts & Figures 2007*

1 car key = approx. 10,000,000

TOP 10 CAR MANUFACTURERS

COMPANY / COUNTRY	PASSENGER CAR PRODUCTION (2006)
1 Toyota (Japan)	6,800,228
2 General Motors (USA)	5,708,038
3 Volkswagen group (Germany)	5,429,896
4 Ford (USA)	3,800,633
5 Honda (Japan)	3,549,787
6 PSA Peugeot Citroën (France)	2,961,437
7 Nissan (Japan)	2,512,519
8 Hyundai (South Korea)	2,231,313
9 Renault-Dacia-Samsung (France)	2,085,837
10 Suzuki (Japan)	2,004,310
World total (including manufacturers outside Top 10)	51,953,234

Source: OICA Statistics Committee

THE 10 COUNTRIES WITH MOST PEOPLE PER CAR

COUNTRY	CARS	PEOPLE PER CAR (2005)
1 Myanmar	7,750	6,012.4
2 Bangladesh	35,950	4,014.5
3 Central African Republic	2,000	2,119.0
4 Tanzania	21,450	1,714.0
5 Mali	8,250	1,379.3
6 Malawi	11,650	1,113.7
7 Sudan	37,800	1,063.1
8 Afghanistan	28,600	1,046.5
9 Ethiopia	73,500	993.9
10 Côte d'Ivoire	21,000	823.7
USA	*132,908,828*	*2.2*
World average	*617,020,169*	*10.0*

Source: *Ward's Motor Vehicle Facts & Figures 2007*

As the total number of vehicles on the world's roads has grown out of proportion to population increases, the average ratio of people to cars has fallen from 23 in 1960 to 10 per car. Despite a recent surge in ownership in China, there are still 146.8 people for every car.

TOP 10 COUNTRIES WITH THE LONGEST ROAD NETWORKS

COUNTRY / TOTAL ROAD NETWORK MILES/KM

1 USA 3,995,644 / 6,430,366

2 India 2,102,312 / 3,383,344

3 China 1,162,375 / 1,870,661

4 Brazil 1,088,560 / 1,751,868

5 Japan 735,082 / 1,183,000

6 Canada 647,655 / 1,042,300

7 France 594,219 / 956,303

8 Russia 541,214 / 871,000

9 Australia 503,709 / 810,641

10 Spain 414,015 / 666,292

Top 10 11,784,785 / 18,965,775
World 20,098,351 / 32,345,165

Source: CIA, *The World Factbook 2008*

The CIA's assessment of road lengths includes both paved (mostly tarmac-surfaced) and unpaved highways (gravel and earth-surfaced). In many developing countries the proportion of unpaved is greater than paved. The world total is equivalent to over 800 times the circumference of the Earth at the Equator.

On Track

THE 10 FIRST UNDERGROUND RAILWAY SYSTEMS

CITY / FIRST LINE ESTABLISHED

1. **London**, UK
Jan 10, 1863

2. **Budapest**, Hungary
May 2, 1896

3. **Glasgow**, UK
Dec 14, 1896

4. **Boston**, USA
Sep 1, 1897

5. **Paris**, France
Jul 19, 1900

6. **Berlin**, Germany
Feb 15, 1902

7. **New York**, USA
Oct 27, 1904

8. **Philadelphia**, USA
Mar 4, 1907

9. **Hamburg**, Germany
Feb 15, 1912

10. **Buenos Aires**, Argentina
Dec 1, 1913

TOP 10 BUSIEST UNDERGROUND RAILWAY NETWORKS

CITY / PASSENGERS PER ANNUM (2006)

1. **Tokyo**, Japan
2,646,000,000

2. **Moscow**, Russia
2,475,000,000

3. **New York**, USA
1,850,000,000

4. **Seoul**, South Korea
1,654,000,000

5. **Mexico City**, Mexico
1,417,000,000

6. **Paris**, France
1,409,000,000

7. **London**, UK
1,094,000,000

8. **Osaka**, Japan
912,000,000

9. **Hong Kong**, China
867,000,000

10. **São Paulo**, Brazil
774,000,000

TOP 10 LONGEST UNDERGROUND RAILWAY NETWORKS

CITY / OPENED / STATIONS / TOTAL TRACK LENGTH MILES/KM

1. **London**, UK
(1863) 268
254 / 408

2. **New York**, USA
(1904) 468
229 / 368

3. **Moscow**, Russia
(1935) 176
182 / 293

4. **Tokyo**, Japan
(1927) 282
182 / 292

5. **Seoul**, South Korea
(1974) 266
179 / 287

6. **Madrid**, Spain
(1919) 316
175 / 282

7. **Paris**, France
(1900) 298
132 / 213

8. **Mexico City**, Mexico
(1969) 175
110 / 177

9. **Hong Kong**, China
(1979) 82
109 / 175

10. **Chicago**, USA
(1943) 144
107 / 173

Mumbai station
The Indian railway system is one of the world's most extensive and busiest, transporting over 15 million passengers a day.

TOP 10 BUSIEST RAIL NETWORKS

	LOCATION	PASSENGER/ KM PER ANNUM*
1	China	606,200,000,000
2	India	575,700,000,000
3	Japan	245,960,000,000
4	Russia	170,900,000,000
5	France	79,400,000,000
6	Germany	74,300,000,000
7	Ukraine	52,660,000,000
8	UK	46,760,000,000
9	Italy	46,440,000,000
10	Egypt	40,840,000,000

* Number of passengers multiplied by distance carried in 2006 or latest year for which figures available; totals include national and local services where applicable

Source: UIC Railisa Database

THE 10 FIRST COUNTRIES WITH RAILWAYS

	COUNTRY	FIRST RAILWAY ESTABLISHED
1	UK	Sep 27, 1825
2	France	Nov 7, 1829
3	USA	May 24, 1830
4	Ireland	Dec 17, 1834
5	Belgium	May 5, 1835
6	Germany	Dec 7, 1835
7	Canada	Jul 21, 1836
8	Russia	Oct 30, 1837
9	Austria	Jan 6, 1838
10	Netherlands	Sep 24, 1839

Although there were earlier horse-drawn railways, the Stockton & Darlington Railway in the UK inaugurated the world's first steam service. In their early years, some of those in the 10 first offered only limited services, often over short distances, but their opening dates mark the generally accepted beginning of each country's steam railroad system.

TOP 10 LONGEST RAIL NETWORKS

		TOTAL RAIL LENGTH	
	LOCATION	MILES	KM
1	USA	141,367	226,656
2	Russia	54,156	87,157
3	China	47,051	75,438
4	India	39,431	63,221
5	Germany	30,072	48,215
6	Canada	29,980	48,068
7	Australia	24,044	38,550
8	Argentina	19,897	31,902
9	France	18,318	29,370
10	Brazil	18,271	29,295
	World	*854,971*	*1,370,782*

Source: CIA, *The World Factbook 2008*

The total length of the world rail networks is equivalent to 34 times round the Earth at the Equator. Several countries have networks of under 62 miles (100 km), among them Nicaragua—3.7 miles (6 km), and Paraguay—22.4 miles (36 km).

Water

TOP 10 **LARGEST OIL TANKERS**

	TANKER	YEAR BUILT	OPERATOR'S COUNTRY	DEADWEIGHT TONNAGE*
1	= TI# Africa	2002	Belgium	441,893
	= TI Asia	2002	USA	441,893
	= TI Europe	2002	Belgium	441,893
4	TI Oceania	2003	USA	441,585
5	Marine Pacific	1979	USA	404,536
6	Enterprise	1981	Hong Kong	360,700
7	Nisa	1983	Saudi Arabia	322,912
8	Settebello	1983	Brazil	322,446
9	Aries Voyager	2006	Greece	320,870
10	Andromeda Voyager	2005	Greece	320,472

* Total weight of vessel, including cargo, crew, passengers, and supplies
\# Tankers International

TOP 10 **LARGEST WOODEN SHIPS***

	SHIP / COUNTRY	LAUNCHED	LENGTH FT	LENGTH M
1	Eureka, USA	1890	299.5	91.3
2	Al Hashemi II, Kuwait	2000	274.8	83.8
3	Zheng He, China	2008	233.3	71.1
4	Jylland, Denmark	1860	233.0	71.0
5	Vasa, Sweden	1627#	226.3	69.0
6	SV Tenacious, UK	2000	213.3	65.0
7	Cutty Sark, UK	1869	212.5	64.8
8	Neptune, Italy	1985	203.0	61.9
9	Zinat Al Bihaar, Oman	1988	200.0	61.0
10	HMS Victory, UK	1765	186.0	56.7

* Surviving vessels only
\# Sunk, recovered 1959

TOP 10 **LARGEST MOTOR YACHTS**

	YACHT	OWNER	BUILT/ REFITTED	LENGTH FT	LENGTH IN	LENGTH M
1	Dubai	Sheikh Mohammed, Dubai	2006	524	10	160.0
2	Sunflower	–	2007	508	6	155.0
3	Eclipse	Roman Abramovich, Russia/UK	2008	482	6	147.1
4	Prince Abdulaziz	King Fahd, Saudi Arabia	1984	482	3	147.0
5	Al Salamah	Prince Sultan bin Abdul Aziz, Saudi Arabia	1999	456	10	139.8
6	Rising Sun	Larry Ellison, USA	2004	452	8	138.4
7	Octopus	Paul Allen, USA	2003	414	0	126.1
8	Savarona	Kahraman Sadikoglu, Turkey (charter)	1931/1992	408	0	124.3
9	Alexander	Latsis family, Greece	1976/1986	400	0	122.0
10	Turama	Latsis family, Greece	1990/2004	381	9	116.9

Sheikh's Star

Formerly the *Golden Star*, Sheikh Mohammed bin Rashid Al Maktoum of Dubai's German-built motor yacht *Dubai* features a helicopter pad, submarine, garage, gym, squash court, cinema, theater, and pool. It is 58 ft (18 m) longer than a British Royal Navy Type 42 destroyer, and has had an island with a berth for it specially built in Dubai.

Berth in Venice
Longer than a football field, Microsoft billionaire Paul Allen's motor yacht Octopus *is one of the world's largest private vessels.*

2008 · 1988

TOP 10 **LARGEST PASSENGER SHIPS**

2008

	SHIP	ENTERED SERVICE	COUNTRY BUILT	PASSENGER CAPACITY	GROSS TONNAGE
1	Independence of the Seas	2008	Finland	4,370	160,000
2 =	Liberty of the Seas	2007	Finland	4,370	154,407
=	Freedom of the Seas	2006	Finland	4,370	154,407
4	Queen Mary 2	2004	France	3,090	148,528
5 =	Mariner of the Seas	2004	Finland	3,840	138,279
=	Navigator of the Seas	2003	Finland	3,840	138,279
7	Explorer of the Seas	2000	Finland	3,840	137,308
8 =	Adventure of the Seas	2001	Finland	3,838	137,276
=	Voyager of the Seas	1999	Finland	3,838	137,276
10	Crown Princess	2006	Italy	3,800	117,477

1988

	SHIP*	ENTERED SERVICE	COUNTRY BUILT	PASSENGER CAPACITY	GROSS TONNAGE#
1	Sovereign of the Seas	1988	France	2,852	73,192
2	Norway†	1961	France	1,944	70,202
3	Queen Elizabeth II	1969	Scotland	1,892	66,450
4 =	Celebration	1987	Sweden	1,486	47,262
=	Jubilee	1986	Sweden	1,950	47,262
6	Holiday	1985	Denmark	–	46,052
7	Canberra	1961	N. Ireland	1,737	44,807
8	Royal Princess	1984	Finland	1,200	44,348
9	Seaward	1988	Finland	1,480	42,276
10	Westerdam	1986	W. Germany	1,494	42,092

* Name in 1988—some later changed
\# In 1988—some were smaller at launch but increased during refitting
† Formerly France

Ocean giant
Cruise line Royal Caribbean's Freedom of the Seas accommodates 4,370 passengers and 1,360 crew on its 15 decks.

Top Flight

THE 10 **FIRST COUNTRIES TO HAVE BALLOON FLIGHTS***

1 France   Nov 21, 1783
The Montgolfier brothers, Joseph and Etienne, tested their
first unmanned hot-air balloon in the French town of Annonay
on June 5, 1783. On November 21, 1783, the first manned
flight of a Montgolfier balloon covered a distance of about
5.5 miles (9 km) in 23 minutes, landing safely near Gentilly.

2 Italy   Feb 25, 1784
The Chevalier Paolo Andreani and the brothers Augustino
and Carlo Giuseppe Gerli (the builders of the balloon) made
the first flight outside France, at Moncucco near Milan, Italy.

3 Austria   Jul 6, 1784
Johann Georg Stuwer made the first Austrian flight from
the Prater, Vienna.

4 Scotland   Aug 27, 1784
James Tytler (known as "Balloon Tytler"), a doctor and
newspaper editor, took off from Comely Gardens, Edinburgh,
in a hot-air balloon, achieving an altitude of 350 ft (107 m)
in a 0.5-mile (0.8-km) hop in a home-made balloon.

5 England   Sep 15, 1784
Watched by a crowd of 200,000, Italian balloonist
Vincenzo Lunardi ascended from the Artillery
Company Ground, Moorfields, London, flying
to Standon near Ware in Hertfordshire.
On October 4, 1784, James Sadler flew a
Montgolfier balloon at Oxford, thereby
becoming the first English-born pilot.

6 Ireland   Jan 19, 1785
Although there are earlier claims, it is likely that Richard
Crosbie's hydrogen balloon flight from Ranelagh Gardens,
Dublin, was the first in Ireland.

7 Holland   Jul 11, 1785
French balloon pioneer Jean-Pierre Blanchard, took off from
The Hague in a hydrogen balloon.

8 Germany   Oct 3, 1785
Blanchard made the first flight in Germany from Frankfurt.

9 Belgium   Oct 20, 1785
Blanchard flew his hydrogen balloon from Ghent.

10 Switzerland   May 5, 1788
Blanchard flew from Basel. As well as flights from other
European cities, Blanchard made the first in the USA,
from Philadelphia, on January 9, 1793, watched by George
Washington—as well as future presidents John Adams,
Thomas Jefferson, and James Monroe.

* Several of the balloonists listed also made subsequent flights, but in each
instance only their first flights are included

Up and Away
On November 21, 1783, François Laurent,
Marquis d'Arlandes and Jean-François Pilâtre
de Rozier took off from the Bois de Boulogne,
Paris, in a Montgolfier hot-air balloon, covering
a distance of about 5.5 miles (9 km).

TOP 10 **BUSIEST AIRPORTS**

2007

	AIRPORT	LOCATION	PASSENGERS
1	Atlanta Hartsfield International	Atlanta, USA	84,846,639
2	Chicago O'Hare	Chicago, USA	77,028,134
3	London Heathrow	London, UK	67,530,197
4	Tokyo International	Tokyo, Japan	65,810,672
5	Los Angeles, International	Los Angeles, USA	61,041,066
6	DFW International	Dallas/Fort Worth, USA	60,226,138
7	Charles De Gaulle	Paris, France	56,849,567
8	Frankfurt	Frankfurt, Germany	52,810,683
9	Beijing	Beijing, China	48,654,770
10	Denver International	Denver, USA	47,325,016

1987

	AIRPORT	LOCATION	PASSENGERS
1	Chicago O'Hare	Chicago, USA	53,338,056
2	Atlanta Hartsfield International	Atlanta, USA	45,191,480
3	Los Angeles, International	Los Angeles, USA	41,417,867
4	DFW International	Dallas/Fort Worth, USA	39,945,326
5	London Heathrow	London, UK	34,700,000
6	Denver International	Denver, USA	34,685,944
7	Newark	New Jersey, USA	29,433,046
8	San Francisco	San Francisco, USA	28,607,363
9	JFK	New York, USA	27,223,733
10	Tokyo International	Tokyo, Japan	27,217,761

Source: Airports Council International

TOP 10 **AIRLINES WITH THE MOST PASSENGERS**

AIRLINE / COUNTRY	PASSENGERS CARRIED (2006)*		
1 American Airlines, USA	99,835,000	**6** Lufthansa, Germany	51,213,000
2 Southwest Airlines, USA	96,277,000	**7** Air France, France	49,411,000
3 Delta Air Lines, USA	73,584,000	**8** All Nippon Airways, Japan	49,226,000
4 United Airlines, USA	69,265,000	**9** Japan Airlines International, Japan	48,911,000
5 Northwest Airlines, USA	55,925,000	**10** China Southern Airlines, China	48,512,000

* Total of international and domestic

Source: International Air Transport Association

Aircrash!

THE 10 WORST AIR COLLISIONS IN THE WORLD

LOCATION / DATE / INCIDENT   NO. KILLED

1 Charkhi Dadrio, India, Nov 12, 1996   349
Soon after taking off from New Delhi's Indira Gandhi International Airport, a Saudi Arabian Airlines Boeing 747 collided with a Kazakh Airlines Ilyushin IL76 cargo aircraft on its descent and exploded, killing all 312 on the Boeing and all 37 on the Ilyushin in the world's worst midair crash.

2 Near Dneprodzerzhinsk, Ukraine, USSR, Aug 11, 1979   178
Two Soviet Tupolev-134 Aeroflot airliners collided in midair.

3 Vrbovec, Croatia, Sep 10, 1976   177
A British Airways Trident and a Yugoslav DC-9 collided, killing all 176 on board and a woman on the ground.

4 Morioko, Japan, Jul 30, 1971   162
An air collision occurred between an All Nippon Boeing 727 and Japanese Air Force F-86F. The student pilot and instructor in the fighter survived, but both were found guilty of negligence and imprisoned.

5 Near Souq as-Sabt, Libya, Dec 22, 1992   157
A Libyan Boeing 747 and a Libyan air force MiG-23 fighter collided. The fighter crew reportedly ejected to safety, but all passengers and crew on the airliner were killed.

6 San Diego, California, USA, Sep 25, 1978   144
A Pacific Southwest Boeing 727 collided in the air with a Cessna 172 light aircraft with a student pilot, killing 135 in the airliner, two in the Cessna, and seven on the ground.

7 New York, USA, Dec 16, 1960   135
A United Airlines DC-8 with 77 passengers and a crew of seven and a TWA Super Constellation with 39 passengers and five crew, collided in a snowstorm. The DC-8 crashed in Brooklyn, killing six on the ground; the Super Constellation crashed in Staten Island harbor, killing all passengers and crew on board.

8 Tehran, Iran, Feb 8, 1993   132
As it took off, a passenger aircraft carrying pilgrims was struck by a military aircraft, causing it to crash, killing all on board.

9 Grand Canyon, Arizona, USA, Jun 30, 1956   128
A United Airlines DC-7 and a TWA Super Constellation collided in the air, killing all on board both airliners in the worst civil aviation disaster to that date, and the first ever commercial aviation accident with more than 100 fatalities.

10 Ankara, Turkey, Feb 1, 1963   104
A Middle East Airlines Viscount 754 and a Turkish Air Force C-47 collided and plunged on to the city. All 14 on the airliner, three in the fighter and 87 on the ground were killed by the crash and fire that followed.

The first air collision resulting in more than 50 deaths occurred on November 1, 1949, when a Bolivian Air Force P-38 fighter and an Eastern Airlines DC-4 collided at Washington, D.C., killing 56.

THE 10 WORST AIR DISASTERS IN THE USA

LOCATION / DATE / INCIDENT   NO. KILLED*

1 New York, Sep 11, 2001   c. 1,622
Following a hijacking by terrorists, an American Airlines Boeing 767 was deliberately flown into the North Tower of the World Trade Center, killing all 81 passengers (including five hijackers), 11 crew on board, and an estimated 1,530 on the ground, both as a direct result of the crash and the subsequent fire and collapse of the building, which also killed 479 rescue workers.

2 New York, Sep 11, 2001   c.677
As part of the coordinated attack, hijackers commandeered a second Boeing 747 and crashed it into the South Tower of the World Trade Center, killing all 56 passengers and nine crew on board, and approximately 612 on the ground.

3 Chicago, Illinois, May 25, 1979   273
The worst air disaster in the US occurred when an engine fell off an American Airlines DC-10 as it took off from Chicago O'Hare airport and the plane plunged out of control, killing all 271 on board and two on the ground.

4 Belle Harbor, New York, Nov 12, 2001   265
An American Airlines Airbus A300 crashed soon after takeoff from New York-JFK killing all 260 passengers and crew and five people on the ground.

5 Off Long Island, New York, Jul 17, 1996   230
Soon after takeoff from JFK, a TWA Boeing 747 en route for Paris exploded in midair and crashed into the Atlantic Ocean nine miles south of Moriches Inlet, Long Island, killing all on board.

6 Off Nantucket Sound, Massachusetts, Oct 31, 1999   217
Soon after takeoff from JFK, New York, an EgyptAir Boeing 767 went out of control, broke up, and crashed into the sea, killing all 202 passengers and 15 crew.

7 Washington, D.C., Sep 11, 2001   189
As part of the 9/11 terrorist attacks, a Boeing 757 was hijacked and deliberately crashed into the Pentagon, killing all 64 on board and a further 125 on the ground.

8 Romulus, Michigan, Aug 16, 1987   156
A Northwest Airlines McDonnell Douglas DC-9 crashed on to a road following an engine fire after takeoff from Detroit. A girl aged four was the only survivor; two were killed on the ground.

9 Kenner, Louisiana, Jul 9, 1982   153
A Pan American Boeing 727 crashed after takeoff from New Orleans for Las Vegas, killing all on board (137 passengers and the crew of eight) and eight on the ground.

10 San Diego, California, Sep 25, 1978   144
A Pacific Southwest Airline Boeing 727 collided in the air with a Cessna 172 light aircraft, killing 135 in the airliner, two in the Cessna and seven on the ground.

* Including ground casualties

THE 10 WORST AIRSHIP DISASTERS

LOCATION / DATE / INCIDENT	NO. KILLED

1 **Coast off New Jersey**, USA, Apr 4, 1933 — 73
US Navy airship *Akron* crashed into the sea in a storm, leaving only three survivors.

2 **Over the Mediterranean**, Dec 21, 1923 — 52
French airship *Dixmude* is assumed to have been struck by lightning, broke up, and crashed into the sea.

3 **Near Beauvais**, France, Oct 5, 1930 — 50
British airship *R101* crashed into a hillside leaving 48 dead, with two dying later, and six survivors.

4 **Coast off Hull**, UK, Aug 24, 1921 — 44
Airship *R38* broke in two on a training and test flight.

5 **Lakehurst**, New Jersey, USA, May 6, 1937 — 36
German zeppelin *Hindenburg* caught fire when mooring. Remarkably, 62 people survived the blaze.

6 **Hampton Roads**, Virginia, USA, Feb 21, 1922 — 34
Roma, an Italian airship bought by the US Army, hit power lines and crashed, killing all but 11 men on board.

7 **Berlin**, Germany, Oct 17, 1913 — 28
The first air disaster with more than 20 fatalities, German airship *LZ18* crashed after engine failure and an explosion during a test flight at Berlin-Johannisthal.

8 **Baltic Sea**, Mar 30, 1917 — 23
German airship *SL9* was struck by lightning on a flight from Seerappen to Seddin, and crashed into the sea.

9 **Mouth of the River Elbe**, Germany, Sep 3, 1915 — 19
German airship *L10* was struck by lightning and plunged into the sea.

10 **Coast off Barnegat City**, New Jersey, USA, Jul 6, 1960 — 18
Largest-ever nonrigid airship US Navy *Goodyear ZPG-3W* crashed into the sea. There were three survivors.

"Oh, the humanity…"
Radio commentator Herbert Morrison's memorable remark summarized the horror of eyewitnesses to the conflagration that engulfed German airship Hindenburg *as it prepared to moor, leaving 36 dead.*

SPORT & LEISURE

Summer Olympics

TOP 10 COUNTRIES WINNING THE MOST GOLD MEDALS AT ONE OLYMPICS*

	COUNTRY	YEAR	GOLD MEDALS
1	USA#	1984	83
2	Soviet Union#	1980	80
3	USA#	1904	79
4	Great Britain#	1908	56
5	Soviet Union	1988	55
6	Soviet Union	1972	50
7	Soviet Union	1976	49
8	East Germany	1980	47
9	= USA	1924	45
	= USA	1968	45
	= Unified Team	1992	45

* All Summer Olympic Games 1896–2004
# Host nation

East Germany (1980) is the only country on the list not to have topped the gold medal-winning table.

TOP 10 LEADING MEDAL-WINNING COUNTRIES, 2004

	COUNTRY	GOLD	SILVER	BRONZE	TOTAL
1	USA	36	39	27	102
2	Russia	27	27	38	92
3	China	32	17	14	63
4	= Australia	17	16	16	49
	= Germany	13	16	20	49
6	Japan	16	9	12	37
7	France	11	9	13	33
8	Italy	10	11	11	32
9	= South Korea	9	12	9	30
	= UK	9	9	12	30

Twelve of the United States' 36 gold medals came in the pool, with the men winning nine golds and the women three. They won a total of 28 medals in swimming events. Their next most successful sport was track and field, in which they won a total of eight golds. In all, the United States won gold medals in 15 different sports.

TOP 10 MEDAL-WINNING COUNTRIES AT THE SUMMER PARALYMPICS

	COUNTRY	GOLD	SILVER	BRONZE	TOTAL
1	USA	665	579	607	1,851
2	UK	470	468	454	1,392
3	Germany/West Germany	437	431	413	1,281
4	Canada	445	275	294	1,014
5	France	326	300	283	909
6	Australia	292	306	272	870
7	Netherlands	238	200	169	607
8	Poland	204	209	167	580
9	Sweden	206	203	145	554
10	Spain	176	166	182	524

The first international games for the disabled took place at Stoke Mandeville, UK, in 1952, when 130 athletes from just two countries—the UK and Netherlands—competed. The first Paralympics to take place at the same venue as the Olympic Games was in Rome in 1960, since when they have been held every four years, and since Seoul in 1988, at the same venue as the Summer Olympics. Some 400 athletes from 23 countries took part in 1960, while at Athens in 2004 a total of 3,806 athletes from 136 nations competed. The most medals won at one Games is 388 by the USA in the "dual" Paralympics of 1984. Their total of 131 gold medals is also a record for one Games.

TOP 10 MOST GOLD MEDALS BY A MALE ATHLETE AT ONE OLYMPIC GAMES*

	ATHLETE / COUNTRY	SPORT	YEAR	GOLDS
1	Mark Spitz, USA	Swimming	1972	7
2	= Vitaly Scherbo, Unified Team	Gymnastics	1992	6
	= Michael Phelps, USA	Swimming	2004	6
4	= Anton Heida, USA	Gymnastics	1904	5
	= Willis Lee, USA	Shooting	1920	5
	= Paavo Nurmi, Finland	Athletics	1924	5
	= Matt Biondi, USA	Swimming	1988	5
8	= Hubert Van Innis, Belgium	Archery	1920	4
	= Carl Osburn, USA	Shooting	1920	4
	= Lloyd Spooner, USA	Shooting	1920	4
	= Ville Ritola, Finland	Athletics	1924	4
	= Viktor Chukarin, USSR	Gymnastics	1956	4
	= Boris Shakhlin, USSR	Gymnastics	1960	4
	= Don Schollander, USA	Swimming	1964	4
	= Akinori Nakayama, Japan	Gymnastics	1968	4
	= Nikolay Andrianov, USSR	Gymnastics	1976	4
	= Carl Lewis, USA	Athletics	1984	4

* All Summer Olympics 1896–2004

TOP 10 **SUMMER OLYMPIC GOLD MEDAL-WINNERS (MEN)**

	ATHLETE / COUNTRY	SPORT	YEARS	GOLDS
1	= Paavo Nurmi, Finland	Athletics	1920–28	9
	= Mark Spitz, USA	Swimming	1968–72	9
	= Carl Lewis, USA	Athletics	1984–96	9
4	= Sawao Kato, Japan	Gymnastics	1968–76	8
	= Matt Biondi, USA	Swimming	1984–92	8
	= Ray Ewry, USA	Athletics	1900–08	8
7	= Nikolay Andrianov, USSR	Gymnastics	1972–80	7
	= Boris Shakhlin, USSR	Gymnastics	1956–64	7
	= Viktor Chukarin, USSR	Gymnastics	1952–56	7
	= Aladàr Gerevich, Hungary	Fencing	1932–60	7

TOP 10 **SUMMER OLYMPIC GOLD MEDAL-WINNERS (WOMEN)**

	ATHLETE / COUNTRY	SPORT	YEARS	GOLDS
1	Larissa Latynina, USSR	Gymnastics	1956–64	9
2	= Birgit Fischer (née Schmidt) East Germany/Germany	Canoeing	1980–2004	8
	= Jenny Thompson, USA	Swimming	1992–2000	8
4	Vera Casalavska, Czechoslovakia	Gymnastics	1964–68	7
5	= Kristin Otto, Germany	Swimming	1988	6
	= Amy van Dyken, USA	Swimming	1996–2000	6
7	= Agnes Keleti, Hungary	Gymnastics	1952–56	5
	= Polina Astakhova, USSR	Gymnastics	1956–64	5
	= Nadia Comaneci, Romania	Gymnastics	1976–80	5
	= Nelli Kim, USSR	Gymnastics	1976–80	5
	= Elisabeta Oleniuc-Lipa, Romania	Rowing	1984–2004	5
	= Krisztina Egerszegi, Hungary	Swimming	1988–96	5

Above: Paddle power
German kayak star Birgit Fischer won eight gold and four silver medals in six consecutive Olympic Games.

Below: Seventh heaven
Carl Lewis's 1992 4 x 100 m relay victory added the seventh gold to his ultimate tally of nine.

Athletics

	COUNTRY	GOLD	SILVER	BRONZE	TOTAL
1	USA	14	4	8	26
2	Russia	4	9	3	16
3	Kenya	5	3	5	13
4	Jamaica	1	6	3	10
5	Germany	2	2	3	7
6	UK	1	1	3	5
7	Ethiopia	3	1	0	4
8	= Bahamas	1	2	0	3
	= Belarus	1	1	1	3
	= China	1	1	1	3
	= Cuba	1	1	1	3
	= Czech Republic	2	1	0	3

Brad Walker
American pole vaulter Brad Walker, winner of the 2007 World Championship gold medal with a vault of 5.86 m. It was just 28 cm short of Sergey Bubka's world record.

TOP 10 **MOST IMPROVED WOMEN'S IAAF WORLD RECORDS, 1988–2008***

	EVENT	1988	2008	% IMPROVEMENT
1	Pole vault	3.59m	5.01m	39.55
2	Hammer throw	58.94m	78.61m	33.37
3	20 km walk	1h 36m 19s	1h 25m 41s	11.04
4	Triple jump	14.04m	15.50m	10.40
5	Javelin throw#	67.09m	71.70m	6.87
6	Marathon	2h 21m 06s	2h 15m 25s	4.03
7	Discus throw	74.56m	76.80m	3.00
8	100 m	10.76s	10.49s	2.51
9	5,000 m	14m 37.33s	14m 16.63	2.36
10	10,000 m	30m 13.74s	29m 31.78s	2.31

* In events as contested at the Olympic Games and outdoor World Championships, based on the IAAF world records as at January 1, 1988 and January 1, 2008
# Based on the present-day weight of the javelin, in force since November 18, 1991

Source: International Association of Athletics Federations (IAAF)

The 800 m, high jump, and shot put are the only three women's world records that were not broken in the period 1988–2008. The women's world record for the discus throw is the only event that is better than the men's world record, as at January 1, 2008.

TOP 10 **MOST IMPROVED MEN'S IAAF WORLD RECORDS, 1988–2008***

	EVENT	1988	2008	% IMPROVEMENT
1	Javelin throw#	91.46m	98.48m	7.68
2	10,000 m	27m 13.81s	26m 17.53s	3.44
3	5,000 m	12m 58.39s	12m 37.35s	2.70
4	20 km walk	1h 19m 12s	1h 17m 16s	2.44
5	3,000 m steeplechase	8m 05.4s	7m 53.63s	2.42
6	Marathon	2h 07m 12s	2h 04m 26s	2.18
7	200 m	19.72s	19.32s	2.03
8	Decathlon	8,847 pts	9,026 pts	2.02
9	100 m	9.93s	9.74s	1.91
10	Pole vault	6.03m	6.14m	1.82

* In events as contested at the Olympic Games and outdoor World Championships, based on the IAAF world records as at January 1, 1988 and January 1, 2008
# Based on the present-day weight of the javelin, in force since November 18, 1991

Source: International Association of Athletics Federations (IAAF)

The discus throw and hammer throw are the only two men's world records that have not been broken in the period 1988–2008. The current discus world record has stood since June 6, 1986.

Haile Gebrselassie
Ethiopia's Haile Gebrselassie, winner of two Olympic golds and four World Championship golds at the 10,000 m. He has also won four indoor World Championship gold medals.

TOP 10 **MOST IAAF WORLD CHAMPIONSHIP MEDALS (MEN)***

	ATHLETE / COUNTRY	YEARS	GOLD	SILVER	BRONZE	TOTAL
1	Carl Lewis, USA	1983–93	8	1	1	10
2	Michael Johnson, USA	1991–99	9	0	0	9
3	Haile Gebrselassie, Ethiopia	1993–2003	4	2	1	7
4	= Sergey Bubka, USSR/Ukraine	1983–97	6	0	0	6
	= Butch Reynolds, USA	1987–95	3	2	1	6
	= Lars Riedel, Germany	1991–2001	5	0	1	6
7	= Colin Jackson, UK	1987–99	2	2	1	5
	= Jan Zelezny, Czechoslovakia/ Czech Republic	1987–2001	3	0	2	5
	= Dennis Mitchell, USA	1991–2001	3	0	2	5
	= Antonio Pettigrew, USA	1991–2001	4	1	0	5
	= Jonathan Edwards, UK	1993–2001	2	1	2	5
	= Bruny Surin, Canada	1995–99	2	2	1	5
	= Allen Johnson, USA	1995–2003	4	0	1	5
	= Maurice Greene, USA	1997–2001	5	0	0	5
	= Hicham El Guerrouj, Morocco	1997–2003	4	1	0	5

* Up to and including the 2007 Championships in Osaka, Japan

TOP 10 **MOST IAAF WORLD CHAMPIONSHIP MEDALS (WOMEN)***

	ATHLETE / COUNTRY	YEARS	GOLD	SILVER	BRONZE	TOTAL
1	Merlene Ottey, Jamaica	1983–95	3	4	7	14
2	Jearl Miles-Clark, USA	1991–2003	4	3	2	9
3	= Gail Devers, USA	1993–2001	5	3	0	8
	= Gwen Torrence, USA	1991–95	3	4	1	8
5	= Heike Daute (née Dreschler), GDR/Germany	1983–93	2	2	2	6
	= Yuliya Pechonkina (née Nosova), Russia	2001–05	2	2	2	6
7	= Inger Miller, USA	1997–2003	3	2	0	5
	= Marion Jones, USA	1997–99	3	1	1	5
	= Maria Lourdes Mutola, Mozambique	1993–2003	3	1	1	5
	= Eunice Barber, France	1999–2005	2	2	1	5

* Up to and including the 2007 Championships in Osaka, Japan

First held at Helsinki in 1983, the IAAF (International Amateur Athletics Federation) outdoor Championships were originally held every four years, but since 1993 have been held every two years. A record 1,981 athletes competed in 2007 at Osaka, Japan.

Baseball

THE 10 LAST PERFECT GAMES IN MAJOR-LEAGUE BASEBALL

	PITCHER	TEAM	OPPONENTS	SCORE	DATE
1	Randy Johnson	Arizona Diamondbacks	Atlanta Braves	2–0	May 18, 2004
2	David Cone	New York Yankees	Montreal Expos	6–0	Jul 18, 1999
3	David Wells	New York Yankees	Minnesota Twins	4–0	May 17, 1998
4	Kenny Rogers	Texas Rangers	California Angels	4–0	Jul 28, 1994
5	Dennis Martinez	Montreal Expos	Los Angeles Dodgers	2–0	Jul 28, 1991
6	Tom Browning	Cincinnati Reds	Los Angeles Dodgers	1–0	Sep 16, 1988
7	Mike Witt	California Angels	Texas Rangers	1–0	Sep 30, 1984
8	Len Barker	Cleveland Indians	Toronto Blue Jays	3–0	May 15, 1981
9	Catfish Hunter	Oakland A's	Minnesota Twins	4–0	May 8, 1968
10	Sandy Koufax	Los Angeles Dodgers	Chicago Cubs	1–0	Sep 9, 1965

* As at end of the 2007 regular season

A perfect game is when a pitcher achieves victory (minimum of nine innings) with none of the opposing players reaching first base. The first pitcher to throw a perfect game was John Lee Richmond of Worcester Worcesters against Cleveland Blues on June 12, 1880.

THE 10 LAST PLAYERS TO HIT FOUR HOME RUNS IN A SINGLE MAJOR-LEAGUE BASEBALL GAME*

	PLAYER	TEAM	OPPONENTS	DATE
1	Carlos Delgado	Toronto Blue Jays	Tampa Bay Devil Rays	Sep 25, 2003
2	Shawn Green	Los Angeles Dodgers	Milwaukee Brewers	May 23, 2002
3	Mike Cameron	Seattle Mariners	Chicago White Sox	May 2, 2002
4	Mark Whiten	St. Louis Cardinals	Cincinnati Reds	Sep 7, 1993
5	Bob Horner	Atlanta Braves	Montreal Expos	Jul 6, 1986
6	Mike Schmidt	Philadelphia Phillies	Chicago Cubs	Apr 17, 1976
7	Willie Mays	San Francisco Giants	Milwaukee Braves	Apr 30, 1961
8	Rocky Colavito	Cleveland Indians	Baltimore Orioles	Jun 10, 1959
9	Joe Adcock	Milwaukee Braves	Brooklyn Dodgers	Jul 31, 1954
10	Gil Hodges	Brooklyn Dodgers	Boston Braves	Aug 31, 1950

* As at the end of the 2007 regular season

TOP 10 MOST HOME RUNS IN A CAREER*

	PLAYER	YEARS	HOMERS
1	Barry Bonds	1986–2007	762
2	Hank Aaron	1954–76	755
3	Babe Ruth	1914–36	714
4	Willie Mays	1951–73	660
5	Sammy Sosa#	1989–2007	609
6	Ken Griffey, Jr.	1989–2007	593
7	Frank Robinson	1956–76	586
8	Mark McGwire	1986–2001	583
9	Harmon Killebrew	1954–75	573
10	Rafael Palmeiro	1986–2005	569

* Up to and including 2007 season
# Inactive during 2006 season

Barry Bonds
A free agent since 2007, outfielder Barry Bonds leads the field in home runs with 762. He also holds a record seven Most Valuable Player awards.

TOP 10 PITCHERS WITH THE MOST CAREER WINS*

	PLAYER	YEARS	WINS
1	Cy Young	1890–1911	511
2	Walter Johnson	1907–27	417
3	= Grover Alexander	1911–30	373
	= Christy Mathewson	1900–16	373
5	Pud Galvin	1879–92	364
6	Warren Spahn	1942–65	363
7	Kid Nichols	1890–1906	361
8	Roger Clemens	1984–2007	354
9	Greg Maddux	1986–2007	347
10	Tim Keefe	1880–93	342

* Up to and including 2007 season

Warren Spahn is the only left-handed pitcher on the list.

TOP 10 **MOST WORLD SERIES WINS***

	TEAM	FIRST	WINS LAST	TOTAL
1	New York Yankees	1923	2000	26
2	St. Louis Cardinals	1926	2006	10
3	Oakland Athletics (5 titles as Philadelphia Athletics)	1910	1989	9
4	Boston Red Sox	1903	2007	7
5	Los Angeles Dodgers (1 title as Brooklyn Dodgers)	1955	1988	6
6 =	San Francisco Giants (all titles as New York Giants)	1905	1954	5
=	Pittsburgh Pirates	1909	1979	5
=	Cincinatti Reds	1919	1990	5
9	Detroit Tigers	1935	1984	4
10 =	Chicago White Sox	1906	2005	3
=	Atlanta Braves (1 title as Boston Braves, 1 as Milwaukee Braves)	1914	1995	3
=	Minnesota Twins (1 title as Washington Senators)	1924	1991	3
=	Baltimore Orioles	1966	1983	3

* Up to and including 2007 World Series

TOP 10 **BIGGEST BALL PARKS***

	TEAM	STADIUM / LOCATION	DISTANCE (FT)
1	Houston Astros	Minute Maid Park, Houston, Texas	436
2	Florida Marlins	Dolphin Stadium, Miami, Florida	434
3	Detroit Tigers	Comerica Park, Detroit, Michigan	420
4	Colorado Rockies	Coors Field, Denver, Colorado	415
5 =	Baltimore Orioles	Oriole Park at Camden Yards, Baltimore, Maryland	410
=	Kansas City Royals	Kauffman Stadium, Kansas City, Missouri	410
=	New York Mets	Shea Stadium, New York City	410
8 =	Minnesota Twins	Hubert H. Humphrey Metrodome, Minneapolis, Minnesota	408
=	New York Yankees	Yankee Stadium, New York City	408
=	Washington Nationals	RFK Stadium, Washington, D.C.	408

* Based on distance from the home plate to the centerfield fence during 2007 season

Ball Games

TOP 10 MOST ALL-IRELAND GAELIC FOOTBALL TITLES*

	TEAM	FIRST WIN	LAST WIN	TOTAL WINS
1	Kerry	1903	2007	35
2	Dublin	1891	1995	22
3	Galway	1925	2001	9
4	Meath	1949	1999	7
5	Cork	1890	1990	6
6	= Wexford	1893	1918	5
	= Cavan	1933	1952	5
	= Down	1960	1994	5
9	= Tipperary	1889	1920	4
	= Kildare	1905	1928	4

* Gaelic Athletic Association (GAA) senior titles 1887–2007

The All-Ireland Final is played at Croke Park, Dublin, on the third or fourth Sunday in September each year. The winning team receives the Sam Maguire Cup, named after the former player and senior member of the GAA who died in 1928. The province of Munster has provided a record 47 winners.

TOP 10 MOST WORLD POOL TITLES*

	PLAYER / COUNTRY	TITLE	YEARS	WINS
1	Sue Thompson, Scotland	Women's 8-Ball	1996–97, 2000, 2002–04, 2006–07	8
2	= Linda Leadbitter (née Moffat), England	Women's 8-Ball	1993–95, 1998	4
	= Allison Fisher, England	Women's 9-Ball	1996–98, 2001	4
4	Earl Strickland, USA	Men's 9-Ball	1990–91, 2002	3
5	= Robin Bell, USA	Women's 9-Ball	1990–91	2
	= Johnny Archer, USA	Men's 9-Ball	1992, 1997	2
	= Rob McKenna, Scotland	Men's 8-Ball	1994, 1997	2
	= Chao Fongpang, Chinese Taipei	Men's 9-Ball	1993, 2000	2
	= Lisa Quick, England	Women's 8-Ball	1999, 2001	2
	= Liu Hsinmei, Chinese Taipei	Women's 9-Ball	1999, 2002	2
	= Jason Twist, England	Men's 8-Ball	2000, 2002	2
	= Chris Melling, England	Men's 8-Ball	2001, 2003	2
	= Kim Ga-Young, South Korea	Women's 9-Ball	2004, 2006	2

* 8-Ball Pool World Championship (men and women) and 9-Ball Pool World Championships (men and women) up to and including all 2007 Championships

The first World 9-Ball Championships were held in 1990 and the inaugural 8-Ball Championships in 1993. The 9-Ball Championships are organized by the WPBA (World Pool-Billiard Association) while the 8-Ball event is under the aegis of the WEPF (World Eight Ball Pool Federation), but their championship is now also recognized by the WPBA.

TOP 10 MOST PBA* TITLES

BOWLER# / FIRST/LAST WINS† / TOTAL

Rank	Bowler	Years	Total
1	Walter Ray Williams Jr.	1986–2007	43
2	Earl Anthony	1970–83	41
3	= Mark Roth	1975–95	34
3	= Pete Weber	1982–2007	34
5	Parker Bohn III	1987–2005	30
6	Mike Aulby	1979–2001	27
7	= Dick Weber	1959–77	26
7	= Don Johnson	1964–77	26
7	= Norm Duke	1983–2007	26
10	Brian Voss	1983–2006	24

* Professional Bowlers Association   # All bowlers from the USA   † As at 1 January 2008   Source: PBA

NOW & THEN

John Higgins

John Higgins beating his fellow Scot Stephen Maguire 17–15 in the 2007 World Championship semifinal.

TOP 10 SNOOKER RANKINGS

2007–08 Season PLAYER / COUNTRY	**1987–88 Season** PLAYER / COUNTRY
1 John Higgins, Scotland	Steve Davis, England
2 Graeme Dott, Scotland	Jimmy White, England
3 Shaun Murphy, England	Neal Foulds, England
4 Ken Doherty, Ireland	Cliff Thorburn, Canada
5 Ronnie O'Sulllivan, England	Joe Johnson, England
6 Peter Ebdon, England	Terry Griffiths, Wales
7 Neil Robertson, Australia	Tony Knowles, England
8 Stephen Hendry, Scotland	Dennis Taylor, Northern Ireland
9 Ding Junhui, China	Alex Higgins, Northern Ireland
10 Stephen Maguire, Scotland	Silvino Francisco, South Africa

Only two players from the Top 10 ranked players of 1987–88 were still in the main tour rankings in 2007–08; Steve Davis was ranked No. 15 and Jimmy White was No. 60.

TOP 10 MOST MEN'S MAJOR FAST PITCH SOFTBALL TITLES*

	TEAM / LOCATION	FIRST WIN	LAST WIN	TOTAL WINS
1	Clearwater Bombers, Florida	1950	1973	10
2	Raybestos Cardinals, Stratford, Connecticut	1955	1976	6
3	Sealmasters, Aurora, Illinois	1959	1967	4
4	= Zollner Pistons, Fort Wayne, Indiana	1945	1947	3
	= Briggs Beautyware, Detroit	1948	1953	3
	= Pay'n Pak, Seattle	1985	1987	3
	= Decatur Pride, Decatur, Illinois	1995	1999	3
8	= Kodak Park, Rochester, New York	1936	1940	2
	= Hammer Air Field, Fresno, California	1943	1944	2
	= Billard Barbell, Reading, Pennsylvania	1977	1978	2
	= Peterbilt Western, Seattle	1980	1982	2
	= Penn Corp, Sioux City, Iowa	1989	1990	2
	= National Health Care, Sioux City, Iowa	1992	1993	2
	= Meierhoffer, St Joseph, Missouri	1998	2000	2
	= Frontier Players Casino, St Joseph, Missouri	2001	2002	2
	= Farm Tavern, Madison, Wisconsin	2003	2004	2
	= Tampa Bay Smokers, Tampa Bay, Florida	1997	2005	2

* Amateur Softball Association of America (ASA) titles 1933–2007

TOP 10 MOST WOMEN'S MAJOR FAST PITCH SOFTBALL TITLES*

	TEAM / LOCATION	FIRST WIN	LAST WIN	TOTAL WINS
1	Raybestos/Stratford Brakettes, Stratford, Connecticut	1958	2007	26
2	Orange Lionettes, California	1950	1970	9
3	Jax Maids, New Orleans	1942	1947	5
4	California Commotion, Woodland Hills	1996	1999	4
5	= Arizona Ramblers, Phoenix	1940	1949	3
	= Redding Rebels, California	1993	1995	3
7	= National Screw & Manufacturing, Cleveland	1936	1937	2
	= J. J. Krieg's, Alameda, California	1938	1939	2
	= Hi-Ho Brakettes, Stratford, Connecticut	1985	1988	2
	= Phoenix Storm, Phoenix, Arizona	2000	2001	2

* Amateur Softball Association of America (ASA) titles 1933–2007

Basketball

TOP 10 **MEDAL-WINNING COUNTRIES IN THE BASKETBALL WORLD CHAMPIONSHIPS***

	COUNTRY	GOLD	SILVER	BRONZE	TOTAL
1	= Yugoslavia	5	3	2	10
	= USA	3	3	4	10
3	USSR/Russia	3	5	1	9
4	Brazil	2	2	1	5
5	= Argentina	1	1	0	2
	= Chile	0	0	2	2
7	= Croatia	0	0	1	1
	= Germany	0	0	1	1
	= Greece	0	1	0	1
	= Phillipines	0	0	1	1
	= Spain	1	0	0	1

* Up to and including the 2006 Championships

The first FIBA World Championship was held at Buenos Aires, Argentina, in 1950. The Women's World Championship was first held at Santiago, Chile, in 1953.

Spain versus Greece
Spain won the 2006 World Championship with a comfortable 70–47 win over Greece in the final.

TOP 10 **MOST POINTS IN A SINGLE NBA GAME***

	PLAYER / TEAM	OPPONENTS	DATE	POINTS
1	Wilt Chamberlain, Philadelphia Warriors	New York Knicks	Mar 2, 1962	100
2	Kobe Bryant, Los Angeles Lakers	Toronto Raptors	Jan 22, 2006	81
3	Wilt Chamberlain, Philadelphia Warriors	Los Angeles Lakers	Dec 8, 1961#	78
4	= Wilt Chamberlain, Philadelphia Warriors	Chicago Packers	Jan 13, 1962	73
	= Wilt Chamberlain, San Francisco Warriors	New York Knicks	Nov 16, 1962	73
	= David Thompson, Denver Nuggets	Detroit Pistons	Apr 9, 1978	73
7	Wilt Chamberlain, San Francisco Warriors	Los Angeles Lakers	Nov 3, 1962	72
8	= David Robinson, San Antonio Spurs	Los Angeles Clippers	Apr 24, 1994	71
	= Elgin Baylor, Los Angeles Lakers	New York Knicks	Nov 15, 1960	71
10	Wilt Chamberlain, San Francisco Warriors	Syracuse Nationals	Mar 10, 1963	70

* As at the end of the 2006–07 season # Including three periods of overtime

TOP 10 **MOST GAMES PLAYED IN THE NBA***

PLAYER / YEARS	GAMES
1 Robert Parish 1976–97	1,611
2 Kareem Abdul-Jabbar# 1969–89	1,560
3 John Stockton 1984–2003	1,504
4 Karl Malone 1985–2004	1,476
5 Kevin Willis† 1984–2007	1,424
6 Reggie Miller 1987–2005	1,389
7 Clifford Robinson 1989–2007	1,380
8 Gary Payton 1990–2007	1,335
9 Moses Malone 1976–95	1,329
10 Buck Williams 1981–99	1,307

* As at the end of 2006–07 season
# Lew Alcindor in 1971
† Active in 2007–08

Source: NBA

TOP 10 **NCAA MEN'S DIVISION 1 BASKETBALL CHAMPIONSHIPS***

	TEAM	FIRST WIN	LAST WIN	TOTAL WINS
1	UCLA	1964	1995	11
2	Kentucky	1948	1998	7
3	Indiana	1940	1987	5
4	North Carolina	1957	2005	4
5	Duke	1991	2001	3
6	=Oklahoma A&M#	1945	1946	2
	=San Francisco	1955	1956	2
	=Cincinnati	1961	1962	2
	=North Carolina State	1974	1983	2
	=Louisville	1980	1986	2
	=Kansas	1952	1988	2
	=Michigan State	1979	2000	2
	=Connecticut	1999	2004	2
	=Florida	2006	2007	2

* Since 1939
# Now Oklahoma State

Karl Malone
After 18 seasons starring for Utah Jazz between 1985 and 2003, Karl Malone finished his career with one season at Los Angeles Lakers in 2003–04.

TOP 10 **ALL-TIME CAREER SCORING LEADERS IN THE NBA***

PLAYER	YEARS	GAMES	POINTS
1 Kareem Abdul-Jabbar#	1969–89	1,560	38,387
2 Karl Malone	1985–2004	1,476	36,928
3 Michael Jordan	1984–2003	1,072	32,292
4 Wilt Chamberlain	1959–73	1,045	31,419
5 Moses Malone	1976–95	1,329	27,409
6 Elvin Hayes	1968–84	1,303	27,313
7 Hakeem Olajuwon	1984–2002	1,238	26,946
8 Oscar Robertson	1960–74	1,040	26,710
9 Dominique Wilkins	1982–99	1,074	26,668
10 John Havlicek	1962–78	1,270	26,395

* As at the end of 2006–07 season
# Lew Alcindor in 1971

Source: NBA

TOP 10 GOLD MEDAL-WINNING COUNTRIES AT THE WORLD AMATEUR BOXING CHAMPIONSHIPS*

COUNTRY	GOLD MEDALS
1 Cuba	62
2 Russia/USSR	32
3 USA	16
4 = Bulgaria	7
= Romania	7
5 Kazakhstan	6
7 Uzbekistan	4
8 = Hungary	3
= Italy	3
= Germany	3

Men's, 1974–2007

The first World Amateur Boxing Championships were held at Havana, Cuba, in 1974 and since 1989 have been staged every two years.

THE 10 LAST FIGHTS OF MUHAMMAD ALI

	OPPONENT / COUNTRY	VENUE	RESULT	DATE
1	Trevor Berbick, Canada	Nassau, Bahamas	Lost—points, 10 rounds	Dec 11, 1981
2	Larry Holmes, USA	Las Vegas, USA	Lost—retired, 10th round	Oct 2, 1980
3	Leon Spinks, USA	New Orleans, USA	Won—points, 15 rounds	Sep 15, 1978
4	Leon Spinks, USA	Las Vegas, USA	Lost—points, 15 rounds	Feb 15, 1978
5	Earnie Shavers, USA	New York, USA	Won—points, 15 rounds	Sep 29, 1977
6	Alfredo Evangelista, Uruguay	Landover, USA	Won—points, 15 rounds	May 16, 1977
7	Ken Norton, USA	New York, USA	Won—points, 15 rounds	Sep 28, 1976
8	Richard Dunn, UK	Munich, West Germany	Won—tko*, 5 rounds	May 24, 1976
9	Jimmy Young, USA	Landover, USA	Won—points, 15 rounds	Apr 30, 1976
10	Jean-Pierre Coopman, Belgium	San Juan, Puerto Rico	Won—knockout, 5 rounds	Feb 20, 1976

* tko = technical knockout

TOP 10 **OLYMPIC FENCING COUNTRIES***

	COUNTRY	GOLD	MEDALS SILVER	BRONZE	TOTAL
1	Italy	42	37	26	105
2	France	36	35	31	102
3	Hungary	34	21	25	80
4	Russia/USSR/Unified Team	27	20	23	70
5	Germany/West Germany	11	15	10	36
6	Poland	4	8	8	20
7	United States	2	5	12	19
8	Romania	3	3	6	12
9	= Belgium	3	3	4	10
	= Great Britain	1	9	0	10

* Based on total medals won by men and women at all Olympics up to and including 2004

TOP 10 **OLYMPIC JUDO COUNTRIES***

	COUNTRY	GOLD	MEDALS SILVER	BRONZE	TOTAL
1	Japan	31	14	13	58
2	Russia/USSR/Unified Team	7	8	20	35
3	= France	10	6	17	33
	= South Korea	8	12	13	33
5	Cuba	5	8	13	26
6	Germany/West Germany	3	5	14	22
7	= Netherlands	4	1	10	15
	= UK	0	6	9	15
9	China	5	2	7	14
10	Brazil	2	3	7	12

* Based on total medals won by men and women at all Olympics up to and including 2004

Judo was first contested at the Tokyo Olympics in 1964. However, it was not held four years later but returned in 1972, and has been featured ever since.

Crossing swords
Aldo Montano (left) of Italy and Zsolt Nemcsik (Hungary) in the saber event at the Athens Olympic Games, 2004. Montano's 15–14 win added to his country's tally of gold medals, plus a silver as a member of his country's saber team.

On Two Wheels

TOP 10 MEDAL-WINNING COUNTRIES IN THE WORLD ROAD-RACE CYCLING CHAMPIONSHIPS*

	NATION	GOLD	SILVER	BRONZE	TOTAL
1	Italy	20	25	22	67
2	Belgium	31	17	15	63
3	France	17	16	17	50
4	Netherlands	14	12	11	37
5	Russia/Soviet Union	3	9	12	24
6	Germany/West Germany	6	8	7	21
7	Spain	5	5	9	19
8	Switzerland	5	8	4	17
9	USA	5	7	3	15
10	Great Britain	4	3	3	10

* Men 1927–2007; women 1958–2007

The first men's champion was Alfredo Binda of Italy, who won the inaugural race at the Nürburgring, Germany, in 1927.

World Championship
The 2007 event took place in Stuttgart, Germany. The men's Road Race was won by Paolo Bettini and the women's race by Marta Bastianelli, both of Italy, further confirming their country's overall pole position in the table.

TOP 10 MOST FINISHERS IN THE TOUR DE FRANCE

	YEAR	WINNING RIDER / COUNTRY	STARTERS	FINISHERS
1	1991	Miguel Indurain, Spain	198	158
2	1990	Greg LeMond, USA	198	156
3	2005	Lance Armstrong, USA	189	155
4	2002	Lance Armstrong, USA	189	153
5	1988	Pedro Delgado, Spain	198	151
6	= 2004	Lance Armstrong, USA	188	147
	= 2003	Lance Armstrong, USA	189	147
8	= 2001	Lance Armstrong, USA	189	144
	= 1985	Bernard Hinault, France	180	144
10	= 1999	Lance Armstrong, USA	180	141
	= 2007	Alberto Contador, Spain	189	141

The first time that 100 riders finished the race was in 1970, when Eddy Merckx (Belgium) headed the field of 150 starters. The 155 finishers from 189 starters in 2005 represents the highest percentage of finishers to starters—82.01 percent. The year with fewest finishers was 1919, when just 11 of the 69 starters completed the race, which was won by Firmin Lambot (Belgium).

Rossi and Hayden
Valentino Rossi handed Nicky Hayden his first world title when he crashed out in the final round of the 2006 MotoGP.

Surtees' Success

The only man to win world titles on two and four wheels is John Surtees (UK). Between 1956 and 1960 Surtees won seven world titles at both 350 and 500cc. He switched to Formula One and made his debut for Lotus at Monaco in 1960. He moved to Ferrari in 1963 and the following year was crowned World Champion.

THE 10 **LATEST US RIDERS TO WIN MOTOR-RACING GRAND PRIX WORLD TITLES***

	RIDER	CLASS	YEAR
1	Nicky Hayden	MotoGP	2006
2	Kenny Roberts, Jr.	500cc	2000
3	Kevin Schwantz	500cc	1993
4	Wayne Rainey	500cc	1992
5	Wayne Rainey	500cc	1991

	RIDER	CLASS	YEAR
6	= Wayne Rainey	500cc	1990
	= John Kocinski	250cc	1990
8	Eddie Lawson	500cc	1989
9	Eddie Lawson	500cc	1988
10	Eddie Lawson	500cc	1986

* Individual champions only; as at the end of the 2007 season

Freddie Spencer is the only US rider to win two world titles in one year, winning the 500cc and 250cc titles in 1985.

TOP 10 **COUNTRIES WITH THE MOST WORLD MOTOR-CYCLING CHAMPIONS***

	COUNTRY	MOTO GP/ 500CC	250CC	125CC	350CC	50/80CC	TOTAL
1	Italy	18	21	23	8	2	72
2	UK	17	9	4	13	–	43
3	Spain	1	6	12	–	12	31
4	USA	15	2	–	–	–	17
5	Germany/ West Germany	–	7	3	2	4	16
6	Australia	7	1	1	1	–	10
7	= Southern Rhodesia	1	2	–	5	–	8
	= Switzerland	–	–	4	–	4	8
9	Japan	–	2	4	1	–	7
10	South Africa	–	2	–	3	–	5

* Individual champions only; as at end of 2007 season

TOP 10 **RIDERS WITH THE MOST MOTOR-CYCLING GRAND PRIX WINS***

	RIDER / COUNTRY	YEARS	WINS
1	Giacomo Agostini, Italy	1965–76	122
2	Angel Nieto, Spain	1969–85	90
3	Valentino Rossi, Italy	1996–2007	88
4	Mike Hailwood, UK	1959–67	76
5	Mick Doohan, Australia	1990–98	54
6	Phil Read, UK	1961–75	52
7	Jim Redman, Southern Rhodesia	1961–66	45
8	= Anton Mang, West Germany	1976–88	42
	= "Max" Biaggi, Italy	1992–2004	42
10	Carlo Ubbiali, Italy	1950–60	39

* Solo classes only; correct as at end of the 2007 season

Hockey

TOP 10 POINTS-SCORERS IN AN NHL CAREER*

	PLAYER	YEARS	GAMES	POINTS
1	Wayne Gretzky	1970–99	1,487	2,857
2	Mark Messier	1979–2004	1,756	1,887
3	Gordie Howe	1946–80	1,767	1,850
4	Ron Francis	1981–2004	1,731	1,798
5	Marcel Dionne	1971–89	1,348	1,771
6	Steve Yzerman	1983–2006	1,514	1,755
7	Mario Lemieux	1984–2006	915	1,723
8	Joe Sakic	1988–2008	1,363	1,629
9	Jaromir Jagr	1990–2008	1,273	1,599
10	Phil Esposito	1963–81	1,282	1,590

* Regular season; as at end of the 2007–08 season

TOP 10 NCAA TITLES*

	TEAM	FIRST WIN	LAST WIN	TOTAL
1	Michigan	1948	1998	9
2	=North Dakota	1959	2000	7
	=Denver	1958	2005	7
4	Wisconsin	1973	2006	6
5	Minnesota	1974	2003	5
6	Boston University	1971	1995	4
7	=Lake Superior	1988	1994	3
	=Michigan Tech	1962	1975	3
	=Michigan State	1966	2007	3
	=Boston College	1949	2008	3

* NCAA Division 1 Champions 1948–2007

The first champions were Michigan, who beat Dartmouth 8–4 in the 1948 final. Originally four teams contested the end-of-season playoffs. Currently 12 teams take part. The biggest win in the final was in 1961 when Denver beat St. Lawrence 12–2. The most goals by one team in a single game is 13 by Colorado College in 1950 (beat Boston University 13–4) and Colorado College, again, in 1957 (beat Michigan 13–6).

TOP 10 COACHES IN THE NHL*

	COACH	YEARS	WINS
1	Scotty Bowman	1967–2002	1,244
2	Al Arbour	1970–1994	781
3	Dick Irvin	1928–56	692
4	Pat Quinn	1978–2006	657
5	Mike Keenan	1984–2008	626
6	Bryan Murray	1981–2008	620
7	Billy Reay	1957–77	542
8	Ray Wilson	1993–2008	518
9	Jacques Martin	1986–2008	517
10	Pat Burns	1988–2004	501

* Based on regular season victories to the end of the 2007–08 season

Mike Keenan came out of retirement to coach the Calgary Flames after three years away from coaching in the NHL. Scotty Bowman also holds the record for winning the most Stanley Cups—nine, one more than Hector "Toe" Blake.

Canada leads the way
Canadian forward Shane Doan ensures Canada's top ranking during a qualification round match for the International Ice Hockey federation World Championship in 2007.

TOP 10 **TEAMS WITH THE MOST STANLEY CUP WINS***

	TEAM	FIRST WIN	LAST WIN	TOTAL
1	Montreal Canadiens	1916	1993	24
2	Toronto Maple Leafs	1918	1967	13
3	Detroit Red Wings	1936	2002	10
4	= Boston Bruins	1929	1972	5
	= Edmonton Oilers	1984	1990	5
6	= New York Islanders	1980	1983	4
	= New York Rangers	1928	1994	4
	= Ottawa Senators	1920	1927	4
9	= Chicago Blackhawks	1934	1961	3
	= New Jersey Devils	1995	2003	3

* Since abolition of challenge match format in 1915; up to and including the 2007 Stanley Cup

Source: NHL

TOP 10 **MEDAL-WINNING COUNTRIES IN THE ICE-HOCKEY WORLD CHAMPIONSHIPS***

	COUNTRY	MEDALS			
		GOLD	SILVER	BRONZE	TOTAL
1	Canada	24	11	9	44
2	Czechoslovakia/Czech Republic	11	13	19	43
3	Sweden	8	18	14	40
4	Russia/USSR	23	8	7	38
5	USA	2	9	5	16
6	= Finland	1	6	2	9
	= Switzerland	0	1	8	9
8	UK	1	2	2	5
9	Germany/West Germany	0	2	2	4
10	Slovakia	1	1	1	3

* Up to and including 2007

In the period 1920–68, the Olympic hockey tournaments were also the World Championships of those years. When Sweden won the Olympic and World titles in 2006, it became the first country to win both titles in the same year.

Golf

TOP 10 **MOST POINTS IN THE RYDER CUP***

	PLAYER / COUNTRY#	TEAM(S)	YEARS	POINTS
1	Nick Faldo, England	GB & I/Europe	1977–97	25
2	Bernhard Langer, Germany	Europe	1981–2002	24
3	=Billy Casper, USA	USA	1961–75	23.5
	=Colin Montgomerie, Scotland	Europe	1991–2006	23.5
5	Arnold Palmer, USA	USA	1961–73	23
6	Seve Ballesteros, Spain	Europe	1979–95	22.5
7	Lanny Wadkins, USA	USA	1977–93	21.5
8	José María Olazábal, Spain	Europe	1987–2006	20.5
9	Lee Trevino, USA	USA	1969–81	20
10	Jack Nicklaus, USA	USA	1969–81	18.5

* Up to and including 2006
# Great Britain (GB): 1921 to 1971; Great Britain and Ireland (GB & I): 1973 to 1977; Europe (E): 1979 to 2006

TOP 10 **MONEY WINNERS ON THE PGA CHAMPIONS TOUR***

	PLAYER	WINNINGS ($)
1	Hale Irwin	24,654,218
2	Gil Morgan	18,383,634
3	Dana Quigley	13,956,074
4	Bruce Fleisher	13,513,100
5	Larry Nelson	13,049,347
6	Allen Doyle	12,590,476
7	Jim Thorpe	12,476,861
8	Jim Colbert	11,623,031
9	Tom Kite	11,593,910
10	Tom Jenkins	11,225,366

* As at January 1, 2008; all golfers from the USA

The Champions Tour was founded in 1980 as the Senior PGA Tour, and changed its name in 2002. Run by the PGA Tour, it is for professional golfers who have reached the age of 50, and many ex-stars of the regular Tour compete on the Champions Tour.

TOP 10 **GOLF COURSES TO HOST THE MOST MAJORS**

	CLUB / LOCATION	YEARS	US MASTERS	BRITISH OPEN	US OPEN	US PGA	TOTAL
1	Augusta National, Georgia	1934–2007	71	0	0	0	71
2	St. Andrews, Fife, Scotland	1873–2005	0	27	0	0	27
3	Prestwick, Ayrshire, Scotland	1860–1925	0	24	0	0	24
4	Muirfield, East Lothian, Scotland	1892–2002	0	15	0	0	15
5	Royal St. George's, Sandwich, Kent	1894–2003	0	13	0	0	13
6	=Royal Liverpool, Hoylake	1897–2006	0	11	0	0	11
	=Oakmont, Pennsylvania	1922–2007	0	0	8	3	11
8	=Baltusrol, New Jersey	1903–2005	0	0	7	1	8
	=Oakland Hills, Michigan	1924–96	0	0	6	2	8
10	Southern Hills, Oklahoma	1958–2007	0	0	3	4	7

The Augusta National is the only course to play host to a Major every year, as the home of the US Masters since its inception in 1934.

Augusta
The Augusta National in Georgia realized the dream of the top amateur golfer Bobby Jones and his friend Clifford Roberts. The course, designed by Scot Dr. Alistair Mackenzie, opened in 1931. Horton Smith won the first Masters at Augusta in 1934.

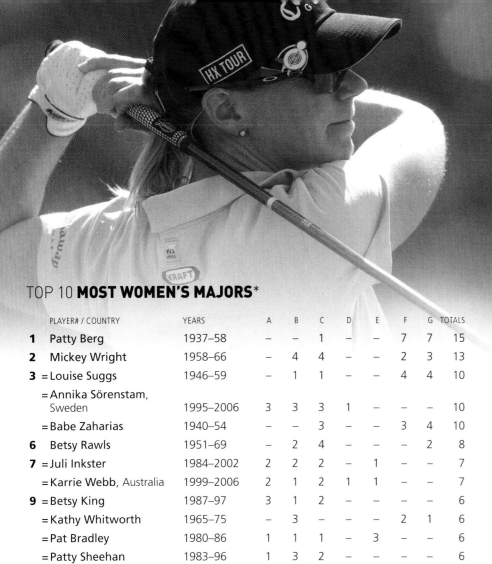

TOP 10 **MOST WOMEN'S MAJORS***

PLAYER# / COUNTRY	YEARS	A	B	C	D	E	F	G	TOTALS
1 Patty Berg	1937–58	–	–	1	–	–	7	7	15
2 Mickey Wright	1958–66	–	4	4	–	–	2	3	13
3 =Louise Suggs	1946–59	–	1	1	–	–	4	4	10
=Annika Sörenstam, Sweden	1995–2006	3	3	3	1	–	–	–	10
=Babe Zaharias	1940–54	–	–	3	–	–	3	4	10
6 Betsy Rawls	1951–69	–	2	4	–	–	–	2	8
7 =Juli Inkster	1984–2002	2	2	2	–	1	–	–	7
=Karrie Webb, Australia	1999–2006	2	1	2	1	1	–	–	7
9 =Betsy King	1987–97	3	1	2	–	–	–	–	6
=Kathy Whitworth	1965–75	–	3	–	–	–	2	1	6
=Pat Bradley	1980–86	1	1	1	–	3	–	–	6
=Patty Sheehan	1983–96	1	3	2	–	–	–	–	6

* As recognized by the Ladies Professional Golf Association (LPGA) up to and including 2007
# All from the USA unless otherwise stated

Women's championships: a—Kraft Nabisco Championship (previously Nabisco Dinah Shore, Nabisco Championship) 1983–2007; b—LPGA Championship 1955–2007; c—US Women's Open 1946–2007; d—Women's British Open 2001–07; e—du Maurier Classic 1979–2000; f—Titleholders Championship 1937–42, 1946–66, 1972; g—Western Open 1930–67

TOP 10 **MOST MEN'S MAJORS IN A CAREER***

PLAYER / COUNTRY	YEARS	US MASTERS	US OPEN	BRITISH OPEN	US PGA	TOTAL
1 Jack Nicklaus	1962–86	6	4	3	5	18
2 Tiger Woods	1997–2007	4	2	3	4	13
3 Walter Hagen	1914–29	0	2	4	5	11
4 =Ben Hogan	1946–53	2	4	1	2	9
=Gary Player, South Africa	1959–78	3	1	3	2	9
6 Tom Watson	1975–83	2	1	5	0	8
7 =Harry Vardon, England	1896–1914	0	1	6	0	7
=Gene Sarazen	1922–35	1	2	1	3	7
=Bobby Jones	1923–30	0	4	3	0	7
=Sam Snead	1942–54	3	0	1	3	7
=Arnold Palmer	1958–64	4	1	2	0	7

* Professional Majors only, up to and including 2007; All golfers from the USA unless otherwise stated

Above: Annika Sörenstam
In 2003 Annika Sörenstam made history as the first woman to play on the men's PGA Tour since 1945.

Below: Jack Nicklaus
Jack Nicklaus won his first major, the US Open, in 1962 at the age of 22 and his last, the Masters, in 1986.

Horse Sports

Equine elegance
The Dutch dressage rider Anky van Grunsven.

TOP 10 **OLYMPIC EQUESTRIAN MEDALLISTS***

	RIDER / COUNTRY	YEARS	MEDALS GOLD	SILVER	BRONZE	TOTAL
1	**Reiner Klimke**, West Germany	1964–88	7	0	2	9
2	**Hans-Günther Winkler**, West Germany	1956–76	5	1	1	7
3	=**Piero d'Inzeo**, Italy	1956–72	0	2	4	6
	=**Raimondo d'Inzeo**, Italy	1956–72	1	2	3	6
	=**Josef Neckerman**, West Germany	1960–72	2	2	2	6
	=**Michael Plumb**, USA	1964–84	2	4	0	6
	=**Isabell Werth**, Germany	1992–2000	4	2	0	6
	=**Anky van Grunsven**, Holland	1992–2004	2	4	0	6
9	=**Earl Thomson**, USA	1932–48	2	3	0	5
	=**André Jousseaumé**, France	1932–52	2	2	1	5
	=**Henri Chammartin**, Switzerland	1952–68	1	2	2	5
	=**Gustav Fischer**, Switzerland	1952–68	0	3	2	5
	=**Liselott Linsenhoff**, West Germany	1956–72	2	2	1	5
	=**Christine Stückelberger**, Switzerland	1976–88	1	3	1	5
	=**Mark Todd**, New Zealand	1984–2000	2	1	2	5

* Up to and including the 2004 Olympics

TOP 10 **TRAINERS IN THE BREEDERS' CUP***

	TRAINER#	YEARS	WINS
1	**D. Wayne Lukas**	1985 (2), 1986 (2), 1987 (2), 1988 (3), 1989, 1994 (2), 1996, 1999 (2), 2000, 2002, 2005	18
2	**"Shug" McGaughey III**	1988–89 (2), 1992–93, 1995 (2), 2002, 2005	9
3	=**Neil Drysdale**, UK	1984–85, 1989, 1992–93, 2000	6
	=**Richard Mandella**	1993 (2), 2003 (4)	6
5	=**Bill Mott**	1987, 1992, 1995, 1997–98	5
	=**Bob Baffert**	1992, 1998, 2002, 2007 (2)	5
	=**Bobby Frankel**	2001–02, 2004–05, 2007	5
8	=**Ron McAnally**	1989–90, 1992, 1995	4
	=**André Fabre**, France	1990, 1993, 2001, 2005	4
	=**Aidan O'Brien**, Ireland	2001–03, 2007	4

* Up to and including the 2007 Breeders Cup races
\# All jockeys from the USA unless otherwise stated

Source: Breeders' Cup

D. Wayne Lukas has saddled 146 horses in the Breeders' Cup and is the only trainer to have had a starter at every meeting. He has had 53 first three finishers and won nearly $20 million in prize money. His last winner was in 2005.

TOP 10 **US JOCKEYS WITH THE MOST CAREER WINS***

	JOCKEY	YEARS	WINS
1	**Russell Baze**	1974–2007	9,957
2	**Laffit Pincay, Jr.**, Panama	1966–2003	9,530
3	**William Shoemaker**	1949–90	8,833
4	**Pat Day**	1973–2005	8,803
5	**David Gall**, Canada	1956–1999	7,396
6	**Chris McCarron**	1974–2002	7,141
7	**Angel Cordero, Jr.**, Puerto Rico	1962–95	7,057
8	**Jorge Velasquez**, Panama	1964–1997	6,795
9	**Sandy Hawley**, Canada	1967–1998	6,449
10	**Earlie Fires**	1964–2007	6,434

* As at January 1, 2008; all jockeys from the USA unless otherwise stated

Russell Baze broke Laffit Pincay's record in the fourth race at Bay Meadows, San Mateo, California, on Friday December 1, 2006 when he came home first riding Butterfly Belle. Pat Day holds the record for the most money won in a career with $297,912,019.

TOP 10 FASTEST WINNING TIMES OF THE KENTUCKY DERBY*

	HORSE	YEAR	TIME MINS:SECS
1	Secretariat	1973	1:59.40
2	Monarchos	2001	1:59.97
3	Northern Dancer	1964	2:00.00
4	Spend A Buck	1985	2:00.20
5	Decidedly	1962	2:00.40
6	Proud Clarion	1967	2:00.60
7	=Grindstone	1996	2:01.00
	=Fusaichi Pegasus	2000	2:01.00
9	War Emblem	2002	2:01.13
10	Funny Cide	2003	2:01.19

* Up to and including 2007

The Kentucky Derby is held on the first Saturday in May at Churchill Downs, Louisville, Kentucky. The opening leg of the Triple Crown, it was first raced in 1875 over a distance of one mile four furlongs.

TOP 10 JOCKEYS WITH THE MOST US TRIPLE CROWN WINS*

	JOCKEY / COUNTRY	YEARS	KENTUCKY DERBY	PREAKNESS STAKES	BELMONT STAKES	TOTAL WINS
1	Eddie Arcaro	1938–57	5	6	6	17
2	Bill Shoemaker	1955–86	4	2	5	11
3	=Bill Hartack	1956–-69	5	3	1	9
	=Earl Sande	1921–30	3	1	5	9
	=Pat Day	1985–2000	1	5	3	9
6	=Jim McLaughlin	1881–88	1	1	6	8
	=Gary Stevens	1988–2001	3	2	3	8
8	=Angel Cordero, Jr., Puerto Rico	1974–85	3	2	1	6
	=Charley Kurtsinger	1931–37	2	2	2	6
	=Ron Turcotte, Canada	1965–73	2	2	2	6

* Up to and including 2007; all jockeys from the USA unless otherwise stated

Eddie Arcaro won his first Triple Crown race, the Kentucky Derby, on Lawrin in 1938. He twice won the Triple Crown, on Whirlaway in 1941 and in 1948 on Citation. Arcaro won 4,779 out of 24,092 races, in which he won a then-record of more than $30 million in prize money. Arcaro retired in 1962 and died in 1997 at the age of 81.

Derby winner
Monarchos on his way to winning the 2001 Kentucky Derby. He raced only 10 times before retiring to stud. His only other major win was the 2001 Florida Derby.

Motor Sports

TOP 10 MOST RACE WINS IN A FORMULA ONE CAREER BY A DRIVER*

	DRIVER / COUNTRY	YEARS	WINS
1	Michael Schumacher, Germany	1992–2006	91
2	Alain Prost, France	1981–93	51
3	Ayrton Senna, Brazil	1985–93	41
4	Nigel Mansell, UK	1985–94	31
5	Jackie Stewart, UK	1965–73	27
6	= Jim Clark, UK	1962–68	25
	= Niki Lauda, Austria	1974–85	25
8	Juan-Manuel Fangio, Argentina	1950–57	24
9	= Nelson Piquet, Brazil	1980–91	23
	= Damon Hill, UK	1993–98	22

* Up to and including the 2007 season

The most career wins by a current driver is 19 by Fernando Alonso.

TOP 10 MOST CAREER WINS IN CHAMP CAR RACES*

	DRIVER#	CAREER	WINS
1	A. J. Foyt	1960–81	67
2	Mario Andretti	1965–93	52
3	Michael Andretti	1986–2003	42
4	Al Unser	1967–87	39
5	Bobby Unser	1966–81	38
6	= Al Unser Jr	1984–95	31
	= Paul Tracy, Canada	1993–2007	31
8	Rick Mears	1978–91	29
9	= Johnny Rutherford	1965–86	27
	= Sébastien Bourdais, France	2003–07	27

* Formerly CART (Championship Auto Racing Teams), Champ Car (short for 'Championship Car') was introduced in 2004; correct as at the end of the 2007 season
# All drivers from the USA unless otherwise stated

TOP 10 MOST FORMULA ONE GRAND PRIX RACE WINS IN A SEASON BY A DRIVER*

	DRIVER / COUNTRY	SEASON	WINS
1	Michael Schumacher, Germany	2004	13
2	Michael Schumacher, Germany	2002	11
3	= Nigel Mansell, UK	1992	9
	= Michael Schumacher, Germany	1995	9
	= Michael Schumacher, Germany	2000	9
	= Michael Schumacher, Germany	2001	9
7	= Ayrton Senna, Brazil	1988	8
	= Michael Schumacher, Germany	1994	8
	= Damon Hill, UK	1996	8
	= Mika Häkkinen, Finland	1998	8

* To the end of the 2007 season

TOP 10 MOST FORMULA ONE GRAND PRIX WINS BY A MANUFACTURER*

	MANUFACTURER / COUNTRY#	FIRST WIN	LAST WIN	TOTAL WINS
1	Ferrari, Italy	1951	2007	201
2	McLaren	1968	2007	156
3	Williams	1979	2003	113
4	Lotus	1960	1987	79
5	Brabham	1964	1985	35
6	Renault, France	1979	2006	33
7	Benetton, Italy	1986	1997	27
8	Tyrrell	1971	1983	23
9	BRM	1959	1972	17
10	Cooper	1958	1967	16

* To the end of the 2007 season
# All manufacturers from the UK unless otherwise stated

Michael Schumacher
Michael Schumacher winning at Imola in his final season, 2006.

Lewis Hamilton
Lewis Hamilton leading the field ahead of his McLaren teammate Fernando Alonso in the United States Grand Prix at Indianapolis. Hamilton went on to win his second Formula One race.

THE 10 **LOWEST STARTING POSITIONS BY WINNERS OF THE INDIANAPOLIS 500***

	DRIVER#	YEAR	POSITION
1	= Ray Harroun	1911	28th
	= Louie Meyer	1936	28th
3	Fred Frame	1932	27th
4	Johnny Rutherford	1974	25th
5	= George Souders	1927	22nd
	= Kelly Petillo	1935	22nd
7	Lora Corum/ Joe Boyer†	1924	21st
8	= Tommy Milton	1921	20th
	= Frank Lockhart	1926	20th
	= Al Unser	1987	20th

* Based on the starting position on the grid
# All drivers from the USA
† Joint drivers

Source: Indianapolis Motor Speedway

THE 10 **FIRST FORMULA ONE GRAND PRIX RACES OF LEWIS HAMILTON**

	GRAND PRIX	VENUE	POSITION	DATE
1	Australian	Albert Park, Melbourne	3rd	Mar 18, 2007
2	Malaysian	Sepang, Kuala Lumpur	2nd	Apr 8, 2007
3	Bahrain	Bahrain International Circuit, Sakhir	2nd	Apr 15, 2007
4	Spanish	Circuit de Catalunya, Barcelona	2nd	May 3, 2007
5	Monaco	Circuit de Monaco, Monte-Carlo	2nd	May 7, 2007
6	Canadian	Circuit Gilles Villeneuve, Montreal	1st	Jun 10, 2007
7	United States	Indianapolis Motor Speedway, Indianapolis	1st	Jun 17, 2007
8	French	Circuit de Nevers, Magny-Cours	3rd	Jul 1, 2007
9	British	Silverstone, England	3rd	Jul 8, 2007
10	European	Nürburgring, Nürburg, Germany	9th	Jul 22, 2007

In addition to his two wins here, Hamilton won two more races, in Hungary and Japan. In 17 races he failed to finish just once, was out of the points on only two occasions, and achieved 12 podium finishes. His total points for the season was 109, one behind the eventual champion Kimi Räikkönen, who captured the title in the last race of the season in Brazil. Whilst Hamilton's 12 podiums is a record for a rookie, it falls five short of the record set by Michael Schumacher in 2002.

Football

TOP 10 MOST TOUCHDOWNS IN A CAREER

	PLAYER	YEARS	TOUCH-DOWNS
1	Jerry Rice	1984–2004	207
2	Emmitt Smith	1990–2004	175
3	Marcus Allen	1982–97	144
4	Marshall Faulk	1994–2006	136
5	Terrell Owens	1996–2007	131
6	Cris Carter	1987–2002	130
7	LaDainian Tomlinson	2001–07	129
8	Jim Brown	1957–65	126
9	Walter Payton	1975–87	125
10	Randy Moss	1998–2007	124

* Up to and including the 2007 regular season

TOP 10 NFL COACHES*

	COACH	TEAM(S)	YEARS	WINS
1	Don Shula	Baltimore Colts, Miami Dolphins	1963–95	347
2	George Halas	Chicago Bears	1920–67	324
3	Tom Landry	Dallas Cowboys	1960–88	270
4	Curly Lambeau	Green Bay Packers, Chicago Cardinals, Washington Redskins	1921–53	229
5	Chuck Noll	Pittsburgh Steelers	1969–91	209
6	Marty Schottenheimer	Cleveland Browns, Kansas City Chiefs, Washington Redskins, San Diego Chargers	1984–2006	205
7	Dan Reeves	Denver Broncos, NY Giants, Atlanta Falcons	1981–2003	201
8	Chuck Knox	Los Angeles Rams, Buffalo Bills, Seattle Seahawks	1973–91	193
9	Bill Parcells	NY Giants, New England Patriots, NY Jets, Dallas Cowboys	1983–2006	183
10	Paul Brown	Cleveland Browns, Cincinnati Bengals	1950–75	170

* Based on most wins in regular- and post-season games

TOP 10 NFL SALARIES, 2007

	PLAYER / TEAM	SALARY ($)
1	Dwight Freeney, Indianapolis Colts	30,750,000
2	Marc Bulger, St Louis Rams	17,502,040
3	Leonard Davis, Dallas Cowboys	17,006,240
4	Gaines Adams, Tampa Bay Buccaneers	15,434,000
5	Robert Geathers, Cincinnati Bengals	14,000,000
6	Cory Redding, Detroit Lions	13,625,000
7	Derrick Dockery, Buffalo Bills	13,504,680
8	Reggie Bush, New Orleans Saints	13,375,960
9	Kris Dielman, San Diego Chargers	13,305,280
10	Larry Johnson, Kansas City Chiefs	13,300,000

TOP 10 MOST SUPER BOWL APPEARANCES*

	TEAM	WON	LOST	APPEARANCES
1	Dallas Cowboys	5	3	8
2 =	Denver Broncos	2	4	6
=	New England Patriots	3	3	6
=	Pittsburgh Steelers	5	1	6
5 =	Miami Dolphins	2	3	5
=	Oakland/ LA Raiders	3	2	5
=	San Francisco 49ers	5	0	5
=	Washington Redskins	3	2	5
9 =	Buffalo Bills	0	4	4
=	Green Bay Packers	3	1	4
=	Minnesota Vikings	0	4	4
=	New York Giants	3	1	4

* Up to and including 2008

Dallas Cowboys, with 221, have also scored more points in the Super Bowl than any other team. Denver Broncos have conceded the most—206.

TOP 10 MOST TOUCHDOWNS IN A SEASON*

	PLAYER / TEAM	SEASON	TOUCH-DOWNS
1	LaDainian Tomlinson, San Diego Chargers	2006	31
2	Shaun Alexander, Seattle Seahawks	2005	28
3	Priest Holmes, Kansas City Chiefs	2003	27
4	Marshall Faulk, St Louis Rams	2000	26
5	Emmitt Smith, Dallas Cowboys	1995	25
6 =	John Riggins, Washington Redskins	1983	24
=	Priest Holmes, Kansas City Chiefs	2002	24
8 =	Randy Moss, New England Patriots	2007	23
=	Terrell Davis, Denver Broncos	1998	23
=	Jerry Rice, San Francisco 49ers	1987	23
=	O. J. Simpson, Buffalo Bills	1975	23

* Up to and including the 2007 regular season

LaDainian Tomlinson set a new NFL record for the most points in a season in 2006.

LaDainian Tomlinson
*In 2006, Tomlinson's tally of 186 overtook the record of 176 set by Paul Hornung
(Green Pay Packers) in 1960.*

TOP 10 MOST POINTS IN AN NFL CAREER*

	PLAYER	YEARS	POINTS
1	Morten Andersen	1982–2007	2,544
2	Gary Anderson	1982–2004	2,434
3	George Blanda	1949–75	2,002
4	Matt Stover	1991–2007	1,822
5	John Carney	1988–2007	1,812
6	Jason Elam	1993–2007	1,786
7	Norm Johnson	1982–99	1,736
8	Nick Lowery	1980–96	1,711
9	Jan Stenerud	1967–85	1,699
10	Jason Hanson	1992–2007	1,659

* To the end of the 2007 regular season

TOP 10 BIGGEST WINNING MARGINS IN THE SUPER BOWL*

	WINNERS	RUNNERS-UP	YEAR	SCORE	MARGIN
1	San Francisco 49ers	Denver Broncos	1990	55–10	45
2	Chicago Bears	New England Patriots	1986	46–10	36
3	Dallas Cowboys	Buffalo Bills	1993	52–17	35
4	Washington Redskins	Denver Broncos	1988	42–10	32
5	Los Angeles Raiders	Washington Redskins	1984	38–9	29
6 =	Baltimore Ravens	New York Giants	2001	34–7	27
=	Tampa Bay Buccaneers	Oakland Raiders	2003	48–21	27
8	Green Bay Packers	Kansas City Chiefs	1967	35–10	25
9	San Francisco 49ers	San Diego Chargers	1995	49–26	23
10	San Francisco 49ers	Miami Dolphins	1985	38–16	22

* Up to and including 2008

Tennis

TOP 10 MOST WINS IN THE DAVIS CUP*

	COUNTRY	YEARS	WINS
1	USA	1978–79, 1981–82, 1990, 1992, 1995	8
2	Sweden	1975, 1984–85, 1987, 1994, 1997–98	7
3	Australia	1973, 1977, 1983, 1986, 1999, 2003	6
4	= Germany	1988–89, 1993	3
	= France	1991, 1996, 2001	3
6	= Spain	2000, 2004	2
	= Russia	2002, 2006	2
8	= South Africa	1974	1
	= Italy	1976	1
	= Czechoslovakia	1980	1
	= Croatia	2005	1

* Since the abolition of the Challenge system in 1972

The Davis Cup was first contested in 1900. From then until 1972 the winners were challenged for the title each year, but it became a knockout tournament between the top 16 nations in 1981.

TOP 10 MOST MEN'S GRAND SLAM TITLES*

	PLAYER / COUNTRY / YEARS	SINGLES	DOUBLES	MIXED	TOTAL
1	Roy Emerson, Australia 1959–71	12	16	0	28
2	John Newcombe, Australia 1965–76	7	17	2	26
3	= Frank Sedgman, Australia 1948–52	5	9	8	22
	= Todd Woodbridge, Australia 1988–2004	0	16	6	22
5	Bill Tilden, USA 1913–30	10	6	5	21
6	Rod Laver, Australia 1960–71	11	6	3	20
7	John Bromwich, Australia 1938–50	2	13	4	19
8	= Jean Borotra, France 1925–36	4	9	5	18
	= Ken Rosewall, Australia 1953–72	8	9	1	18
	= Neale Fraser, Australia 1957–62	3	11	4	18

* Up to and including 2007

THE 10 LONGEST SETS IN A GRAND SLAM FINAL*

	YEAR	TOURNAMENT	EVENT	SET WINNERS	OPPONENTS	SCORE
1	1946	US Open	Men's doubles	Gardnar Mulloy (US) Bill Talbert (US)	Don McNeil (US) Frank Guernsey (US)	20–18
2	1992	Wimbledon	Men's doubles	John McEnroe (US) Michael Stich (Germany)	Jim Grabb (US) Richey Reneberg (US)	19–17
3	= 1927	Australian Open	Men's singles	Gerald Patterson (Australia)	John Hawkes (Australia)	18–16
	= 1949	US Open	Men's singles	Ted Schroeder (US)	Pancho Gonzales (US)	18–16
	= 2000	Australian Open	Men's doubles	Ellis Ferrera (South Africa) Rick Leach (US)	Wayne Black (Zimbabwe) Andrew Kratzmann (Australia)	18–16
6	1959	Wimbledon	Men's doubles	Rod Laver (Australia) Bob Mark (Australia)	Roy Emerson (Australia) Neale Fraser (Australia)	16–14
7	= 1911	US Open	Men's doubles	Fred Alexander (US Harold Hackett (US)	Raymond Little (US) Gus Touchard (US)	15–13
	= 1930	US Open	Men's doubles	George Lott (US) Johnny Doeg (US)	Wilmer Allison (US) John Von Ryn (US)	15–13
	= 1959	US Open	Mixed doubles	Bob Mark (Australia) Janet Hopps (US)	Neale Fraser (Australia) Margaret Osborne duPont (US)	15–13
	= 1971	Wimbledon	Mixed doubles	Owen Davidson (Australia) Billie Jean King (US)	Marty Riessen (US) Margaret Court (Australia)	15–13

* Up to and including all 2007 Grand Slam events

The first-named player(s) won the set, not necessarily the match.

For Pete's sake
Pete Sampras won a record 14 Grand Slam singles titles—the most by a male player.

Below: Court's triumph
Margaret Court's four singles titles in a year and total of 24 remains an unbeaten record.

TOP 10 **MOST GRAND SLAM SINGLES TITLES***

	PLAYER / COUNTRY	YEARS	A	F	W	US	TOTAL
1	Margaret Court (*née* Smith), Australia	1960–73	11	5	3	5	24
2	Steffi Graf, Germany	1987–99	4	6	7	5	22
3	Helen Wills-Moody, USA	1923–38	0	4	8	7	19
4	= Chris Evert-Lloyd, USA	1974–86	2	7	3	6	18
	= Martina Navratilova, Czechoslovakia/USA	1978–90	3	2	9	4	18
6	Pete Sampras, USA	1990–2002	2	0	7	5	14
7	= Roy Emerson, Australia	1961–67	6	2	2	2	12
	= Billie Jean King, USA	1966–75	1	1	6	4	12
	= Roger Federer, Switzerland	2003–07	3	0	5	4	12
10	= Rod Laver, Australia	1960–69	3	2	4	2	11
	= Bjorn Borg, Sweden	1974–81	0	6	5	0	11

* Up to and including 2007

A = Australian Open; F = French Open; W = Wimbledon; US = US Open

Suzanne Lenglen (France) won eight Grand Slam singles titles, but if her total of four French singles titles (1920–23) were included, she would be in joint seventh place with 12. However, because the French Championships up to 1925 were for members of French clubs only, they are not regarded as official Grand Slam events.

Water Sports

TOP 10 **MEDAL-WINNING COUNTRIES AT THE WORLD AQUATIC CHAMPIONSHIPS***

	COUNTRY	GOLD	MEDALS SILVER	BRONZE	TOTAL
1	USA	144	120	78	342
2	Australia	58	45	34	137
3	East Germany	50	40	25	115
4	Russia/USSR	31	38	38	107
5	Germany/West Germany	25	36	40	101
6	China	33	17	17	67
7 =	Hungary	17	12	14	43
=	UK	6	10	27	43
9	Netherlands	7	16	17	40
10	Japan	3	10	24	37

* At the FINA World Long Course Championships 1973–2007

The first World Swimming Championships were held at Belgrade, Yugoslavia, in 1973 and held sporadically to 1998. Since 2001 they have been held every two years and the next championships will be in Rome, Italy, in 2009.

TOP 10 **OLYMPIC ROWING COUNTRIES***

	COUNTRY	GOLD	MEDALS SILVER	BRONZE	TOTAL
1	USA	30	29	21	80
2	Germany/West Germany	26	21	21	68
3	East Germany	33	7	7	47
4 =	UK	21	17	8	46
=	Russia/USSR/Unified Team	13	20	13	46
6	Italy	10	13	13	36
7	Romania	18	10	7	35
8	Canada	7	13	12	32
9	France	6	11	10	27
10	Australia	8	7	11	26

* Up to and including the 2004 Olympics

TOP 10 **FASTEST WINNING TIMES OF THE MEN'S 100-METERS FREESTYLE FINAL AT THE OLYMPIC GAMES**

	SWIMMER / COUNTRY	YEAR	TIME (SECS)
1	Pieter van den Hoogenband, Netherlands	2004	48.17
2	Pieter van den Hoogenband, Netherlands	2000	48.30
3	Matt Biondi, USA	1988	48.63
4	Aleksandr Popov, Russia	1996	48.74
5	Aleksandr Popov, Unified Team	1992	49.02
6	Rowdy Gaines, USA	1984	49.80
7	Jim Montgomery, USA	1976	49.99
8	Jörg Woithe, East Germany	1980	50.40
9	Mark Spitz, USA	1972	51.22
10	Mike Wenden, Australia	1968	52.20

* At all Olympic finals up to and including 2004

Pulling together
Lisa Schlenker and Stacey Borgman (USA), winners of the women's lightweight double sculls "B" final at the 2004 Athens Olympics.

Record-breaker
In his semifinal at the 2000 Sydney Olympics, Pieter van den Hoogenband set a new world record time of 47.84 seconds, still standing in 2008.

TOP 10 MOST GOLD MEDALS AT THE FINA WORLD AQUATICS CHAMPIONSHIPS*

	SWIMMER / COUNTRY	YEARS COMPETED	INDIVIDUAL GOLDS	RELAY GOLDS	TOTAL GOLDS
1	Michael Phelps, USA	2001–07	11	4	15
2	Ian Thorpe, Australia	1998–2003	6	5	11
3	Grant Hackett, Australia	1998–2005	7	3	10
4 =	Kornelia Ender, East Germany	1973–75	4	4	8
=	Aaron Peirsol, USA	2001–07	6	2	8
=	Libby Lenton, Australia	2003–07	4	4	8
7 =	Kristin Otto, East Germany	1982–86	3	4	7
=	Jenny Thompson, USA	1998–2003	3	4	7
=	Leisel Jones, USA	2001–07	4	3	7
10 =	Aleksandr Popov, Russia	1994–2003	5	1	6
=	Brendan Hansen, USA	2001–07	4	2	6
=	Katie Hoff, USA	2005–07	4	2	6

* Individual medals at the FINA World Long Course Championships, 1973–2007

TOP 10 OLYMPIC SWIMMING GOLD MEDALS*

	SWIMMER / COUNTRY	YEAR(S)	INDIVIDUAL	RELAY	TOTAL
1	Mark Spitz, USA	1968–72	4	5	9
2 =	Matt Biondi, USA	1984–92	2	6	8
=	Jenny Thompson, USA	1992–2004	0	8	8
4 =	Kristin Otto, East Germany	1988	4	2	6
=	Amy van Dyken, USA	1996–2000	2	4	6
=	Michael Phelps, USA	2004	4	2	6
7 =	Charles Daniels#, USA	1904–08	4	1	5
=	Johnny Weismuller, USA	1924–28	3	2	5
=	Don Schollander, USA	1964–68	2	3	5
=	Tom Jager, USA	1984–92	0	5	5
=	Krizstina Egerszegi, Hungary	1988–96	5	0	5
=	Gary Hall, Jr., USA	1996–2004	2	3	5
=	Ian Thorpe, Australia	2000–04	3	2	5

* Up to and including the 2004 Olympics
# Includes one gold medal won at the 1906 Intercalated Olympic Games in Athens

Winter Sports

TOP 10 ICE HOCKEY NATIONS AT THE OLYMPIC GAMES*

1 Canada

2 = United States

  = USSR/Russia

4 = Czechoslovakia/ Czech Republic

  = Sweden

6 Finland

7 = Great Britain

  = West Germany/ Germany

  = Switzerland

10 Unified Team

GOLD
SILVER
BRONZE

* Up to and including the 2006 Turin Olympics

Ice hockey was first contested at the Summer Olympics in 1920, and at the Winter Olympics since 1924 for men and since 1998 for women.

TOP 10 OLYMPIC BOBSLEIGH NATIONS*

	COUNTRY	GOLD	SILVER	BRONZE	TOTAL
1	Switzerland	9	10	11	30
2	Germany/West Germany	10	6	8	24
3	United States	6	6	6	18
4	East Germany	5	5	3	13
5	Italy	4	4	4	12
6	= UK	1	1	2	4
	= USSR/Russia	1	1	2	4
8	= Canada	2	1	0	3
	= Austria	1	2	0	3
10	Belgium	0	1	1	2

* Up to and including the 2006 Turin Olympics

The two-man bobsleigh event made its debut at the 1932 Olympics and has been held at every Games since, with the exception of 1960 as there was no bob run at Squaw Valley, California, USA. The four-man event made its debut at the 1928 Games in St. Moritz. The two-women bobsleigh event was held for the first time at the 2002 Olympics, when it was won by the USA.

TOP 10 MEDAL-WINNING COUNTRIES AT THE WINTER OLYMPICS*

	COUNTRY	GOLD	SILVER	BRONZE	TOTAL
1	Russia/USSR/Unified Team	122	89	86	297
2	Norway	96	102	84	282
3	USA	78	81	59	218
4	Germany/West Germany	76	78	57	211
5	Austria	50	64	71	185
6	Finland	42	57	52	151
7	Sweden	46	32	44	122
8	Canada	38	38	44	120
9	Switzerland	37	37	43	117
10	East Germany	39	37	35	111

* Up to and including the 2006 Turin Games

Totals include medals won at figure skating and ice hockey included in the Summer Olympics prior to the inauguration of the Winter Games in 1924. From 1924 to 1992, they were held in the same year as the Summer Olympics but since 1994 they have been held in the two years in between the Summer Games.

TOP 10 **MOST SKIING WORLD CUP RACE WINS IN A CAREER (MEN)***

SKIER / COUNTRY	FIRST WIN	LAST WIN	TOTAL WINS
1 Ingemar Stenmark, Sweden	1974–75	1988–89	86
2 Hermann Maier, Austria	1997–97	2005–06	53
3 Alberto Tomba, Italy	1987–88	1997–98	50
4 Marc Girardelli, Luxembourg	1982–83	1995–96	46
5 Pirmin Zurbriggen, Switzerland	1981–82	1989–90	40
6 Bode Miller, USA	2001–02	2007–08	31
7 Benjamin Raich, Austria	1998–99	2007–08	30
8 Stephan Eberharter, Austria	1997–98	2003–04	29
9 Phil Mahre, USA	1976–77	1982–83	27
10 Franz Klammer, Austria	1973–74	1983–84	26

* Up to and including the 2007–08 season

TOP 10 **MOST SKIING WORLD CUP RACE WINS IN A CAREER (WOMEN)***

SKIER / COUNTRY	FIRST WIN	LAST WIN	TOTAL WINS
1 Annemarie Pröll, Austria	1969–70	1979–80	62
2 Vreni Schneider, Switzerland	1984–85	1994–95	55
3 Renate Goetschl, Austria	1992–93	2006–07	46
4 Anja Paerson, Sweden	1998–99	2007–08	38
5 Katja Seizinger, Germany	1991–92	1997–98	36
6 Hanni Wenzel, Liechtenstein	1973–74	1983–84	33
7 Erika Hess, Switzerland	1980–81	1986–87	31
8 Janica Kostelic, Croatia	1998–99	2005–06	30
9 Michela Figini, Switzerland	1983–84	1989–90	26
10 = Maria Walliser, Switzerland	1982–83	1989–90	25
= Michaela Dorfmeister, Austria	1995–96	2005–06	25

* Up to and including the 2007–08 season

Alpine champion
Sweden's Anja Paerson has also won an Olympic gold medal, in the slalom in 2006, and won seven World Championship golds between 2001 and 2007 in slalom, giant slalom, super-g, combined, and downhill.

Leisure Pursuits

TOP 10 **HIGHEST-EARNING SPORTSMEN**

	SPORTSMAN / COUNTRY*	SPORT	EARNINGS ($)
1	Tiger Woods	Golf	100,000,000
2	Oscar de la Hoya	Boxing	43,000,000
3	Phil Mickelson	Golf	42,200,000
4	Kimi Raikkonen, Finland	Motor racing	40,000,000
5	Michael Schumacher, Germany	Motor racing	36,000,000
6	David Beckham, UK	Football	33,000,000
7	Kobe Bryant	Basketball	32,900,000
8	Shaquille O'Neal	Basketball	31,900,000
9 =	Michael Jordan	Basketball	31,000,000
=	Ronaldinho, Brazil	Football	31,000,000

* All from the USA unless otherwise stated

Source: *Forbes* magazine

Winner of 13 Majors and 61 Tour events (to January 1, 2008), Tiger Woods has won over $75 million since turning professional in 1996—$25 million more than the second-placed golfer. His annual income includes payments for endorsements for companies such as Nike.

$351-million team
Manchester United players celebrating after beating Chelsea 4-0 on penalties, after the game ended 1-1, to win the 2007 FA Community Shield at Wembley Stadium.

TOP 10 **MOST VALUABLE SPORTS TEAM BRANDS**

	TEAM / COUNTRY	SPORT	VALUE 2007 ($)
1	Manchester United/UK	Soccer	351,000,000
2	Real Madrid/Spain	Soccer	288,000,000
3	Bayern Munich/Germany	Soccer	255,000,000
4	New York Yankees/USA	Baseball	217,000,000
5	Arsenal/UK	Soccer	185,000,000
6	AC Milan/Italy	Soccer	184,000,000
7	Dallas Cowboys/USA	American football	175,000,000
8	Barcelona/Spain	Soccer	130,000,000
9	Boston Red Sox/USA	Baseball	125,000,000
10	Washington Redskins/USA	American football	120,000,000

Source: *Forbes* magazine

Manchester United has one of the biggest fans bases with supporters in all corners of the globe. It is estimated that more than 50 percent of their supporters are based in Asia. Their estimated merchandise revenue was nearly $25 million in 2007, but their overall value falls well short of the most valuable sports brand, ESPN, which is estimated to be worth $7.5 billion.

TOP 10 SPORTS PROVIDING THE MOST WINNERS OF THE *SPORTS ILLUSTRATED* SPORTSMAN OF THE YEAR AWARD

	SPORT	WINNERS
1	Baseball	15
2	Track and field	8
3	= Golf	7
	= Professional basketball	7
	= Professional football	7
6	Hockey	4
7	= Boxing	3
	= College basketball	3
	= College football	3
	= Tennis	3

Source: *Sports Illustrated*

$200-million film
Hillary Swank, as Maggie Fitzgerald, a waitress who decides to change her life by becoming a boxer, in Million Dollar Baby. Directed by Clint Eastwood, it won four Oscars, including those for Best Picture, Best Director and Best Actress—and earned over $200 million worldwide.

TOP 10 PARTICIPATION SPORTS IN THE USA

	SPORT	TOTAL*
1	Exercise walking	87,500,000
2	Swimming	56,500,000
3	Exercising with equipment	52,400,000
4	Camping (vacation/overnight)	48,600,000
5	Bowling	44,800,000
6	Fishing	40,600,000
7	Bicycle riding	35,600,000
8	Aerobic exercising	33,700,000
9	Weightlifting	32,900,000
10	Billiards/pool	31,800,000

* Seven years of age and older who participated more than once during 2006

Source: National Sporting Goods Association

TOP 10 SPORT FILMS

	FILM	YEAR	SPORT
1	Cars*	2006	Car racing
2	Rocky IV	1985	Boxing
3	Million Dollar Baby	2004	Boxing
4	Space Jam*	1996	Basketball
5	The Longest Yard	2005	American footbal
6	The Waterboy	1998	American footbal
7	Dodgeball: A True Underdog Story	2004	Dodgeball
8	Days of Thunder	1990	Stock car racing
9	Talladega Nights: The Ballad of Ricky Bobby	2006	NASCAR racing
10	Rocky Balboa	2006	Boxing

* Animated

Further Information

THE UNIVERSE & THE EARTH

Astronautics
www.astronautix.com
Spaceflight news and reference

Caves
www.caverbob.com
Lists of long and deep caves

Disasters
www.emdat.be
Emergency Events Database covering major disasters since 1900

Elements
www.webelements.com
Detailed data on every element

Islands
islands.unep.ch
Information on the world's islands

Mountains
peaklist.org
Lists of the world's tallest mountains

NASA
www.nasa.gov
The main website for the US space program

Ocean
www.oceansatlas.org
The UN's resource on oceanographic issues

Planets
www.nineplanets.org
A multimedia tour of the Solar System

Space
www.space.com
Reports on events in space exploration

LIFE ON EARTH

American Forests
www.americanforests.org
A website covering all aspects of forests and trees in the USA

Animals
animaldiversity.ummz.umich.edu
A wealth of animal data

Birds
www.bsc-eoc.org/avibase
A database on the world's birds

Conservation
cms.iucn.org
The leading nature conservation site

Endangered
www.cites.org
Lists of endangered species of flora and fauna

Environment
www.unep.ch
The UN's Earthwatch and other programs

Fish
www.fishbase.org
Global information on fish

Food and Agriculture Organization
www.fao.org
Statistics from the UN's FAO website

Insects
ufbir.ifas.ufl.edu
The University of Florida Book of Insect Records

Sharks
www.flmnh.ufl.edu/fish/sharks
The Florida Museum of Natural History's shark data files

THE HUMAN WORLD

Death penalty
www.deathpenaltyinfo.org
Facts and statistics from the Death Penalty Information Center

Bureau of Justice
ojp.usdoj.gov/bjs
US Crime statistics

FBI
www.fbi.gov
Information and links on crime in the USA

Health
www.cdc.gov/nchs
Information and links on health for US citizens

Leaders
www.terra.es/personal2/monolith/00index.htm
Facts about world leaders since 1945

Names
www.ssa.gov/OACT/babynames
Most common names since 1879 from the Social Security Administration

Prisons
www.bop.gov
Public information on all aspects of the US prison system

Religions
www.worldchristiandatabase.org
World religion data

Rulers
rulers.org
A database of the world's rulers and political leaders

US presidents
www.whitehouse.gov/history/presidents
Biographies, facts and figures from the White House

TOWN & COUNTRY

Bridges and tunnels
en.structurae.de
Facts and figures on the world's buildings, tunnels and other structures

Countries
www.theodora.com/wfb
Country data, rankings, etc.

Country and city populations
www.citypopulation.de
A searchable guide to the world's countries and major cities

Country data
www.cia.gov/library/publications/the-world-factbook
The CIA World Factbook

Country populations
www.un.org/esa/population/unpop
The UN's worldwide data on population issues

Development
www.worldbank.org
Development and other statistics from around the world

Population
www.census.gov/ipc/www
International population statistics

Steel bridges
www.sbi.se/default_en.asp
A downloadable list of the world's steel bridges

Skyscrapers
www.emporis.com/en
The Emporis database of high-rise buildings

Tunnels
home.no.net/lotsberg
A database of the longest rail, road, and canal tunnels

CULTURE & LEARNING

The Art Newspaper
www.theartnewspaper.com
News and views on the art world

Books
www.publishersweekly.com
Publishers Weekly, the trade journal of American publishers

Education
nces.ed.gov
The home of federal education data

Languages of the world
www.ethnologue.com
Online reference work on the world's 6,912 living languages

Libraries
www.ala.org
US library information and book awards from the American Library Association

The Library of Congress
www.loc.gov
The gateway to one of the world's greatest collections of words and pictures

The New York Public Library
www.nypl.org
One of the country's foremost libraries, with an online catalog

The Pulitzer Prizes
www.pulitzer.org
A searchable guide to the prestigious US literary prize

Translations
databases.unesco.org/xtrans/stat/xTransList.a
UNESCO's lists of the most translated books and authors

UNESCO
www.unesco.org
Comparative international statistics on education and culture

MUSIC

All Music Guide
www.allmusic.com
A comprehensive guide to all genres of music

American Society of Composers, Authors, and Publishers
www.ascap.com
ASCAP songwriter and other awards

Billboard
www.billboard.com
US music news and charts data

Classical music
classicalusa.com
An online guide to classical music in the USA

Country Music Hall of Fame
www.countrymusichalloffame.com
The history of and information about Country music

Grammy Awards
www.naras.org
The official site for the famous US music awards

MTV
www.mtv.com
The online site for the MTV music channel

Recording Industry Association of America
www.riaa.org
Searchable data on gold and platinum disk award winners

Rock and Roll Hall of Fame
www.rockhall.com
The museum of the history of rock

Rolling Stone magazine
www.rollingstone.com
Features on popular music since 1967

ENTERTAINMENT

Academy Awards
www.oscars.org
The official "Oscars" website

Emmy Awards
www.emmyonline.org
Emmy TV awards from the National Television Academy site

Golden Globe Awards
www.goldenglobes.org
Hollywood Foreign Press Association's Golden Globes site

Hollywood
www.hollywood.com
A US cinema site with details on all the new releases

Internet Movie Database
www.imdb.com
The best of the publicly accessible film websites; IMDbPro is available to subscribers

Internet Broadway Database
www.ibdb.com
Broadway theater information

Internet Theatre Database
www.theatredb.com
A Broadway-focused searchable stage site

Tony Awards
www.tonyawards.com
Official website of the American Theatre Wing's Tonys

Variety
www.variety.com
Extensive entertainment information (extra features available to subscribers)

Yahoo! Movies
movies.yahoo.com
Charts plus features, trailers, and links to the latest movie releases

THE COMMERCIAL WORLD

The Economist
www.economist.com
Global economic and political news

Energy
www.eia.doe.gov
Official US energy statistics

Gold
www.gold.org
The website of the World Gold Council

Organization for Economic Co-operation and Development
www.oecd.org
World economic and social statistics

Rich lists
www.forbes.com
Forbes magazine's celebrated lists of the world's wealthiest people

Telecommunications
www.itu.int
Worldwide telecommunications statistics

Travel industry
www.tia.org
Stats on travel to and within the USA

The World Bank
www.worldbank.org
World development, trade, and labor statistics

World Tourism Organization
www.world-tourism.org
The world's principal travel and tourism organization

United Nations Development Program
www.undp.org
Country GDPs and other development data

ON THE MOVE

Air disasters
www.airdisaster.com
Reports on aviation disasters

Airports
www.airports.org
Statistics on the world's busiest airports

Air speed records
www.fai.org/records
The website of the official air speed record governing body

Aviation
www.aerofiles.com
Information on a century of American aviation

Balloons
www.eballoon.org
History and information on hot-air ballooning

Car manufacture
www.oica.net
The International Organization of Motor Vehicle Manufacturers' website

Land and water speed records
www.bluebird-electric.net/bluebird_site_navigator.htm
Wide range of resources, 1901–2006

Railroads
www.railwaygazette.com
The world's railway business in depth from *Railway Gazette International*

Water speed records
www.geocities.com/Colosseum/Sideline/8707
List of record-holders, 1919 to the present

Yachts
powerandmotoryacht.com
Includes the annual *Power & Motoryacht* guide to the world's megayachts

SPORT & LEISURE

Baseball
mlb.mlb.com
The official website of Major League Baseball

Basketball
www.nba.com
The official website of the NBA

Cycling
www.uci.ch
The Union Cycliste Internationale, the competitive cycling governing body

Football
www.nfl.com
The official website of the NFL

Golf
www.pgatour.com
The Professional Golfers' Association (PGA) Tour

Hockey
www.nhl.com
The official website of the NHL

Olympics
www.olympic.org
The official website of the International Olympic Committee

Skiing
www.fis-ski.com
Fédèration Internationale de Ski, the world governing body of skiing and snowboarding

Sports Illustrated
sportsillustrated.cnn.com
Sports Illustrated's comprehensive coverage of all major sports

Track and field
www.iaaf.org
The world governing body of athletics

Index

T

tea *see under* drink

telephones
  countries with the most 186
  countries with the most cell 186

tennis
  Davis Cup, most wins 238
  Grand Slam
    longest sets 238
    most men's titles 238
    most singles titles 239

theatre
  longest-running mysteries and thrillers on Broadway 138
  longest-running comedies on Broadway 138
  longest-running musicals on Broadway 139
  longest-running nonmusicals on Broadway 138
  longest-running Rogers & Hammerstein productions on Broadway 139
  shows of all time 138

Tour de France
  most finishers 226

tourism
  art galleries and museums in the USA 189
  countries earning the most from 188
  countries of origin of visitors to the USA 189
  countries spending most on 188
  countries with biggest increase in 189
  destinations 188

trees
  most common in the UK 47

tunnels
  longest canal 98
  longest rail 99
  longest road 99
  longest subsea 98
  longest water-supply 98

turkeys
  countries with the most 43

TV
  audiences in the USA 163
  cable countries 163
  Emmy award for Comedy Series 162
  Emmy award for Outstanding Lead Actor in a Drama 162
  Emmy award for Outstanding Lead Actress in a Drama 162
  satellite countries 162

U

universities
  largest 104
  oldest in the USA 105

uranium
  countries producing the most 175

urbanization
  least urbanized countries 88
  most urbanized countries 88

V

vegetables
  countries producing the most 44

videos
  cities in the USA 165

vitamins and dietary supplements
  countries consuming most 52

volcanoes
  largest volcanic islands 21
  worst eruptions 27

W

water-speed record
  latest holders of 200

water sports
  fastest winning times of the men's 100-meters freestyle at the Olympics 240
  medal-winning countries at World Aquatic Championships 240
  most gold medals at the FINA World Aquatic Championships 241
  Olympic rowing countries 240
  Olympic swimming gold medals 241

waterfalls
  highest 19
  widest 19

wealth
  government
    areas of federal government expenditure 170
    coins and notes in the UK 170
    countries with highest inflation 170
    poorest countries 171
    richest countries 171
    sources of US income 170
  personal
    countries with most dollar billionaires 172
    highest-earning celebrities 173
    highest-earning dead celebrities 173
    highest-earning sportsmen 173
    richest men 172

weather
  coldest places—average 25
  driest places—average 25
  heaviest daily downpours 24
  hottest places—average 25
  most contrasting seasons 25
  wettest places—average 24

whales
  largest 33

wind power
  countries generating most 192

wine *see under* drink

words
  longest in the *Oxford English Dictionary* 102

work
  companies with most employees 168
  countries with highest proportion of workers 169
  countries with most fatalities at 196
  countries with most workers 169
  countries working longest hours 168
  occupations in the USA 168

World War I
  countries suffering greatest losses 74
  largest armed forces 74

World War II
  British and Commonwealth air aces 75
  countries suffering greatest losses 74
  largest armed forces 74
  Luftwaffe aces 75

Y

yachts
  largest motor 206

Acknowledgments

Special research: Ian Morrison (sport); Dafydd Rees (music)

Peter Bond, Richard Braddish, Thomas Brinkhoff, Philip Eden, Christopher Forbes, Russell E. Gough, Robert Grant, Bob Gulden, Dr Benjamin Lucas, Chris Mead, Roberto Ortiz de Zarate, Emil Pocock, Robert Senior, Lucy T. Verma

Academy of Motion Picture Arts and Sciences—Oscar statuette is the registered trademark and copyrighted property of the Academy of Motion Picture Arts and Sciences
Advertising Age
Airports Council International
Alexa
Amateur Softball Association of America (ASA)
American Forests
The American Kennel Club
Amnesty International
Animated Film Society (Annie Awards)
Arbitron
Artnet
The Art Newspaper
Association of Tennis Professionals
Audit Bureau of Circulations Ltd (ABC)
Billboard
Box Office Mojo
BP Statistical Review of World Energy 2007
Breeders' Cup
The BRIT Awards
British Library
Bureau of Federal Prisons
Bureau of Justice Statistics
Bureau of Labor Statistics
BusinessWeek
The Cat Fanciers' Association
Central Intelligence Agency, *World Factbook*
Championship Auto Racing Teams (CART)
Channel Swimming Association
Chinese Academy of Sciences
Christie's
Computer Industry Almanac
Consumer Federation of America
Consumer Product Safety Council
Crime in the United States 2006
Death Penalty Information Center
De Beers
Department of Trade and Industry
The Diamond Registry
Drama Desk Awards
DVD Release Report
EarthTrends
The Economist
Editor and Publisher Year Book
EM-DAT, CRED, University of Louvain
Emporis
Energy Information Administration
Environmental Performance Index (EPI)
Environmental Protection Agency
Ethnologue
Euromonitor International, Global Market Information Database
FBI Uniform Crime Reports
Federal Bureau of Investigation
Federal Bureau of Prisons

Fédération Internationale de Motorcyclisme
Fédération Internationale de Ski
Food and Agriculture Organization of the United Nations (FAO)
Forbes magazine
Fortune
The Gallup Organization
Global Education Digest (UNESCO)
Global Forest Resources Assessment (FAO)
Global Wind 2006 Report
Gold Fields Mineral Services, *Gold Survey 2007*
Human Development Report (United Nations)
Imperial War Museum, UK
Index Translationum (UNESCO)
Indianapolis Motor Speedway
Interbrand
International Air Transport Association
International Association of Athletics Federations
International Atomic Energy Agency
International Centre for Prison Studies
International Federation of Audit Bureaux of Circulations
International Federation of Organic Agriculture Movements
International Game Fish Association
The International Institute for Strategic Studies, *The Military Balance 2008*
International Iron & Steel Institute
International Labour Organization
International Monetary Fund (IMF)
International Obesity Task Force
International Olympic Committee
International Organization of Motor Vehicle Manufacturers
International Shark Attack File, Florida Museum of Natural History
International Telecommunication Union
International Union for Conservation of Nature and Natural Resources (IUCN)
Internet Movie Database
Internet World Stats
Kentucky Derby
Kirin
Ladies Professional Golf Association
Library Journal
Library of Congress
Lipmann Walton
Magazine Publishers of America
Major League Baseball
Metropolitan Opera House, New York
MTV
Music Information Database
National Academy of Recording Arts and Sciences (NARAS) (Grammy Awards)
National Academy of Television Arts & Sciences (Emmy Awards)
National Aeronautics and Space Administration (NASA)
National Association of Broadcasters (NAB)
National Audubon Society
National Basketball Association (NBA)
National Center for Education Statistics
National Football League (NFL)
National Hockey League
National Phobics Society, UK
National Public Radio (NPR)
National Sporting Goods Association
Nationwide Mercury Prize

Natural History Museum, UK
Newspaper Association of America
Nielsen Media Research
Nielsen SoundScan
Nobel Foundation
NSS GEO2 Committee on Long and Deep Caves
The Official Museums Directory
Online Computer Library Center
Organisation for Economic Co-operation and Development (OECD)
Organisation Internationale des Constructeurs d'Automobiles (OICA)
Oxford English Dictionary
George Foster Peabody Awards
Point Topic
Population Reference Bureau
Power & Motoryacht
Professional Bowlers Association
Professional Golfers' Association
Recording Industry Association of America (RIAA)
River Systems of the World
Royal Aeronautical Society, UK
Royal Astronomical Society, UK
Royal Opera House, Covent Garden
Screen Digest
Screen International
Siemens, *International Telecom Statistics*
The Silver Institute, World Silver Survey 2007
Social Security Administration
Sotheby's
Sports Illustrated
Statistical Abstract of the United States
Stockholm International Peace Research Institute (SIPRI)
Stores
Top500
Tour de France
UIC Railisa Database
United Nations
United Nations Educational, Scientific and Cultural Organization (UNESCO)
United Nations Environment Programme (UNEP)
United Nations Office on Drugs and Crime
United Nations Population Division
United States Postal Service
Universal Postal Union
US Census Bureau
US Census Bureau International Data Base
US Department of Agriculture, Economic Research Service
US Geological Survey
US Justice Department
US Mint
US Treasury
Variety
Video Business
Ward's Motor Vehicle Facts & Figures 2007
Wine Institute
World Association of Newspapers
World Bank
World Christian Database
World Development Indicators (World Bank)
World Gold Council
World Health Organization
World Nuclear Association
World of Learning
World Population Reference Bureau
World Tourism Organization

Picture Credits

AKG Images: 75t Ullstein Bild, 158 Walt Disney Pictures/Album, 165tr Disney Enterprises/Album.

Catherine Benson: 7

Christie's Images Limited: 114l.

Corbis: 10-11 Farhad Parsa/zefa, 11b, 95c, 121, 211, 231b, 239b Bettmann, 16 Michael S. Lewis, 18, 22t Galen Rowell, 19 George Steinmetz, 21 Wayne Lawler; Ecoscene, 23tr David Muench, 27t & b, 62l Corbis, 30t Louie Psihoyos, 31t Theo Allofs, 32b Denis Scott, 34b (inset) Stephen Frink, 35t, 39t Paul Souders, 35b Renee Lynn, 37r Serge Kozak/zefa, 38b Manfred Danegger/zefa, 40b, 84b Yann Arthus-Bertrand, 42b Ricardo Azoury, 43b, 63tr, 128c, 134t, 191t, 196, 209t, 215t, 232tl, 233b, 239t Reuters, 45br Phil Schermeister, 46-47, 47t Rickey Rogers/Reuters, 53br Pierre Perrin Sygma, 56t Ali Jarekji/Reuters, 59tl Larry Williams, 59bl Jack Hollingsworth, 60br, 171c Michel Setboun, 61 epa, 65tl PoodlesRock, 66 Ted Spiegel, 67tr Kieran Doherty/Reuters, 68br Creasource, 71t Matt Rainey/Star Ledger, 73b Scott Houston, 76b KCNA/epa, 78b Eyal Ofer, 79b Punit Paranjpe/Reuters, 82-83b Hamid Sardar, 83t, 86 Kevin R. Morris, 85tr Gideon Mendel/ActionAid, 87 China Daily Information Corp - CDIC/Reuters, 88b Ken Straiton, 89 Peter Adams, 91l Ladislav Janicek/zefa, 91r Nick Smyth; Cordaiy Photo Library Ltd., 92-93t Momatiuk - Eastcott, 92-93b, 115t Nik Wheeler, 94 Juergen Effner/dpa, 95b Anwar Mirza/Reuters, 99tr Martin Ruetschi/epa, 103 Keren Su, 107bl John Springer Collection, 108tl Nancy Kaszerman/ZUMA, 108-109t & b Jim Zuckerman, 109r Massimo Listri, 110b Simon Marcus, 112b Tony Kurdzuk/Star Ledger, 113b Mike Segar/Reuters, 118cl Contographer ®, 120c Neal Preston, 124tl Gary Hershorn/Reuters, 125b John Hayes/Reuters, 126 Federico Gambarini/epa, 127 Bruno Bebert/Pool/Reuters, 130 Jose Manuel Ribeiro/Reuters, 131 Alessia Pierdomenico/Reuters, 135c Robbie Jack, 142cl Phil McCarten/Reuters, 150-151 Patrik Giardino, 160b Jutta Klee, 161 Lester Lefkowitz, 168l China Newsphoto/Reuters, 169r Sherwin Crasto/Reuters, 171b Lynsey Addario, 173tl Jodi Hilton, 177t Raj Patidar/Reuters, 180 José Fuste Raga/zefa, 181 Gideon Mendel, 183 Dave G. Houser, 185t Emilio Suetone/Hemis, 186 Tokyo Space Club, 187t David Pillinger, 188cr Owen Franken, 189cr Jose Fuste Raga, 190br Rick Wilking/Reuters, 192-193t Du Huaju/Xinhua Press, 192-193b Karl-Heinz Haenel/zefa, 194ct Gilles Sabrié, 195t Jeremy Horner, 197 Sergio Dorantes/Sygma, 200t Wolfgang Deuter/zefa, 200b Skyscan, 202b Matthias Hiekel/dpa, 203 Jim Sugar, 205t Fred Derwal/Hemis, 206b Chris Helgre/Reuters, 207b Robert Sciarrino/Star Ledger, 214tr Duomo, 215b Jean-Yves Ruszniewski/TempSport, 216c Kimimasa Mayama/epa, 219 Rhona Wise/epa, 222b Franck Robichon/epa, 223b Eric Miller/Reuters, 224-225 Jason Reed/Reuters, 229 Toms Kalnins/epa, 230b Tony Roberts, 231t Greg Fiume/NewSport, 234b Schlegelmilch, 235 Gero Breloer/epa, 237 Molly Riley/reuters, 243b Eddy Risch/epa, 244b Andy Rain/epa.

Fotolia: 20t Imageman Rez, 22-23c Nikolay Titov, 24b Georgios Alexandris, 25tr Antony McAulay, 26 Robert Paul van Beets, 32t Zampa, 33b Olivier Lantzendörffer, 34t Fotoflash, 38t Ichtor, 40tl,

233tl Edsweb, 40tr Stefan Hermans, 41tl Luchschen, 41tr EastWest Imaging, 41b Jody Snelgrove, 46t Andrzej Tokarski, 46b Piter PKruger, 51bl Olga Lyubkina, 51br Stephen Finn, 52-53 Karin Lau, 56b Nymph, 60l Roman Dekan, 62-63 Granitepeaker, 64t Nikolay Okhitin, 64tr Mikhail Perfilov, 64-65b Irmine van der Geest, 66tl Mashe, 68 PhotoBristol, 68tl Photlook, 69 Kmit, 70tl, 175b Irochka, 70c Sergey Lavrentev, 71c Sascha Burkard, 74b Slobodan Djajic, 77l, 156b Kirsty Pargeter, 77tr Xygo, 78tl Drizzd, 78tr Georgios Kollidas, 79tl, 175t Jean-Louis Bouzou, 79tc Dmitry Rukhlenko, 79tr MM, 84-85t Leslie Hender, 88t Robert, 90b Claudio Baldini, 96-97b ManicBlu, 102t Douglas Freer, 102bl Gudellaphoto, 106-107, 129b Mr. Lightning, 110-111t Jo Ann Snover, 111br Paul Turner, 112t JChMedinger, 113t Andrey Chmelyov, 118b Dino O., 118-119t Mark Huls, 119br Marlee, 120t Pierre-Jean G., 120b Carsten Reisinger, 122-123, 245b Franck Boston, 124b, 129t OH, 124-125t U.P.images, 128t Vladimir Mucibabic, 128b, 178t Dotshock, 135t, 142l, 143r Ferenc Szelepcsenyi, 135b Alex Staroseltsev, 138-139 James Steidl, 140l Milosluz, 141, 244t ktsdesign, 144t, 145r Olga Mishyna, 144-145 Joyful_Girl, 148-149 Lorelyn Medina, 152-153b Tritooth, 156t Michanolimit, 157b Tatyana Nyshko, 160t Adam Gryko, 162-163 Laura, 163br Ljupco Smokovski, 165 Claudio Divizia, 165br Adam Borkowski, 170t Ploum1, 170b Stachu343, 171t Georgios Kollidas, 172t Mikhail Tolstoy, 172cl Gino Santa Maria, 172-173b Orlando Florin Rosu, 174tl PhotoCreate, 174tr Sir_Eagle, 174b Aleksandr Ugorenkov, 179b Objectsforall, 182tl Tom Perkins, 182tc Joe Gough, 182tr Elnur, 184t Celso Pupo, 184cl Steve Cukrov, 184cr Luka, 184-185b Pandore, 187b Sdraskovic, 188-189 Mathieu Viennet, 190bl Stefano Maccari, 190-191 Juan Jose Gutierrez Barrow, 194t Hazel Proudlove, 194cb Clivia, 194b BilderBox, 195 Nickos, 205b Gina Sanders, 206-207t Stephanie Bandmann, 210 Stasys Eidiejus, 214b TFphotos, 216t Jeffrey van Daele, 216b jStock, 218 Albo, 220t Jean-Luc Cochonneau, 220b TimurD, 221b Bryce Newell, 222t, 223t Albo, 228 Denis Pepin, 230t Ant Clausen, 232 Sean Gladwell, 236 GoodMood Photo, 238t Vincenzo Novello, 242-243 Imagine-Nation.

Getty Images: 51t Hank Walker/Time Life Pictures, 55 Per-Anders Pettersson, 63br Alex Wong, 69tc Time Life Pictures/FBI/Time Life Pictures, 73t Ruslan Alkhanov/AFP, 74t Mansell/Time & Life Pictures, 75b Topical Press Agency, 96-97t Liu Song/ChinaFotoPress, 104t Choo Youn-Kong/AFP, 106bl Popperfoto, 119c Alexander Tamargo, 122bl, 129c Michael Ochs Archives, 122br Ed Clark/Time & Life Pictures, 123b Frank Driggs Collection, 173tr Fotos International, 179t AFP, 217 Hugo Philpott/AFP, 219 Jewel Samad/AFP, 221c Laurence Griffiths, 226 David Hecker/AFP, 227 Teh Eng Koon/AFP, 240br Robert Laberge, 241t Phil Walter.

Ivan Hissey: 66t, 174b, 177cr, 187l, 240bl

iStockphoto: 10br Carolina K. Smith, 11c, 16-17 Shawn Gearhart, 20b Edwin van Wier, 22-23b Dmytro Korolov, 23t Mikael Damkier, 24t Amanda Rohde, 24c John Rodriguez, 25cl & cr Fred De Bailliencourt, 25b Ilker Canikligil, 30b Victor Soares, 31b, 43tl, tcll, tclr, tc & tr Eric Isselée, 34b Michal Rozanski, 39b Scott Morgan, 42tl Editorial12, 42tr Narvikk, 43tcrl Jiri Vaclavek, 43tcrr

Chepko Danil, 44t Ceneri, 44cl Christine Balderas, 44cr Spauln, 44b Bluestocking, 45t Naphtalina, 45bl Jaroslaw Wojcik, 52br Ferran Traite Soler, 54t & b Corey Weiner, 54c Cole Vineyard, 57 Rob Blackburn, 58 Sandramo, 59tr, 69tl & tr, 71b, 202tr, 238-239 iStockphoto.com, 59br Blackred, 60bc Stefan Hermans, 65tl Michel de Nijs, 66b Tatiana Morozova, 70tr & br Andrew Brown, 70bl Robyn Mackenzie, 72 Christian Pound, 76t, 77br Simon Spoon, 77 Phil Morley, 90t Anton Seleznev, 92l, 93r, 105b Lisa Thornberg, 95t DaddyBit, 98-99 Andrea Sturm, 102br Milos Luzanin, 104-105 Perefu, 114-115 Laura Eisenberg, 134b Oscar Durand, 147b Izabela Habur, 154t Kirill Putchenko, 164l Steve Jacobs, 168r Chris Schmidt, 168-169t Ryan KC Wong, 172cr Vik Thomas, 176tl, tr & b Mark Evans, 177b Scott Maxwell, 178b Hans F. Meier, 182b, 245t YinYang, 187cr Matt Knannlein, 188t Vito Elefante, 189t Lidian Neeleman, 193br Svetlana Tebenkova, 202tl kkgas, 209b Goldmund, 214tl Brian Wilke, 221t Slawomir Kruz, Simon Askham, 234t Kativ, 238b Sean Warren, 240bl Neeley Spotts, 240-241 Peter Evans.

The Kobal Collection: 132-133 New Line/James, David, 133r MGM/UA, 141t Walt Disney/Mountain, Peter, 142-143t Marvel/Sony Pictures, 142-143b Dreamworks/Paramount, 144b New Line/Avery Pix/Cartwright, Richard, 145l Bonne Pioche/Buena Vista/APC/Maison, Jerome, 146 New Line, 147t Sony/Columbia/Bennett, Tracy, 148tr 20th Century Fox/Paramount, 149t Paramount/Miramax, 152t Warner Bros./Gordon, Melinda Sue, 154tl New Line/Saul Zaentz/Wing Nut/Vinet, Pierre, 155 Warner Bros./James, David, 156t (inset) Columbia/Mein, Simon, 157t Warner Bros/DC Comics, 159 20th Century Fox/Groening, Matt, 150tl MGM/ Bull, Clarence Sinclair, 151t Paramount/Vantage, 164r Warner Bros./Cooper, Andrew, 245c Warner Bros./Wallace, Merie W.

Mary Evans Picture Library: 65tr, 208.

Moviestore Collection Ltd.: 140tl, 151br, 153t.

NASA: 10bl, 83c Goddard Space Flight Center, 12 European Space Agency and A. Nota (STScI/ESA), 13tl, bl, bcr & br, 192t Jet Propulsion Laboratory, 13tc European Space Agency, J. Clarke (Boston University), and Z. Levay (STScI), 13tr Solar and Heliospheric Observatory (European Space Agency & NASA), 13ct, 201 NASA, 13cb & bcl Headquarters - Great Images in NASA, 13bc Steve Lee University of Colorado, Jim Bell Cornell University, 14 Kennedy Space Center, 14br, 15 Marshall Space Flight Center.

Naturepl: 33t Doug Perrine, 36 Daniel Gomez.

Photolibrary: 37l Howard Hall.

Science Photo Library: 30c Joe Tucciarone, 50 Scott Camazine.

TopFoto: 138tl Marilyn Kingwill/ArenaPAL, 139t Michael le Poer Trench/ArenaPAL.

Publisher's Acknowledgements
Cover design: Ron Callow at Design 23.

Packager's Acknowledgements
Palazzo Editions would like to thank Richard Constable and Robert Walster for their design contributions.